17th Conference on Computational Natural Language Learning (CoNLL 2013)

Shared Task

Sofia, Bulgaria
8 – 9 August 2013

ISBN: 978-1-62748-982-9

Printed from e-media with permission by:

Curran Associates, Inc.
57 Morehouse Lane
Red Hook, NY 12571

Some format issues inherent in the e-media version may also appear in this print version.

Printed by Curran Associates, Inc. (2013)

For permission requests, please contact the Association for Computational Linguistics at the address below.

Association for Computational Linguistics
209 N. Eighth Street
Stroudsburg, Pennsylvania 18360

Phone: 1-570-476-8006
Fax: 1-570-476-0860

acl@aclweb.org

Additional copies of this publication are available from:

Curran Associates, Inc.
57 Morehouse Lane
Red Hook, NY 12571 USA
Phone: 845-758-0400
Fax: 845-758-2634
Email: curran@proceedings.com
Web: www.proceedings.com

CoNLL-2013

Seventeenth Conference on Computational Natural Language Learning

Proceedings of the Shared Task

August 8-9, 2013
Sofia, Bulgaria

Introduction

This volume contains papers describing the CoNLL-2013 Shared Task and the participating systems. This year, we continue the tradition of the Conference on Computational Natural Language Learning (CoNLL) of having a high profile shared task in natural language processing, centered on automatic grammatical error correction of English essays. This task has gained popularity recently with the organization of the HOO (Helping Our Own) shared tasks in 2011 and 2012. The grammatical error correction task is impactful since it is estimated that hundreds of millions of people in the world are learning English as a second language, and they benefit directly from an automated grammar checker.

In the recent HOO shared task in 2012, only two error types, i.e., determiner and preposition, are considered. In contrast, the CoNLL-2013 shared task has included a more comprehensive list of error types, including noun number, verb form, and subject-verb agreement errors in addition to determiner and preposition errors. Extending into more error types introduces the possibility of correcting multiple interacting errors.

For this shared task, we have only one track in which shared task participants are provided with an annotated training corpus, but are allowed to use additional resources as long as they are publicly available. The training corpus, NUCLE (NUS Corpus of Learner English), is a large collection of English essays written by students at the National University of Singapore (NUS) who are non-native speakers of English. The essays were annotated by professional English instructors at the NUS. As in other shared tasks, we provide a common test set with gold-standard annotations, and a scorer to evaluate the submitted system output.

A total of 17 participating teams submitted system output and 16 of them submitted system description papers. Many different approaches were adopted to perform grammatical error correction. We hope that these approaches help to advance the state of the art in grammatical error correction, and that the test set and scorer, which are freely available after the shared task, can be useful resources for those interested in grammatical error correction.

Hwee Tou Ng, Joel Tetreault, Siew Mei Wu, Yuanbin Wu, and Christian Hadiwinoto
Organizers of the CoNLL-2013 Shared Task
June 2013

Organizers:

Hwee Tou Ng, National University of Singapore
Joel Tetreault, Nuance Communications
Siew Mei Wu, National University of Singapore
Yuanbin Wu, National University of Singapore
Christian Hadiwinoto, National University of Singapore

Program Committee:

Pushpak Bhattacharyya, Indian Institute of Technology Bombay
Francis Bond, Nanyang Technological University
Ted Briscoe, University of Cambridge
Aoife Cahill, Educational Testing Service
Martin Chodorow, City University of New York
Daniel Dahlmeier, SAP Singapore
Markus Dickinson, Indiana University
Dan Flickinger, Stanford University
Jennifer Foster, Dublin City University
Michael Heilman, Educational Testing Service
Yuji Matsumoto, Nara Institute of Science and Technology
Detmar Meurers, University of Tübingen
Alla Rozovskaya, University of Illinois at Urbana-Champaign
Mark Sammons, University of Illinois at Urbana-Champaign
Antal van den Bosch, Radboud University Nijmegen
Veronika Vincze, Hungarian Academy of Sciences
Torsten Zesch, University of Darmstadt

Table of Contents

Conference Program

Friday August 9, 2013

Session 1: Oral Presentation

10:00–10:30 *The CoNLL-2013 Shared Task on Grammatical Error Correction*
Hwee Tou Ng, Siew Mei Wu, Yuanbin Wu, Christian Hadiwinoto and Joel Tetreault

10:30–11:00 Coffee Break

11:00–11:10 *The University of Illinois System in the CoNLL-2013 Shared Task*
Alla Rozovskaya, Kai-Wei Chang, Mark Sammons and Dan Roth

11:10–11:20 *CoNLL-2013 Shared Task: Grammatical Error Correction NTHU System Description*
Ting-hui Kao, Yu-wei Chang, Hsun-wen Chiu, Tzu-Hsi Yen, Joanne Boisson, Jiancheng Wu and Jason S. Chang

11:20–11:30 *NAIST at 2013 CoNLL Grammatical Error Correction Shared Task*
Ippei Yoshimoto, Tomoya Kose, Kensuke Mitsuzawa, Keisuke Sakaguchi, Tomoya Mizumoto, Yuta Hayashibe, Mamoru Komachi and Yuji Matsumoto

11:30–11:40 *UM-Checker: A Hybrid System for English Grammatical Error Correction*
Junwen Xing, Longyue Wang, Derek F. Wong, Lidia S. Chao and Xiaodong Zeng

11:40–11:50 *A Tree Transducer Model for Grammatical Error Correction*
Jan Buys and Brink van der Merwe

11:50–12:00 *Constrained Grammatical Error Correction using Statistical Machine Translation*
Zheng Yuan and Mariano Felice

12:00–12:30 Shared Task Discussion

Friday August 9, 2013 (continued)

Session 2: Poster Presentation

The CoNLL-2013 Shared Task on Grammatical Error Correction

Hwee Tou Ng
Department of Computer Science
National University of Singapore
nght@comp.nus.edu.sg

Siew Mei Wu
Centre for English Language Communication
National University of Singapore
elcwusm@nus.edu.sg

Yuanbin Wu and **Christian Hadiwinoto**
Department of Computer Science
National University of Singapore
{wuyb,chrhad}@comp.nus.edu.sg

Joel Tetreault
Nuance Communications, Inc.
Joel.Tetreault@nuance.com

Abstract

The CoNLL-2013 shared task was devoted to grammatical error correction. In this paper, we give the task definition, present the data sets, and describe the evaluation metric and scorer used in the shared task. We also give an overview of the various approaches adopted by the participating teams, and present the evaluation results.

1 Introduction

Grammatical error correction is the shared task of the Seventeenth Conference on Computational Natural Language Learning in 2013 (CoNLL-2013). In this task, given an English essay written by a learner of English as a second language, the goal is to detect and correct the grammatical errors present in the essay, and return the corrected essay.

This task has attracted much recent research interest, with two shared tasks Helping Our Own (HOO) 2011 and 2012 organized in the past two years (Dale and Kilgarriff, 2011; Dale et al., 2012). In contrast to previous CoNLL shared tasks which focused on particular subtasks of natural language processing, such as named entity recognition, semantic role labeling, dependency parsing, or coreference resolution, grammatical error correction aims at building a complete end-to-end application. This task is challenging since for many error types, current grammatical error correction systems do not achieve high performance and much research is still needed. Also, tackling this task has far-reaching impact, since it is estimated that hundreds of millions of people worldwide are learning English and they benefit directly from an automated grammar checker.

The CoNLL-2013 shared task provides a forum for participating teams to work on the same grammatical error correction task, with evaluation on the same blind test set using the same evaluation metric and scorer. This overview paper contains a detailed description of the shared task, and is organized as follows. Section 2 provides the task definition. Section 3 describes the annotated training data provided and the blind test data. Section 4 describes the evaluation metric and the scorer. Section 5 lists the participating teams and outlines the approaches to grammatical error correction used by the teams. Section 6 presents the results of the shared task. Section 7 concludes the paper.

2 Task Definition

The goal of the CoNLL-2013 shared task is to evaluate algorithms and systems for automatically detecting and correcting grammatical errors present in English essays written by second language learners of English. Each participating team is given training data manually annotated with corrections of grammatical errors. The test data consists of new, blind test essays. Preprocessed test essays, which have been sentence-segmented and tokenized, are also made available to the participating teams. Each team is to submit its system output consisting of the automatically corrected essays, in sentence-segmented and tokenized form.

Grammatical errors consist of many different types, including articles or determiners, prepositions, noun form, verb form, subject-verb agreement, pronouns, word choice, sentence structure, punctuation, capitalization, etc. Of all the error types, determiners and prepositions are among the most frequent errors made by learners of English. Not surprisingly, much published research on grammatical error correction focuses on article and preposition errors (Han et al., 2006; Gamon, 2010; Rozovskaya and Roth, 2010; Tetreault et al., 2010; Dahlmeier and Ng, 2011b), with relatively less work on correcting word choice errors (Dahlmeier and Ng, 2011a). Article and preposition errors were also the only error types featured in the HOO 2012 shared task. Likewise, although all error types were included in the HOO 2011 shared task, almost all participating teams dealt with article and preposition errors only (besides spelling and punctuation errors).

In the CoNLL-2013 shared task, it was felt that the community is now ready to deal with more error types, including noun number, verb form, and subject-verb agreement, besides articles/determiners and prepositions. Table 1 shows examples of the five error types in our shared task.

Since there are five error types in our shared task compared to two in HOO 2012, there is a greater chance of encountering multiple, interacting errors in a sentence in our shared task. This increases the complexity of our shared task relative to that of HOO 2012. To illustrate, consider the following sentence:

> Although we have to admit some bad *effect* which *is* brought by the new technology, still the advantages of the new technologies cannot be simply discarded.

The noun number error *effect* needs to be corrected (effect → effects). This necessitates the correction of a subject-verb agreement error (is → are). A pipeline system in which corrections for subject-verb agreement errors occur strictly before corrections for noun number errors would not be able to arrive at a fully corrected sentence for this example. The ability to correct multiple, interacting errors is thus necessary in our shared task. The recent work of (Dahlmeier and Ng, 2012a), for example, is designed to deal with multiple, interacting errors.

Note that the essays in the training data and the test essays naturally contain grammatical errors of all types, beyond the five error types focused in our shared task. In the automatically corrected essays returned by a participating system, only corrections necessary to correct errors of the five types are made. The other errors are to be left uncorrected.

3 Data

This section describes the training and test data released to each participating team in our shared task.

3.1 Training Data

The training data provided in our shared task is the NUCLE corpus, the NUS Corpus of Learner English (Dahlmeier et al., 2013). As noted by (Leacock et al., 2010), the lack of a manually annotated and corrected corpus of English learner texts has been an impediment to progress in grammatical error correction, since it prevents comparative evaluations on a common benchmark test data set. NUCLE was created precisely to fill this void. It is a collection of 1,414 essays written by students at the National University of Singapore (NUS) who are non-native speakers of English. The essays were written in response to some prompts, and they cover a wide range of topics, such as environmental pollution, health care, etc. The grammatical errors in these essays have been hand-corrected by professional English instructors at NUS. For each grammatical error instance, the start and end character offsets of the erroneous text span are marked, and the error type and the correction string are provided. Manual annotation is carried out using a graphical user interface specifically built for this purpose. The error annotations are saved as stand-off annotations, in SGML format.

To illustrate, consider the following sentence at the start of the first paragraph of an essay:

> From past to the present, many important innovations have surfaced.

There is an article/determiner error (past → the past) in this sentence. The error annotation, also called *correction* or *edit*, in SGML format is shown in Figure 1. `start_par` (`end_par`) denotes the paragraph ID of the start (end) of the erroneous text span (paragraph ID starts from 0 by convention). `start_off` (`end_off`) denotes the character offset of the start (end) of the erroneous text span (again, character offset starts from 0 by convention). The error tag is `ArtOrDet`, and the correction string is `the past`.

Error tag	Error type	Example sentence	Correction (edit)
ArtOrDet	Article or determiner	In *late* nineteenth century, there was a severe air crash happening at Miami international airport.	late → the late
Prep	Preposition	Also tracking people is very dangerous if it has been controlled by bad men *in* a not good purpose.	in → for
Nn	Noun number	I think such powerful *device* shall not be made easily available.	device → devices
Vform	Verb form	However, it is an achievement as it is an indication that our society is *progressed* well and people are living in better conditions.	progressed → progressing
SVA	Subject-verb agreement	People still *prefers* to bear the risk and allow their pets to have maximum freedom.	prefers → prefer

Table 1: The five error types in our shared task.

```
<MISTAKE start_par="0" start_off="5" end_par="0" end_off="9">
<TYPE>ArtOrDet</TYPE>
<CORRECTION>the past</CORRECTION>
</MISTAKE>
```

Figure 1: An example error annotation.

The NUCLE corpus was first used in (Dahlmeier and Ng, 2011b), and has been publicly available for research purposes since June 2011[1]. All instances of grammatical errors are annotated in NUCLE, and the errors are classified into 27 error types (Dahlmeier et al., 2013).

To help participating teams in their preparation for the shared task, we also performed automatic preprocessing of the NUCLE corpus and released the preprocessed form of NUCLE. The preprocessing operations performed on the NUCLE essays include sentence segmentation and word tokenization using the NLTK toolkit (Bird et al., 2009), and part-of-speech (POS) tagging, constituency and dependency tree parsing using the Stanford parser (Klein and Manning, 2003; de Marneffe et al., 2006). The error annotations, which are originally at the character level, are then mapped to error annotations at the word token level. Error annotations at the word token level also facilitate scoring, as we will see in Section 4, since our scorer operates by matching tokens. Note that although we released our own preprocessed version of NUCLE, the participating teams were however free to perform their own preprocessing if they so preferred.

[1]http://www.comp.nus.edu.sg/~nlp/corpora.html

3.1.1 Revised version of NUCLE

NUCLE release version 2.3 was used in the CoNLL-2013 shared task. In this version, 17 essays were removed from the first release of NUCLE since these essays were duplicates with multiple annotations.

In the original NUCLE corpus, there is not an explicit preposition error type. Instead, preposition errors are part of the Wcip (wrong collocation/idiom/preposition) and Rloc (local redundancy) error types. The Wcip error type combines errors concerning collocations, idioms, and prepositions together into one error type. The Rloc error type annotates extraneous words which are redundant and should be removed, and they include redundant articles, determiners, and prepositions.

	Training data (NUCLE)	Test data
# essays	1,397	50
# sentences	57,151	1,381
# word tokens	1,161,567	29,207

Table 2: Statistics of training and test data.

In our shared task, in order to facilitate the detection and correction of article/determiner errors and preposition errors, we performed automatic mapping of error types in the original NUCLE corpus. The mapping relies on POS tags, constituent parse trees, and error annotations at the word token level. Specifically, we map the error types Wcip and Rloc to Prep, Wci, ArtOrDet, and Rloc−. Prepositions in the error type Wcip or Rloc are mapped to a new error type Prep, and redundant articles or determiners in the error type Rloc are mapped to ArtOrDet. The remaining unaffected Wcip errors are assigned the new error type Wci and the remaining unaffected Rloc errors are assigned the new error type Rloc−. The code that performs automatic error type mapping was also provided to the participating teams.

The statistics of the NUCLE corpus (release 2.3 version) are shown in Table 2. The distribution of errors among the five error types is shown in Table 3. The newly added noun number error type in our shared task accounts for the second highest number of errors among the five error types. The five error types in our shared task constitute 35% of all grammatical errors in the training data, and 47% of all errors in the test data. These figures support our choice of these five error types to be the focus of our shared task, since they account for a large percentage of all grammatical errors in English learner essays.

While the NUCLE corpus is provided in our shared task, participating teams are free to not use NUCLE, or to use additional resources and tools in building their grammatical error correction systems, as long as these resources and tools are publicly available and not proprietary. For example, participating teams are free to use the Cambridge FCE corpus (Yannakoudakis et al., 2011; Nicholls, 2003) (the training data provided in HOO 2012 (Dale et al., 2012)) as additional training data.

Error tag	Training data (NUCLE)	%	Test data	%
ArtOrDet	6,658	14.8	690	19.9
Prep	2,404	5.3	312	9.0
Nn	3,779	8.4	396	11.4
Vform	1,453	3.2	122	3.5
SVA	1,527	3.4	124	3.6
5 types	15,821	35.1	1,644	47.4
all types	45,106	100.0	3,470	100.0

Table 3: Error type distribution of the training and test data.

3.2 Test Data

25 NUS students, who are non-native speakers of English, were recruited to write new essays to be used as blind test data in the shared task. Each student wrote two essays in response to the two prompts shown in Table 4, one essay per prompt. Essays written using the first prompt are present in the NUCLE training data, while the second prompt is a new prompt not used previously. As a result, 50 test essays were collected. The statistics of the test essays are shown in Table 2.

Error annotation on the test essays was carried out by a native speaker of English who is a lecturer at the NUS Centre for English Language Communication. The distribution of errors in the test essays among the five error types is shown in Table 3. The test essays were then preprocessed in the same manner as the NUCLE corpus. The preprocessed test essays were released to the participating teams.

Unlike the test data used in HOO 2012 which was proprietary and not available after the shared task, the test essays and their error annotations in the CoNLL-2013 shared task are freely available after the shared task.

4 Evaluation Metric and Scorer

A grammatical error correction system is evaluated by how well its proposed corrections or edits match the gold-standard edits. An essay is first sentence-segmented and tokenized before evaluation is carried out on the essay. To illustrate, consider the following tokenized sentence S written by an English learner:

There is no **a doubt**, tracking **system**

ID	Prompt
1	Surveillance technology such as RFID (radio-frequency identification) should not be used to track people (e.g., human implants and RFID tags on people or products). Do you agree? Support your argument with concrete examples.
2	Population aging is a global phenomenon. Studies have shown that the current average life span is over 65. Projections of the United Nations indicate that the population aged 60 or over in developed and developing countries is increasing at 2% to 3% annually. Explain why rising life expectancies can be considered both a challenge and an achievement.

Table 4: The two prompts used for the test essays.

> **has** brought many benefits in this information age .

The set of gold-standard edits of a human annotator is $\mathbf{g}$ = {a doubt → doubt, system → systems, has → have}. Suppose the tokenized output sentence H of a grammatical error correction system given the above sentence is:

> There is no doubt, tracking system has brought many benefits in this information age .

That is, the set of system edits is $\mathbf{e}$ = {a doubt → doubt}. The performance of the grammatical error correction system is measured by how well the two sets $\mathbf{g}$ and $\mathbf{e}$ match, in the form of recall R, precision P, and F_1 measure: $R = 1/3, P = 1/1, F_1 = 2RP/(R+P) = 1/2$.

More generally, given a set of n sentences, where $\mathbf{g}_i$ is the set of gold-standard edits for sentence i, and $\mathbf{e}_i$ is the set of system edits for sentence i, recall, precision, and F_1 are defined as follows:

$$R = \frac{\sum_{i=1}^{n} |\mathbf{g}_i \cap \mathbf{e}_i|}{\sum_{i=1}^{n} |\mathbf{g}_i|} \quad (1)$$

$$P = \frac{\sum_{i=1}^{n} |\mathbf{g}_i \cap \mathbf{e}_i|}{\sum_{i=1}^{n} |\mathbf{e}_i|} \quad (2)$$

$$F_1 = \frac{2 \times R \times P}{R + P} \quad (3)$$

where the intersection between $\mathbf{g}_i$ and $\mathbf{e}_i$ for sentence i is defined as

$$\mathbf{g}_i \cap \mathbf{e}_i = \{e \in \mathbf{e}_i | \exists g \in \mathbf{g}_i, match(g, e)\} \quad (4)$$

Evaluation by the HOO scorer (Dale and Kilgarriff, 2011) is based on computing recall, precision, and F_1 measure as defined above.

Note that there are multiple ways to specify a set of gold-standard edits that denote the same corrections. For example, in the above learner-written sentence S, alternative but equivalent sets of gold-standard edits are {a → ϵ, system → systems, has → have}, {a → ϵ, system has → systems have}, etc. Given the same learner-written sentence S and the same system output sentence H shown above, one would expect a scorer to give the same R, P, F_1 scores regardless of which of the equivalent sets of gold-standard edits is specified by an annotator.

However, this is not the case with the HOO scorer. This is because the HOO scorer uses GNU `wdiff`[2] to extract the differences between the learner-written sentence S and the system output sentence H to form a set of system edits. Since in general there are multiple ways to specify a set of gold-standard edits that denote the same corrections, the set of system edits computed by the HOO scorer may not match the set of gold-standard edits specified, leading to erroneous scores. In the above example, the set of system edits computed by the HOO scorer for S and H is {a → ϵ}. Given that the set of gold-standard edits $\mathbf{g}$ is {a doubt → doubt, system → systems, has → have}, the scores computed by the HOO scorer are $R = P = F_1 = 0$, which are erroneous.

The *MaxMatch* (M^2) scorer[3] (Dahlmeier and Ng, 2012b) was designed to overcome this limitation of the HOO scorer. The key idea is that the set of system edits automatically computed and used in scoring should be the set that maximally matches the set of gold-standard edits specified by the annotator. The M^2 scorer uses an efficient algorithm to search for such a set of system edits using an edit lattice. In the above example, given S, H, and $\mathbf{g}$, the M^2 scorer is able to come up with the best matching set of system edits $\mathbf{e}$ = {a doubt → doubt}, thus giving the correct scores $R = 1/3, P = 1/1, F_1 = 1/2$. We use the M^2

[2]http://www.gnu.org/s/wdiff/

[3]http://www.comp.nus.edu.sg/~nlp/software.html

scorer in the CoNLL-2013 shared task.

The original M^2 scorer implemented in (Dahlmeier and Ng, 2012b) assumes that there is one set of gold-standard edits $\mathbf{g}_i$ for each sentence i. However, it is often the case that multiple alternative corrections are acceptable for a sentence. As we allow participating teams to submit alternative sets of gold-standard edits for a sentence, we also extend the M^2 scorer to deal with multiple alternative sets of gold-standard edits.

Based on Equations 1 and 2, Equation 3 can be re-expressed as:

$$F_1 = \frac{2 \times \sum_{i=1}^{n} |\mathbf{g}_i \cap \mathbf{e}_i|}{\sum_{i=1}^{n} (|\mathbf{g}_i| + |\mathbf{e}_i|)} \quad (5)$$

To deal with multiple alternative sets of gold-standard edits $\mathbf{g}_i$ for a sentence i, the extended M^2 scorer chooses the $\mathbf{g}_i$ that maximizes the cumulative F_1 score for sentences $1, \ldots, i$. Ties are broken based on the following criteria: first choose the $\mathbf{g}_i$ that maximizes the numerator $\sum_{i=1}^{n} |\mathbf{g}_i \cap \mathbf{e}_i|$, then choose the $\mathbf{g}_i$ that minimizes the denominator $\sum_{i=1}^{n} (|\mathbf{g}_i| + |\mathbf{e}_i|)$, finally choose the $\mathbf{g}_i$ that appears first in the list of alternatives.

5 Approaches

54 teams registered to participate in the shared task, out of which 17 teams submitted the output of their grammatical error correction systems by the deadline. These teams are listed in Table 5. Each team is assigned a 3 to 4-letter team ID. In the remainder of this paper, we will use the assigned team ID to refer to a participating team. Every team submitted a system description paper (the only exception is the SJT2 team).

Many different approaches are adopted by participating teams in the CoNLL-2013 shared task, and Table 6 summarizes these approaches. A commonly used approach in the shared task and in grammatical error correction research in general is to build a classifier for each error type. For example, the classifier for noun number returns the classes {singular, plural}, the classifier for article returns the classes {a/an, the, ϵ}, etc. The classifier for an error type may be learned from training examples encoding the surrounding context of an error occurrence, or may be specified by deterministic hand-crafted rules, or may be built using a hybrid approach combining both machine learning and hand-crafted rules. These approaches are denoted by M, R, and H respectively in Table 6.

The machine translation approach (denoted by T in Table 6) to grammatical error correction treats the task as "translation" from bad English to good English. Both phrase-based translation and syntax-based translation approaches are used by teams in the CoNLL-2013 shared task. Another related approach is the language modeling approach (denoted by L in Table 6), in which the probability of a learner sentence is compared with the probability of a candidate corrected sentence, based on a language model built from a background corpus. The candidate correction is chosen if it results in a corrected sentence with a higher probability. In general, these approaches are not mutually exclusive. For example, the work of (Dahlmeier and Ng, 2012a; Yoshimoto et al., 2013) includes elements of machine learning-based classification, machine translation, and language modeling approaches.

When different approaches are used to tackle different error types by a system, we break down the error types into different rows in Table 6, and specify the approach used for each group of error types. For instance, the HIT team uses a machine learning approach to deal with article/determiner, noun number, and preposition errors, and a rule-based approach to deal with subject-verb agreement and verb form errors. As such, the entry for HIT is sub-divided into two rows, to make it clear which particular error type is handled by which approach.

Table 6 also shows the linguistic features used by the participating teams, which include lexical features (i.e., words, collocations, n-grams), parts-of-speech (POS), constituency parses, dependency parses, and semantic features (including semantic role labels).

While all teams in the shared task use the NUCLE corpus, they are also allowed to use additional external resources (both corpora and tools) so long as they are publicly available and not proprietary. The external resources used by the teams are also listed in Table 6.

6 Results

All submitted system output was evaluated using the M^2 scorer, based on the error annotations provided by our annotator. The recall (R), precision (P), and F_1 measure of all teams are shown in Table 7. The performance of the teams varies greatly,

Team ID	Affiliation
CAMB	University of Cambridge
HIT	Harbin Institute of Technology
IITB	Indian Institute of Technology, Bombay
KOR	Korea University
NARA	Nara Institute of Science and Technology
NTHU	National Tsing Hua University
SAAR	Saarland University
SJT1	Shanghai Jiao Tong University (Team #1)
SJT2	Shanghai Jiao Tong University (Team #2)
STAN	Stanford University
STEL	Stellenbosch University
SZEG	University of Szeged
TILB	Tilburg University
TOR	University of Toronto
UAB	Universitat Autònoma de Barcelona
UIUC	University of Illinois at Urbana-Champaign
UMC	University of Macau

Table 5: The list of 17 participating teams.

Rank	Team	R	P	F_1
1	UIUC	23.49	46.45	31.20
2	NTHU	26.35	23.80	25.01
3	HIT	16.56	35.65	22.61
4	NARA	18.62	27.39	22.17
5	UMC	17.53	28.49	21.70
6	STEL	13.33	27.00	17.85
7	SJT1	10.96	40.18	17.22
8	CAMB	10.10	39.15	16.06
9	IITB	4.99	28.18	8.48
10	STAN	4.69	25.50	7.92
11	TOR	4.81	17.67	7.56
12	KOR	3.71	43.88	6.85
13	TILB	7.24	6.25	6.71
14	SZEG	3.16	5.52	4.02
15	UAB	1.22	12.42	2.22
16	SAAR	1.10	27.69	2.11
17	SJT2	0.24	13.33	0.48

Table 7: Scores (in %) without alternative answers.

from barely half a per cent to 31.20% for the top team.

The nature of grammatical error correction is such that multiple, different corrections are often acceptable. In order to allow the participating teams to raise their disagreement with the original gold-standard annotations provided by the annotator, and not understate the performance of the teams, we allow the teams to submit their proposed alternative answers. This was also the practice adopted in HOO 2011 and HOO 2012. Specifically, after the teams submitted their system output and the error annotations on the test essays were released, we allowed the teams to propose alternative answers (gold-standard edits), to be submitted within four days after the initial error annotations were released. The same annotator who provided the error annotations on the test essays also judged the alternative answers proposed by the teams, to ensure consistency. In all, five teams (NTHU, STEL, TOR, UIUC, UMC) submitted alternative answers.

The same submitted system output was then evaluated using the extended M^2 scorer, with the original annotations augmented with the alternative answers. Table 8 shows the recall (R), precision (P), and F_1 measure of all teams under this new evaluation setting.

The F_1 measure of every team improves when

Team	Error	Approach	Description of Approach	Linguistic Features	External Resources
CAMB	ANPSV	T	factored phrase-based translation model with IRST language model	lexical, POS	Cambridge Learner Corpus
HIT	ANP	M	maximum entropy with confidence tuning, and genetic algorithm for feature selection	lexical, POS, constituency parse, dependency parse, semantic	WordNet, Longman dictionary
	SV	R	rule-based	POS, dependency parse, semantic	
IITB	AN	M	maximum entropy	lexical, POS, noun properties	Wiktionary
	S	R	rule-based	POS, constituency parse, dependency parse	
KOR	ANP	M	maximum entropy	lexical, POS, head-modifier, dependency parse	(none)
NARA	AP	T	phrase-based statistical machine translation	lexical	Lang-8
	N	M	adaptive regularization of weight vectors	lexical, lemma, constituency parse	Gigaword
	SV	L	treelet (tree-based) language model	lexical, POS, constituency parse	Penn Treebank, Gigaword
NTHU	ANPV	L	n-gram-based and dependency-based language model	lexical, POS, constituency parse, dependency parse	Google Web-1T
SAAR	A	M	multi-class SVM and naive Bayes	lexical, POS, constituency parse	CMU Pronouncing Dictionary
	S	R	rule-based	POS, dependency parse	
SJT1	ANPSV	M	maximum entropy (with LM post-filtering)	lexical, lemma, POS, constituency parse, dependency parse	Europarl
STAN	ANPSV	H	English Resource Grammar (ERG), head-driven phrase structure, extended with hand-coded mal-rules	lexical, POS, constituency parse, semantic	English Resource Grammar
STEL	ANPSV	T	tree-to-string with GHKM transducer	constituency parse	Wikipedia, WordNet
SZEG	AN	M	maximum entropy	LFG, lexical, constituency parse, dependency parse	(none)
TILB	ANPSV	M	binary and multi-class IGTree	lexical, lemma, POS	Google Web-1T, Gigaword
TOR	ANPSV	T	noisy channel model involving transformation of single words	lexical, POS	Wikipedia
UAB	ANPSV	R	rule-based	lexical, dependency parse	Top 250 uncountable nouns, FreeLing morphological dictionary
UIUC	ANPSV	M	A: multi-class averaged perceptron; others: naive Bayes	lexical, POS, shallow parse	Google Web-1T, Gigaword
UMC	ANPSV	H	pipeline: rule-based filter → semi-supervised multi-class maximum entropy classifier → LM confidence scorer	lexical, POS, dependency parse	News corpus, JMySpell dictionary, Google Web-1T, Penn Treebank

Table 6: Profile of the participating teams. The *Error* column shows the error type, where each letter denotes the error type beginning with that initial letter. The *Approach* column shows the approach adopted by each team, sometimes broken down according to the error type: H denotes a hybrid classifier approach, L denotes a language modeling-based approach, M denotes a machine learning-based classifier approach, R denotes a rule-based classifier (non-machine learning) approach, and T denotes a machine translation approach

evaluated with alternative answers. Not surprisingly, the teams which submitted alternative answers tend to show the greatest improvements in their F_1 measure. Overall, the UIUC team (Rozovskaya et al., 2013) achieves the best F_1 measure, with a clear lead over the other teams in the shared task, under both evaluation settings (without and with alternative answers).

For future research which uses the test data of the CoNLL-2013 shared task, we recommend that evaluation be carried out in the setting that does *not* use alternative answers, to ensure a fairer evaluation. This is because the scores of the teams which submitted alternative answers tend to be higher in a biased way when evaluated with alternative answers.

Rank	Team	R	P	F_1
1	UIUC	31.87	62.19	42.14
2	NTHU	34.62	30.57	32.46
3	UMC	23.66	37.12	28.90
4	NARA	24.05	33.92	28.14
5	HIT	20.29	41.75	27.31
6	STEL	18.91	37.12	25.05
7	CAMB	14.19	52.11	22.30
8	SJT1	13.67	47.77	21.25
9	TOR	8.77	30.67	13.64
10	IITB	6.55	34.93	11.03
11	STAN	5.86	29.93	9.81
12	KOR	4.78	53.24	8.77
13	TILB	9.29	7.60	8.36
14	SZEG	4.07	6.67	5.06
15	UAB	1.81	17.39	3.28
16	SAAR	1.68	40.00	3.23
17	SJT2	0.33	16.67	0.64

Table 8: Scores (in %) with alternative answers.

We are also interested in the analysis of scores of each of the five error types. To compute the recall of an error type, we need to know the error type of each gold-standard edit, which is provided by the annotator. To compute the precision of each error type, we need to know the error type of each system edit, which however is not available since the submitted system output only contains the corrected sentences with no indication of the error type of the system edits.

In order to determine the error type of system edits, we first perform POS tagging on the submitted system output using the Stanford parser (Klein and Manning, 2003). We also make use of the POS tags assigned in the preprocessed form of the test essays. We then assign an error type to a system edit based on the automatically determined POS tags, as follows:

- ArtOrDet: The system edit involves a change (insertion, deletion, or substitution) of words tagged as article/determiner, i.e., DT or PDT.
- Prep: The system edit involves a change of words tagged as preposition, i.e., IN or TO.
- Nn: The system edit involves a change of words such that a word in the source string is a singular noun (tagged as NN or NNP) and a word in the replacement string is a plural noun (tagged as NNS or NNPS), or vice versa. Since a word tagged as JJ (adjective) can serve as a noun, a system edit that involves a change of POS tags from JJ to one of {NN, NNP, NNS, NNPS} or vice versa also qualifies.
- Vform/SVA: The system edit involves a change of words tagged as one of the verb POS tags, i.e., VB, VBD, VBG, VBN, VBP, and VBZ.

The verb form and subject-verb agreement error types are grouped together into one category, since it is difficult to automatically distinguish the two in a reliable way.

The scores when distinguished by error type are shown in Tables 9 and 10. Based on the F_1 measure of each error type, the noun number error type gives the highest scores, and preposition errors remain the most challenging error type to correct.

7 Conclusions

The CoNLL-2013 shared task saw the participation of 17 teams worldwide to evaluate their grammatical error correction systems on a common test set, using a common evaluation metric and scorer. The five error types included in the shared task account for at least one-third to close to one-half of all errors in English learners' essays. The best system in the shared task achieves an F_1 score of 42%, when it is scored with multiple acceptable answers. There is still much room for improvement, both in the accuracy of grammatical error correction systems, and in the coverage of systems to deal with a more comprehensive set of error

Team	ArtOrDet			Prep			Nn			Vform/SVA		
	R	P	F_1	R	P	F_1	R	P	F_1	R	P	F_1
CAMB	15.07	38.66	21.69	3.54	40.74	6.51	7.58	55.56	13.33	8.54	31.82	13.46
HIT	24.20	42.82	30.93	2.89	28.12	5.25	17.17	29.69	21.76	11.38	26.42	15.91
IITB	1.30	21.43	2.46	(not done)			9.85	28.68	14.66	13.82	30.09	18.94
KOR	4.78	53.23	8.78	0.32	4.76	0.60	6.82	49.09	11.97	(not done)		
NARA	20.43	34.06	25.54	12.54	29.10	17.53	16.41	48.87	24.57	24.80	14.81	18.54
NTHU	21.01	35.80	26.48	12.86	12.01	12.42	45.96	40.90	43.28	26.83	12.22	16.79
SAAR	0.72	62.50	1.43	(not done)			(not done)			5.28	23.21	8.61
SJT1	16.81	47.15	24.79	1.29	12.50	2.33	13.64	42.19	20.61	2.44	14.63	4.18
SJT2	0.00	0.00	0.00	0.00	0.00	0.00	1.01	13.33	1.88	0.00	0.00	0.00
STAN	3.91	20.45	6.57	0.32	20.00	0.63	6.06	29.63	10.06	10.16	32.05	15.43
STEL	12.61	27.71	17.33	9.32	25.66	13.68	18.18	46.75	26.18	12.60	17.61	14.69
SZEG	1.16	1.70	1.38	(not done)			11.11	13.62	12.24	(not done)		
TILB	4.49	4.49	4.49	10.61	5.07	6.86	7.07	21.21	10.61	10.98	9.57	10.23
TOR	8.55	25.54	12.81	2.25	5.38	3.17	1.77	31.82	3.35	2.44	12.24	4.07
UAB	0.00	0.00	0.00	0.00	0.00	0.00	0.00	0.00	0.00	8.13	12.42	9.83
UIUC	25.65	47.84	33.40	4.18	26.53	7.22	38.38	52.23	44.25	17.89	38.94	24.51
UMC	21.01	30.27	24.81	1.93	35.29	3.66	23.23	27.96	25.38	18.29	28.85	22.39

Table 9: Scores (in %) without alternative answers, distinguished by error type. If a team indicates that its system does not handle a particular error type, its entry for that error type is marked as "(not done)".

Team	ArtOrDet			Prep			Nn			Vform/SVA		
	R	P	F_1	R	P	F_1	R	P	F_1	R	P	F_1
CAMB	19.62	49.81	28.15	5.04	50.00	9.15	9.50	69.09	16.70	16.52	54.41	25.34
HIT	27.41	47.44	34.74	4.58	37.50	8.16	19.95	35.37	25.51	17.90	38.32	24.40
IITB	1.79	28.57	3.37	(not done)			11.91	35.29	17.81	18.67	36.84	24.78
KOR	5.95	64.52	10.90	1.53	19.05	2.83	7.52	54.55	13.22	(not done)		
NARA	25.79	43.34	32.34	17.60	34.56	23.33	19.15	57.04	28.68	34.62	19.10	24.62
NTHU	25.30	42.54	31.73	20.45	16.17	18.06	52.35	50.87	51.60	43.03	19.22	26.57
SAAR	1.04	87.50	2.06	(not done)			(not done)			8.60	33.93	13.72
SJT1	19.65	54.07	28.82	1.92	15.62	3.42	16.46	52.34	25.05	4.05	21.95	6.84
SJT2	0.00	0.00	0.00	0.00	0.00	0.00	1.26	16.67	2.35	0.00	0.00	0.00
STAN	4.91	24.81	8.20	0.38	20.00	0.75	6.78	33.33	11.27	13.51	37.97	19.93
STEL	16.23	35.69	22.31	12.83	29.82	17.94	26.05	70.00	37.97	20.52	26.55	23.15
SZEG	1.50	2.13	1.76	(not done)			12.87	15.95	14.25	(not done)		
TILB	5.78	5.64	5.71	13.91	5.68	8.07	8.25	24.26	12.31	16.36	12.77	14.34
TOR	13.10	39.13	19.63	5.97	12.31	8.04	3.52	63.64	6.67	8.14	35.29	13.24
UAB	0.00	0.00	0.00	0.00	0.00	0.00	0.00	0.00	0.00	12.61	17.39	14.62
UIUC	31.99	59.84	41.69	8.81	46.94	14.84	46.88	70.00	56.15	28.57	60.71	38.86
UMC	25.88	36.74	30.37	3.47	56.25	6.55	30.61	38.64	34.16	26.81	40.13	32.14

Table 10: Scores (in %) with alternative answers, distinguished by error type. If a team indicates that its system does not handle a particular error type, its entry for that error type is marked as "(not done)".

types. The evaluation data sets and scorer used in our shared task serve as a benchmark for future research on grammatical error correction[4].

Acknowledgments

This research is supported by the Singapore National Research Foundation under its International Research Centre @ Singapore Funding Initiative and administered by the IDM Programme Office.

References

Steven Bird, Ewan Klein, and Edward Loper. 2009. *Natural Language Processing with Python*. O'Reilly Media.

Daniel Dahlmeier and Hwee Tou Ng. 2011a. Correcting semantic collocation errors with L1-induced paraphrases. In *Proceedings of the 2011 Conference on Empirical Methods in Natural Language Processing*, pages 107–117.

Daniel Dahlmeier and Hwee Tou Ng. 2011b. Grammatical error correction with alternating structure optimization. In *Proceedings of the 49th Annual Meeting of the Association for Computational Linguistics*, pages 915–923.

Daniel Dahlmeier and Hwee Tou Ng. 2012a. A beam-search decoder for grammatical error correction. In *Proceedings of the 2012 Joint Conference on Empirical Methods in Natural Language Processing and Computational Natural Language Learning*, pages 568–578.

Daniel Dahlmeier and Hwee Tou Ng. 2012b. Better evaluation for grammatical error correction. In *Proceedings of the 2012 Conference of the North American Chapter of the Association for Computational Linguistics: Human Language Technologies*, pages 568–572.

Daniel Dahlmeier, Hwee Tou Ng, and Siew Mei Wu. 2013. Building a large annotated corpus of learner English: The NUS Corpus of Learner English. In *Proceedings of the Eighth Workshop on Innovative Use of NLP for Building Educational Applications*, pages 22–31.

Robert Dale and Adam Kilgarriff. 2011. Helping Our Own: The HOO 2011 pilot shared task. In *Proceedings of the 13th European Workshop on Natural Language Generation*, pages 242–249.

Robert Dale, Ilya Anisimoff, and George Narroway. 2012. HOO 2012: A report on the preposition and determiner error correction shared task. In *Proceedings of the 7th Workshop on the Innovative Use of NLP for Building Educational Applications*, pages 54–62.

[4]http://www.comp.nus.edu.sg/∼nlp/conll13st.html

Marie-Catherine de Marneffe, Bill MacCartney, and Christopher D. Manning. 2006. Generating typed dependency parses from phrase structure parses. In *Proceedings of the Fifth Conference on Language Resources and Evaluation*, pages 449–454.

Michael Gamon. 2010. Using mostly native data to correct errors in learners' writing: A meta-classifier approach. In *Proceedings of the Annual Meeting of the North American Chapter of the Association for Computational Linguistics*, pages 163–171.

Na-Rae Han, Martin Chodorow, and Claudia Leacock. 2006. Detecting errors in English article usage by non-native speakers. *Natural Language Engineering*, 12(2):115–129.

Dan Klein and Christopher D. Manning. 2003. Accurate unlexicalized parsing. In *Proceedings of the 41st Annual Meeting of the Association for Computational Linguistics*, pages 423–430.

Claudia Leacock, Martin Chodorow, Michael Gamon, and Joel Tetreault. 2010. *Automated Grammatical Error Detection for Language Learners*. Morgan & Claypool Publishers.

Diane Nicholls. 2003. The Cambridge Learner Corpus: Error coding and analysis for lexicography and ELT. In *Proceedings of the Corpus Linguistics 2003 Conference*, pages 572–581.

Alla Rozovskaya and Dan Roth. 2010. Generating confusion sets for context-sensitive error correction. In *Proceedings of the 2010 Conference on Empirical Methods in Natural Language Processing*, pages 961–970.

Alla Rozovskaya, Kai-Wei Chang, Mark Sammons, and Dan Roth. 2013. The University of Illinois system in the CoNLL-2013 shared task. In *Proceedings of the Seventeenth Conference on Computational Natural Language Learning: Shared Task*.

Joel Tetreault, Jennifer Foster, and Martin Chodorow. 2010. Using parse features for preposition selection and error detection. In *Proceedings of the ACL 2010 Conference Short Papers*, pages 353–358.

Helen Yannakoudakis, Ted Briscoe, and Ben Medlock. 2011. A new dataset and method for automatically grading ESOL texts. In *Proceedings of the 49th Annual Meeting of the Association for Computational Linguistics*, pages 180–189.

Ippei Yoshimoto, Tomoya Kose, Kensuke Mitsuzawa, Keisuke Sakaguchi, Tomoya Mizumoto, Yuta Hayashibe, Mamoru Komachi, and Yuji Matsumoto. 2013. NAIST at 2013 CoNLL grammatical error correction shared task. In *Proceedings of the Seventeenth Conference on Computational Natural Language Learning: Shared Task*.

The University of Illinois System in the CoNLL-2013 Shared Task

Alla Rozovskaya **Kai-Wei Chang** **Mark Sammons** **Dan Roth**
Cognitive Computation Group
University of Illinois at Urbana-Champaign
Urbana, IL 61801
{rozovska,kchang10,mssammon,danr}@illinois.edu

Abstract

The CoNLL-2013 shared task focuses on correcting grammatical errors in essays written by non-native learners of English. In this paper, we describe the University of Illinois system that participated in the shared task. The system consists of five components and targets five types of common grammatical mistakes made by English as Second Language writers. We describe our underlying approach, which relates to our previous work, and describe the novel aspects of the system in more detail. Out of 17 participating teams, our system is ranked first based on both the original annotation and on the revised annotation.

1 Introduction

The task of correcting grammar and usage mistakes made by English as a Second Language (ESL) writers is difficult for several reasons. First, many of these errors are context-sensitive mistakes that confuse valid English words and thus cannot be detected without considering the context around the word. Second, the relative frequency of mistakes is quite low: for a given type of mistake, an ESL writer will typically make mistakes in only a small proportion of relevant structures. For example, determiner mistakes usually occur in 5% to 10% of noun phrases in various annotated ESL corpora (Rozovskaya and Roth, 2010a). Third, an ESL writer may make multiple mistakes in a single sentence, which may give misleading local cues for individual classifiers. In the example shown in Figure 1, the agreement error on the verb "tend" interacts with the noun number error on the word "equipments".

> Therefore , the **equipments/equipment* of biometric identification **tend/tends* to be inexpensive .

Figure 1: Representative ESL errors in a sample sentence from the training data.

The CoNLL-2013 shared task (Ng et al., 2013) focuses on the following five common mistakes made by ESL writers:

- article/determiner
- preposition
- noun number
- subject-verb agreement
- verb form

Errors outside this target group are present in the task corpora, but are not evaluated.

In this paper, we present a system that combines a set of statistical models, where each model specializes in correcting one of the errors described above. Because the individual error types have different characteristics, we use several different approaches. The article system builds on the elements of the system described in (Rozovskaya and Roth, 2010c). The preposition classifier uses a combined system, building on work described in (Rozovskaya and Roth, 2011) and (Rozovskaya and Roth, 2010b). The remaining three models are all Naïve Bayes classifiers trained on the Google Web 1T 5-gram corpus (henceforth, Google corpus, (Brants and Franz, 2006)).

We first briefly discuss the task (Section 2) and give the overview of our system (Section 3). We then describe the error-specific components (Sections 3.1, 3.2 and 3.3). The sections describing individual components quantify their performance on splits of the training data. In Section 4, we evaluate the complete system on the training data using 5-fold cross-validation (hereafter, "*5-fold CV*") and in Section 5 we show the results we obtained on test.

We close with a discussion focused on error analysis (Section 6) and our conclusions (Section 7).

2 Task Description

The CoNLL-2013 shared task focuses on correcting five types of mistakes that are commonly made by non-native speakers of English. The training data released by the task organizers comes from the NUCLE corpus (Dahlmeier et al., 2013), which contains essays written by learners of English as a foreign language and is corrected by English teachers. The test data for the task consists of an additional set of 50 student essays. Table 1 illustrates the mistakes considered in the task and Table 2 illustrates the distribution of these errors in the released training data and the test data. We note that the test data contains a much larger proportion of annotated mistakes. For example, while only 2.4% of noun phrases in the training data have determiner errors, in the test data 10% of noun phrases have mistakes.

Error type	**Percentage of errors**	
	Training	**Test**
Articles	2.4%	10.0%
Prepositions	2.0%	10.7%
Noun number	1.6%	6.0%
Subject-verb agreement	2.0%	5.2%
Verb form	0.8%	2.5%

Table 2: **Statistics on error distribution in training and test data.** Percentage denotes the erroneous instances with respect to the total number of relevant instances in the data. For example, 10% of noun phrases in the test data have determiner errors.

Since the task focuses on five error types, only annotations marking these mistakes were kept. Note that while the other error annotations were removed, the errors still remain in the data.

3 System Components

Our system consists of five components that address individually article[1], preposition, noun verb form and subject-verb agreement errors.

Our article and preposition modules build on the elements of the systems described in Rozovskaya and Roth (2010b), Rozovskaya and Roth (2010c) and Rozovskaya and Roth (2011). The article system is trained using the Averaged Perceptron (AP) algorithm (Freund and Schapire, 1999), implemented within Learning Based Java (Rizzolo and Roth, 2010). The AP system is trained using the *inflation* method (Rozovskaya et al., 2012). Our preposition system is a Naïve Bayes (NB) classifier trained on the Google corpus and with prior parameters adapted to the learner data.

The other modules – those that correct noun and verb errors – are all NB models trained on the Google corpus.

All components take as input the corpus documents preprocessed with a part-of-speech tagger[2] and shallow parser[3] (Punyakanok and Roth, 2001). Note that the shared task data already contains comparable pre-processing information, in addition to other information, including dependency parse and constituency parse, but we chose to run our own pre-processing tools. The article module uses the POS and chunker output to generate some of its features and to generate candidates (likely contexts for missing articles). The other system components use the pre-processing tools only as part of candidate generation (e.g., to identify all nouns in the data for the noun classifier) because these components are trained on the Google corpus and thus only employ word n-gram features.

During development, we split the released training data into five parts. The results in Sections 3.1, 3.2, and 3.3 give performance of 5-fold CV on the training data. In Section 4 we report the development 5-fold CV results of the complete model and the performance on the test data. Note that the performance reported for the overall task on the test data in Section 4 reflects the system that makes use of the entire training corpus. It is also important to remark that only the determiner system is trained on the ESL data. The other models are trained on native data, and the ESL training data is only used to optimize the decision thresholds of the models.

[1]We will use the terms 'article-' and 'determiner errors' interchangeably: article errors constitute the majority of determiner errors, and we address only article mistakes.

[2]http://cogcomp.cs.illinois.edu/page/software_view/POS

[3]http://cogcomp.cs.illinois.edu/page/software_view/Chunker

Error type	Examples
Article	"It is also important to create **a/∅* better material that can support *the/∅ buildings despite any natural disaster like earthquakes."
Preposition	"As the number of people grows, the need **of/for* habitable environment is unquestionably essential.
Noun number	Some countries are having difficulties in managing a place to live for their **citizen/citizens* as they tend to get overpopulated."
Subject-verb agreement	"Therefore , the equipments of biometric identification **tend/tends* to be inexpensive.
Verb form	"...countries with a lot of deserts can terraform their desert to increase their habitable land and **using/use* irrigation.." "it was not **surprised/surprising* to observe an increasing need for a convenient and cost effective platform."

Table 1: **Example errors.** Note that only the errors exemplifying the relevant phenomena are marked in the table; the sentences may contain other mistakes. Errors marked as verb form include multiple grammatical phenomena that may characterize verbs.

3.1 Determiners

There are three types of determiner error: omitting a determiner; choosing an incorrect determiner; and adding a spurious determiner. Even though the majority of determiner errors involve article mistakes, some of these errors involve personal and possessive pronouns.[4] Most of the determiner errors, however, involve omitting an article (these make up over 60% in the training data). Similar error patterns have been observed in other ESL corpora (Rozovskaya and Roth, 2010a).

Our system focuses on article errors. The system first extracts from the data all articles, and all spaces at the beginning of a noun phrase where an article is likely to be omitted (Han et al., 2006; Rozovskaya and Roth, 2010c). Then we train a multiclass classifier with features described in Table 3. These features were used successfully in previous tasks in error correction (Rozovskaya et al., 2012; Rozovskaya et al., 2011).

The original word choice (the source article) used by the writer is also used as a feature. Since the errors are sparse, this feature causes the model to abstain from flagging a mistake, which results in low recall. To avoid this problem, we adopt the approach proposed in (Rozovskaya et al., 2012), the *error inflation* method, and add artificial article errors in the training data based on the error distribution on the training set. This method prevents the source feature from dominating the context features, and improves the recall of the system.

We experimented with two types of classifiers: Averaged Perceptron (AP) and an L1-generalized logistic regression classifier (LR). Since the article system is trained on the ESL data, of which we have a limited amount, we also experimented with adding a language model (LM) feature to the LR learner. This feature indicates if the correction is accepted by a language model trained on the Google corpus. The performance of each classifier on 5-fold CV on the training data is shown in Table 4. The results show that AP performs better than LR. We observed that adding the LM feature improves precision but results in lower F1, so we chose the AP classifier without the LM feature for our final system.

Model	Precision	Recall	F1
AP (inflation)	0.17	0.31	0.22
AP (inflation+LM)	0.26	0.15	0.19
LR (inflation)	0.17	0.29	0.22
LR (inflation+LM)	0.24	0.21	0.22

Table 4: **Article development results** Results on 5-fold CV. AP With Inflation achieves the best development using an inflation constant of 0.85. AP achieves higher performance without using the language model feature.

3.2 Prepositions

The most common preposition errors are replacements, i.e., where the author correctly recognized the need for a preposition, but chose the wrong one to use.

[4] e.g. "Pat apologized to me for not keeping *the*/my* secrets."

Feature Type	Description
Word n-grams	wB, w_2B, w_3B, wA, w_2A, w_3A, $wBwA$, w_2BwB, wAw_2A, w_3Bw_2BwB, w_2BwBwA, $wBwAw_2A$, wAw_2Aw_3A, $w_4Bw_3Bw_2BwB$, w_3w_2BwBwA, $w_2BwBwAw_2A$, $wBwAw_2Aw_3A$, $wAw_2Aw_3w_4A$
POS features	pB, p_2B, p_3B , pA, p_2A, p_3A, $pBpA$, p_2BpB, pAp_2A, $pBwB$, $pAwA$, p_2Bw_2B, p_2Aw_2A, p_2BpBpA, $pBpAp_2A$, pAp_2Ap_3A
NP_1	$headWord$, *npWords*, *NC*, *adj&headWord*, *adjTag&headWord*, *adj&NC*, *adjTag&NC*, *npTags&headWord*, *npTags&NC*
NP_2	*headWord&headPOS*, *headNumber*
wordsAfterNP	*headWord&wordAfterNP*, *npWords&wordAfterNP*, *headWord&2wordsAfterNP*, *npWords&2wordsAfterNP*, *headWord&3wordsAfterNP*, *npWords&3wordsAfterNP*
wordBeforeNP	$wB\&f_i\ \forall i \in NP_1$
Verb	$verb$, *verb*&$f_i\ \forall i \in NP_1$
Preposition	*prep*&$f_i\ \forall i \in NP_1$
Source	the word used by the original writer
LM	a binary feature assigned by a language model

Table 3: **Features used in the article error correction system.** wB and wA denote the word immediately before and after the target, respectively; and pB and pA denote the POS tag before and after the target. *headWord* denotes the head of the NP complement. NC stands for noun compound and is active if second to last word in the NP is tagged as a noun. *Verb* features are active if the NP is the direct object of a verb. *Preposition* features are active if the NP is immediately preceded by a preposition. *adj* feature is active if the first word (or the second word preceded by an adverb) in the NP is an adjective. *npWords* and *npTags* denote all words (POS tags) in the NP.

3.2.1 Preposition Features

All features used in the preposition module are lexical: word n-grams in the 4-word window around the target preposition. The NB-priors classifier, which is part of our model, can only make use of the word n-gram features; it uses n-gram features of lengths 3, 4, and 5. Note that since the NB model is trained on the Google corpus, the annotated ESL training data is used only to replace the prior parameters of the model (see Rozovskaya and Roth, 2011 for more details).

3.2.2 Training the Preposition System

Correcting preposition errors requires more data to achieve performance comparable to article error correction due to the task complexity (Gamon, 2010). We found that training an AP model on the ESL training data with more sophisticated features is not as effective as training on a native English dataset of larger size. The ESL training data contains slightly over 100K preposition examples, which is several orders of magnitude smaller than the Google n-gram corpus. We use the shared task training data to replace the prior parameters of the model (see Rozovskaya and Roth, 2011 for more details). The NB-priors model does not target preposition omissions and insertions: it corrects only preposition replacements that involve the 12 most common English prepositions. The task includes mistakes that cover 36 prepositions but we found that the model performance drops once the confusion set becomes too large. Table 5 shows the performance of the system on the 5-fold CV on the training data, where each time the classifier was trained on 80% of the documents.

Model	Precision	Recall	F1
NB-priors	0.14	0.14	0.14

Table 5: **Preposition results: NB with priors.** Results on 5-fold CV. The model is trained on the Google corpus.

3.3 Correcting Nouns and Verbs

The three remaining types of errors – noun number errors, subject-verb agreement, and the various verb form mistakes – are corrected using separate NB models also trained on the Google corpus. We focus here on the selection of candidates for correction, as this strongly affects performance.

3.3.1 Candidate Selection

This stage selects the set of words that are presented as input to the classifier. This is a crucial step because it limits the performance of any system: those errors that are missed at this stage have no chance of being detected by the later stages. This is also a challenging step as the class of verbs and nouns is open, with many English verbs and nouns being compatible with multiple parts of speech. This problem does not arise in preposition and article error correction, where candidates are determined by surface form (i.e. can be determined using a closed list of prepositions or articles).

We use the POS tag and the shallow parser output to identify the set of candidates that are input to the classifiers. In particular, for nouns, we collect all words tagged as NN or NNS. Since preprocessing tools are known to make more mistakes on ESL data than on native data, this procedure does not have a perfect result on the identification of all noun mistakes. For example, we miss about 10% of noun errors due to POS/shallow parser errors. For verbs, we compared several candidate selection methods. Method (1) extracts all verbs heading a verb phrase, as identified by the shallow parser. Method (2) expands this set to words tagged with one of the verb POS tags {VB,VBN,VBG,VBD,VBP,VBZ}. However, generating candidates by selecting only those tagged as verbs is not good enough, since the POS tagger performance on ESL data is known to be suboptimal (Nagata et al., 2011), especially for verbs containing errors. For example, verbs lacking agreement markers are likely to be mistagged as nouns (Lee and Seneff, 2008). Erroneous verbs are exactly the cases that we wish to include. Method (3) adds words that are in the lemma list of common English verbs compiled using the Gigaword corpus. The last method has the highest recall on the candidate identification; it misses only 5% of verb errors, and also has better performance in the complete model. We thus use this method.

3.3.2 Noun-Verb Correction Performance

Table 6 shows the performance of the systems based on 5-fold CV on the training data. Each model is trained individually on the Google corpus, and is individually processed to optimize the respective thresholds.

Model	Precision	Recall	F1
Noun number	0.17	0.38	0.23
Subject-verb agr.	0.19	0.24	0.21
Verb form	0.07	0.20	0.10

Table 6: **Noun, subject-verb agreement and verb form results.** Results on 5-fold CV. The models are trained on the Google corpus.

4 Combined Model

In the previous sections, we described the individual components of the system developed to target specific error types. The combined model includes all of these modules, which are each applied to examples individually: there is no pipeline, and the individual predictions of the modules are then pooled.

The combined system also includes a post-processing step where we remove certain corrections of noun and verb forms that we found occur quite often but are never correct. This happens when both choices – the writer's selection and the correction – are valid but the latter is observed more frequently in the native training data. For example, the phrase "developing country" is changed to "developed country" even though both are legitimate English expressions. If a correction is frequently proposed but always results in a false alarm, we add it to a list of changes that is ignored when we generate the system output. When we generate the output on Test set, 8 unique pairs of such changes are ignored (36 pairs of changes in total).

We now show the combined results on the training data by conducting 5-fold CV, where we add one component at a time. Table 8 shows that the recall and the F1 scores improve when each component is added to the system. The final system achieves an F1 score of 0.21 on the training data in 5-fold CV.

Model	Precision	Recall	F1
Articles	0.16	0.12	0.14
+Prepositions	0.16	0.14	0.15
+Noun number	0.17	0.23	0.20
+Subject-verb agr.	0.18	0.25	0.21
+Verb form (All)	0.18	0.27	0.21

Table 7: **Results on 5-fold CV on the training data**. The article model is trained on the ESL data using AP. The other models are trained on the Google corpus. The last line shows the results, when all of the five modules are included.

5 Test Results

The previous section showed the performance of the system on the training data. In this section, we show the results on the test set. As previously, the performance improves when each component is added into the final system. However, we also note that the precision is much higher while the recall is only slightly lower. We attribute this increased precision to the observed differences in the percentage of annotated errors in training vs. test (see Section 3) and hypothesize that the training data may contain additional relevant errors that were not included in the annotation.

Besides the original official annotations announced by the organizers, another set of annotations is offered based on the combination of revised official annotations and accepted alternative annotations proposed by participants. We show in Table 8 when our system is scored based on the revised annotations, both the precision and the recall are higher. Our system achieves the highest scores out of 17 participating teams based on both the original and revised annotations.

Model	Precision	Recall	F1
Scores based on the original annotations			
Articles	0.48	0.11	0.18
+Prepositions	0.45	0.12	0.19
+Noun number	0.48	0.21	0.29
+Subject-verb agr.	0.48	0.22	0.30
+Verb form (All)	**0.46**	**0.23**	**0.31**
Scores based on the revised annotations			
All	**0.62**	**0.32**	**0.42**

Table 8: **Results on Test**. The article model is trained on the ESL data using AP. The other models are trained on the Google corpus. *All* denotes the results of the complete model that includes all of the five modules.

6 Discussion and Error Analysis

Here, we present some interesting errors that our system makes.

6.1 Error Analysis

Incorrect verb form correction: *Safety is one of the crucial problems that many countries and companies* *concerned/concerns.

Here, the phrasing requires multiple changes; to maintain the same word order, this correction would be needed in tandem with the insertion of the auxiliary "*have*" to create a passive construction.

Incorrect determiner insertion: *In this era, Engineering designs can help to provide more habitable accommodation by designing a stronger material so it's possible to create a taller and safer building, a better and efficient sanitation system to prevent* *∅/the *disease, and also by designing a way to change the condition of the inhabitable environment.*

This example requires a model of discourse at the level of recognizing when a specific disease is a focus of the text, rather than disease in general. The use of a singular construction "*a taller and safer building*" in this context is somewhat unconventional and potentially makes this distinction even harder to detect.

Incorrect verb number correction:

One current human *need/needs *that should be given priority is the search for renewable resources.*

This appears to be the result of the system heuristics intended to mitigate POS tagging errors on ESL text, where the word "*need*" is considered as a candidate verb rather thana noun; this results in an incorrect change to make the "verb" agree in number with the phrase "one human".

Incorrect determiner deletion: *This had shown that the engineering design process is essential in solving problems and it ensures that the problem is thoroughly looked into and ensure that the engineers are generating ideas that target the main problem,* *the/∅ *depletion and harmful fuel.*

In this example, local context may suggest a list structure, but the wider context indicates that the comma represents an appositive structure.

6.2 Discussion

Note that the presence of multiple errors can have very negative effects on preprocessing. For example, when an incorrect verb form is used that results in a word form commonly used as a noun, the outputs of the parsers tend to be incorrect. This limits the potential of rule-based approaches.

Machine learning approaches, on the other hand, require sufficient examples of each error type to allow robust statistical modeling of contextual features. Given the general sparsity of ESL errors, together with the additional noise introduced into more sophisticated preprocessing components by errors with overlapping contexts, it appears hard to leverage these more sophisticated tools to generate features for machine learning approaches. This motivates our use of just POS and shallow parse analysis, together with language-modeling approaches that can use counts derived from very large native corpora, to provide robust inputs for machine learning algorithms.

The interaction between errors suggests that constraints could be used to improve results by ensuring, for example, that verb number, noun number, and noun phrase determiner are consistent. This is more difficult than it may first appear for two reasons. First, the noun that is the subject of the verb under consideration may be relatively distant in the sentence (due to the presence of intervening relative clauses, for example). Second, the constraint only limits the possible correction options: the correct number for the noun in focus may depend on the form used in the preceding sentences – for example, to distinguish between a general statement about some type of entity, and a statement about a specific entity.

These observations suggest that achieving very high performance in the task of grammar correction requires sophisticated modeling of deep structure in natural language documents.

7 Conclusion

We have described our system that participated in the shared task on grammatical error correction and ranked first out of 17 participating teams. We built specialized models for the five types of mistakes that are the focus of the competition. We have also presented error analysis of the system output and discussed possible directions for future work.

Acknowledgments

This material is based on research sponsored by DARPA under agreement number FA8750-13-2-0008. The U.S. Government is authorized to reproduce and distribute reprints for Governmental purposes notwithstanding any copyright notation thereon. The views and conclusions contained herein are those of the authors and should not be interpreted as necessarily representing the official policies or endorsements, either expressed or implied, of DARPA or the U.S. Government. This research is also supported by a grant from the U.S. Department of Education and by the DARPA Machine Reading Program under Air Force Research Laboratory (AFRL) prime contract no. FA8750-09-C-018.

References

T. Brants and A. Franz. 2006. *Web 1T 5-gram Version 1*. Linguistic Data Consortium, Philadelphia, PA.

D. Dahlmeier, H.T. Ng, and S.M. Wu. 2013. Building a large annotated corpus of learner english: The nus corpus of learner english. In *Proc. of the NAACL HLT 2013 Eighth Workshop on Innovative Use of NLP for Building Educational Applications*, Atlanta, Georgia, June. Association for Computational Linguistics.

Yoav Freund and Robert E. Schapire. 1999. Large margin classification using the perceptron algorithm. *Machine Learning*.

M. Gamon. 2010. Using mostly native data to correct errors in learners' writing. In *NAACL*, pages 163–171, Los Angeles, California, June.

N. Han, M. Chodorow, and C. Leacock. 2006. Detecting errors in English article usage by non-native speakers. *Journal of Natural Language Engineering*, 12(2):115–129.

J. Lee and S. Seneff. 2008. Correcting misuse of verb forms. In *ACL*, pages 174–182, Columbus, Ohio, June. Association for Computational Linguistics.

R. Nagata, E. Whittaker, and V. Sheinman. 2011. Creating a manually error-tagged and shallow-parsed learner corpus. In *ACL*, pages 1210–1219, Portland, Oregon, USA, June. Association for Computational Linguistics.

H. T. Ng, S. M. Wu, Y. Wu, Ch. Hadiwinoto, and J. Tetreault. 2013. The conll-2013 shared task on grammatical error correction. In *Proc. of the Seventeenth Conference on Computational Natural Language Learning*. Association for Computational Linguistics.

V. Punyakanok and D. Roth. 2001. The use of classifiers in sequential inference. In *NIPS*.

N. Rizzolo and D. Roth. 2010. Learning Based Java for Rapid Development of NLP Systems. In *LREC*.

A. Rozovskaya and D. Roth. 2010a. Annotating ESL errors: Challenges and rewards. In *Proceedings of the NAACL Workshop on Innovative Use of NLP for Building Educational Applications*.

A. Rozovskaya and D. Roth. 2010b. Generating confusion sets for context-sensitive error correction. In *Proceedings of the Conference on Empirical Methods in Natural Language Processing (EMNLP)*.

A. Rozovskaya and D. Roth. 2010c. Training paradigms for correcting errors in grammar and usage. In *NAACL*.

A. Rozovskaya and D. Roth. 2011. Algorithm selection and model adaptation for esl correction tasks. In *ACL*.

A. Rozovskaya, M. Sammons, J. Gioja, and D. Roth. 2011. University of Illinois system in HOO text correction shared task.

A. Rozovskaya, M. Sammons, and D. Roth. 2012. The UI system in the hoo 2012 shared task on error correction.

CoNLL-2013 Shared Task: Grammatical Error Correction NTHU System Description

Ting-Hui Kao[+], Yu-Wei Chang[*], Hsun-Wen Chiu[*], Tzu-Hsi Yen[+], Joanne Boisson[*], Jian-Cheng Wu[+], Jason S. Chang[+]

* Institute of Information Systems and Applications
\+ Department of Computer Science

National Tsing Hua University
HsinChu, Taiwan, R.O.C. 30013
{ maxis1718, teer1990, chiuhsunwen, joseph.yen, Joanne.boisson, wujc86, jason.jschang} @gmail.com

Abstract

Grammatical error correction has been an active research area in the field of Natural Language Processing. This paper describes the grammatical error correction system developed at NTHU in participation of the CoNLL-2013 Shared Task. The system consists of four modules in a pipeline to correct errors related to determiners, prepositions, verb forms and noun number. Although more types of errors are involved that than last year's Shared Task, leading to more complicated problem this year, our system still obtain higher F-score as compared to last year. We received an overall F-measure score of 0.325, which put our system in second place among 17 systems evaluated.

1 Introduction

Grammatical error correction is a task involving automatically detecting and correcting grammatical errors and improper choices. Grammatical error correction in writing of English as a second language (L2) or foreign language (EFL) is an important issue, for there are 375 million L2 speakers and 750 million EFL speakers around the world (Graddol, 2006). Most of these non-native speakers tend to make many kinds of error in their writing. An error correction system has the short-term benefit of helping writers improve the quality of writing. In the long run, non-native writers might learn from the corrections and thus gradually gain better command of grammar and word choice.

The HOO shared task of 2012 is aimed at detecting and correcting misuse of determiners and prepositions, two types of errors accounting for only 38% of all errors. Therefore, there are a lot more errors related to other parts of speech that we have to address in this year's shared task. In this paper, we describe the system submission from NTHU. The system reads and processes a given sentence through a pipeline of four distinct modules dealing with determiners, prepositions, verb forms and noun plurality. The output of one module feeds into the next module as input. The system finally produces possibly corrected sentences.

The rest of the article is organized as follows. Section 2 describes detection and correction approach of each module in detail. Section 3 describes experiment setting and results. Then in Section 4, we discuss strengths and limitations of the proposed system and directions of future work. We conclude in Section 5.

2 System Description

The system is designed to read a sentence and process each type of errors in terms and finally produce a corrected sentence. In Section 2.1, we give an overview of the system. Then, in Sections 2.2-2.5, we describe how to correct errors related to noun number, determiner, verb tense, and preposition.

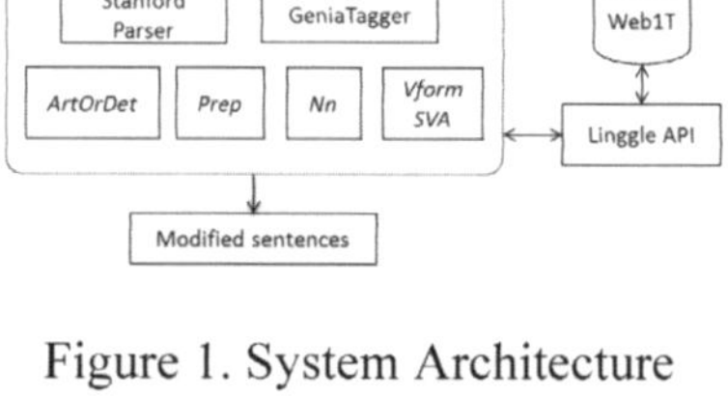

Figure 1. System Architecture

Table 1. Moving windows of '*location*'

Moving Window	*n-grams*
MW_5	track based on the **location**
	based on the **location** of
	on the **location** of cell
	the **location** of cell phone
	location of cell phone by
MW_4	based on the **location**
	on the **location** of
	the **location** of cell
	location of cell phone
MW_3	on the **location**
	the **location** of
	location of cell
MW_2	the **location**
	location of

2.1 Overview

In this section, we give an overview of our system. Figure 1 shows the architecture of the error correction system. In this study, we focus on five different grammatical error types, including the improper usage of Determiner (*ArtOrDet*), Noun Number (*Nn*), Verb-Tenses (*Vform*), Subject-Verb Agreement (*SVA*), and Preposition (*Prep*). In order to deal with these different types of errors systematically, we propose a back-off model based on the moving window approach.

Moving Window

A moving window *MW* of certain word w_i is defined as below. (Leacock et al., 2010; Rozovskaya et al., 2010)

$$MW_{i,k}(w) = \{w_{i-j}, \dots, w_{i-j+(k-1)}, j = 0, k-1\} \quad (1)$$

where *i* denotes the position of word, *k* the window size, and *w* the original or replacement word at position *i*. In our approach, the window size is set to 2 to 5 words.

For example, consider the target word "*location*" in the sentence, "*Children can easily be track based on the location of cell phone by parents.*" The n-grams in moving windows of related to "*location*" of sizes 2 to 5 are shown in Table 1.

Back-off Model

To determine whether the target word needs to be changed to a different form (e.g, from "*location*" to "*locations*"), we first replace the target word with its variant forms (e.g., '*locations*' for '*location*') in all *MW* n-grams and

Table 2. Trigram information of '*location*' and '*locations*' in back-off model

MW_3	*n-gram*	*Freq.*	S_3
location	on the **location**	304,400	4 M
	the **location** of	3,794,400	
	location of cell	1,400	
locations	on the **locations**	18,200	0.04 M
	the **locations** of	374,000	
	locations of cell	200	

then measure the ratio of the counts of the original and replaced n-grams in a corpus. The frequency counts are obtained by querying a linguistic search engine *Linggle* (Joanne Boisson et al. 2013), a web-scale linguistic search engine based on Google Web1T (Brants and Franz, 2006). The sum of n-gram counts, S_k with the word *w* (original or replacement) in the ith position is defined as

$$S_{i,k}(w) = \sum_{ngram \in MW_k(w)} count(ngram) \quad (2)$$

With *MW* and *S*, we design a `Replace` function to determine whether is necessary to replace w_i with its variant form, w':

```
function Replace(i, k, w')
    r = S_{i,k}(w')/S_{i,k}(w_i)
    if r > λ
        return True
    else if k > 2 and r > ε:
        return Replace (i, k-1, w')
    else:
        return False
```

Figure 2. The function `Replace` for determining whether to replace a word in location *i* using moving windows of size *k*.

The parameters λ and ε in `Replace` are set empirically.

For instance, in the given sentence "*Children can easily be track based on the location of cell phone by parents*", the target word w_i is '*location*' and the candidate is '*locations*' for the *Nn* type error. According to Equation 2, the sums $S_{9,3}$("*location*") of the original trigrams is about 4 million, whereas $S_{9,3}$("*locations*") of the replaced trigrams is only 0.4 million (see Table 2 for more details). The value of *r* is 0.096, and depending on the threshold, `Replace` either returns *False* or back off to consider again the ratio *r* of $S_{9,2}$("*location*") of the original bigrams and $S_{9,2}$("*locations*") of the replacement bigrams for confidence in replacing the word "*location*."

2.2 The number module

The number module is designed to correct error related to noun number (i.e., *Nn*). Two types of error are included, errors of singular noun and plural noun.

To correct errors, we identify heads of base noun phrase (i.e., NP consisting of maximal contiguous sequence of tokens without containing another noun phrase or clause) in the given sentence by using part-of-speech tags and *GeniaTagger* (Tsuruoka et al., 2006), then use the `Replace` function to replace the original nouns (either singular or plural) to a different form (i.e., singular to plural, or plural to singular). We use two methods in the number module: combining voting with back-off, and using dependency relations.

Combining voting with back-off

Each n-gram in a moving window of various sizes described in Section 2.1 gets to cast a vote. When the sum of frequency counts related to the original noun is higher than that related to the replacement noun, the original noun gets one vote and vise versa. Voting method determines whether to replace the noun based on majority of the votes. For example, all of the 14 replacement n-grams ($MW_{i,k}$, $k = 2, 5$) in Table 1 get a vote, because the n-gram with "*location*" has higher frequency count that the same n-gram replaced with "*locations*". Intuitively, we should be confident enough to decide to stay with the original noun, i.e., '*location.*'

Back-off model described in Section 2.1 make a decision to permit the `Replace` module to change the original noun depend on threshold λ. Both of voting and back-off model need to show that alternative noun number is better. For the scheme of voting and back-off model, we also require the top count ratio and absolute count of 0.95 and 60,000 based on empirical evidence.

Using dependency relations

In some cases, the noun number depends on subject-verb agreement. We use part-of-speech information of subject and governing verb obtained from a tagger to handle such cases. For that, we use 3rd person singular present (i.e., VBZ) and other verb forms (e.g., VBP) to detect noun number mistakes.

Consider the sentence, "*In the society today, there are many ideas or concept that are currently in the stages of research and development.*", where "*concept*" is a singular noun, but should be plural according to syntactic dependency information. The dependency parser typically produces *nsubj*(*are-7, concept-11*) among other relations and the word "*are*" is tagged as VBP. Accordingly, we can replace the original noun, '*concept*' to its plural form, '*concepts.*'

2.3 Determiners module

The determiner is aimed at correcting determiner errors (i.e., errors annotated as *ArtOrDet*). Given a sentence, we first identify the base noun phrases and their determiners (or lack of determiner) and using the moving window approach to decide whether there is an error and which alternative form to use. For determiner errors, the variant form of a base NP with a determiner is simple the same NP with determiner removed, while the variant form of a base NP without a determiner is simple the same NP with a determiner added.

In addition to the moving window and back-off model, we also use dependency relations to check if a determiner is required for a base noun phrase.

Frequency of n-grams

We adopt the moving window approach and combine it with the back-off model mentioned in Section 2.1 with slight modification for the cases specific to determiner errors. When the head of given Base-NP is the last word of the n-gram, (as in "*Prepare meals for the elderly is my duty.*"), the head can often be used as an modifier (as in "*for elderly people*" leading to higher counts unrelated to the our case of the word being used as the head.

Therefore, while we adopting the moving window approach, the count of such n-gram is not counted. We set the threshold in the `Replace` function empirically: λ=5 and ε=0.35.

Dependency

In some cases, the frequency information of n-grams provides limited evidence for identifying mistakes. Therefore, we use more effective rules based on dependency relations to recognize the determiner errors in a way similar to the number module.

Table 3. Verb form n-grams with PMIs.

Verb Form	n-grams	PMI	Sum
happening	crash **happening**	21.5	59.7
	happening at	38.2	
happen	crash **happen**	24.0	59.7
	happen at	35.7	
happened	crash **happened**	30.5	184.7
	happened at	43.0	
	air crash **happened**	36.2	
	happened at Miami	31.8	
	crash **happened** at	43.2	
happens	crash **happens**	27.9	107.3
	happens at	42.4	
	crash **happens** at	37.0	

We remove a determiner from a noun phrase with a plural head and an existing determiner. Otherwise, this module adds an appropriate determiner before the current noun phrase. For a conjunction (i.e., *X and/or Y*) of two base NPs, the rules favor adding a determiner such that both NPs have the same kind of determiner.

2.4 The verb-tense module

In this section, we mainly concentrate on providing more proper verb tenses. Besides moving window, we introduce accumulated point-wise mutual information (PMI) (Church and Hanks, 1990) to improve the performance of this module. Applying PMI to this topic is based on the hypothesis that an appropriate verb form has a higher PMI measure with the context.

To achieve more flexibility than the standard PMI, we use the modified PMI, which is an extension of standard PMI allowing an n-gram s of arbitrary length as input

$$PMI(s) = \log \frac{P(s|k)}{\prod_{i=1}^{k} P(w_i)} \quad (3)$$

where w_i denotes the i-th word in s, $k = |s|$, and $P(w_i)$ the probability of w_i estimated using a very large corpus. $P(s|k)$ is the probability based on maximal likelihood estimation:

$$P(s|k) = \frac{count(s)}{\sum_{t \in S} count(t)} \quad (4)$$

where S denotes all n-grams of length k. The PMI value of n-grams related to the original and alternative tense forms of a give verb are then calculated to attempt to correct the verb in question with a decision in favor of highest PMI.

Table 4. Sample search results of "being ?$PP a dangerous situation" *

N-gram	Count
being **in a** dangerous situation	161
being a dangerous situation	0
being **at a** dangerous situation	0
being **on a** dangerous situation	0
...	0
being **about** a dangerous situation	0

* Note:? denotes option word and $PP denotes wildcard prepositions

With this extended notion of PMI, we proceed as follows. First, we select each verb in a sentence and extract n-grams in moving window method as described in Section 2.2. Next, we generate more alternative n-grams by substituting all the related verb forms for the selected verb. After that, for all these n-grams, we calculate PMIs and accumulate the measures for each group of verb forms. Finally, if the accumulated PMI of the original verb is lower than the mean value of PMI of all verb forms, the verb in question will be replaced with the verb form associated the highest PMI value.

Consider the sentence, "*In late nineteenth century, there was a severe air crash happening at Miami international airport.*" We attempt to correct the verbs "*was*" and "*happening*" in the sentence. Table 3 shows n-grams and corresponding PMIs of each verb form. The accumulated PMI of "*happened*" has the maximum value. So, the module changes "*happening*" to "*happened.*"

2.5 The prepositions module

For preposition, we attempt to handle the two types of error: DELETE and REPLACE, and leave the INSERT errors for future work. For DELETE errors, the preposition in question should be deleted from the given sentence, whereas for REPLACE errors the preposition should be replaced with a more appropriate alternative. The third error type of preposition, INSERT, is left for future study. The proposed solution is based on the hypothesis that the usage of preposition often depends on the collocation relation of verb or noun. Therefore, we propose a back-off model, which utilizes the dependency relations to identify the related words of the preposition in question.

We proceed as follows: For a target preposition in a given sentence, we extract the n-gram containing the preposition, its prepositional object, and the content word before the preposition. For example, the n-gram "*being in a dangerous situation*" is extracted from the sentence "*This can protect the students from being in a dangerous situation in particularly for the small children who are studying in nursery.*" The n-gram "*being in a dangerous situation*" is then transformed into a query for a linguistic search engine (e.g., *Linggle* as described in Joanne et al. 2013) to obtain the counts of all preposition variant forms, including NULL (for DELETE) or other prepositions (for REPLACE).

The transformation process is very simple involving changing the proposition to a wild part of speech symbol. For example, "*being in a dangerous situation*" is transformed to "*being ?$PP a dangerous situation.*" The sample search results are shown in Table 4. From the results, we could confirm that the preposition "*in*" is used correctly.

Although we use the web-scale n-gram for validation of usage of preposition, however, data sparseness still poses a problem. Furthermore, we cannot obtain information for n-grams with length more than 5, since the Web 1T we used only contains 1 to 5-grams. In order to cope with the data sparseness problem, we transform a query into a more general form, if no result could be obtained in the first round of search. To generalize the query, we remove the modifiers of the prepositional object one after another. Additionally, we also attempt to change the modifiers with the most frequent modifier of the object. Consider the n-gram "*in modern digit world.*" The generalized n-grams "*in digit world*" and "*in new world*" will then be transformed into queries in turns until the results are sufficient for the model to make a decision. To avoid false alarm, empirically determined thresholds are used to measure the ratio of count of a preposition variant form to the original preposition.

3 Experiment

To assess the effectiveness of the proposed method, we used the official training and testing data of CoNLL-2013 Shared Task. We also exploited several tools including *Linggle*, *Stanford Parser* and *Geniatagger* in the proposed system.

Linggle supports flexible linguistic queries with wild part of speech and returns matching n-grams counts in Google Web 1T 5gram. *Stanford Parser* and *Geniatagger* produce syntactical information including dependency relations, part-of-speech tags, and phrase boundary. The evaluation scorer, which computes precision, recall, and F-score, is provided by National University of Singapore, the organizer of CoNLL-2013 Shared Task.

On the test data, our system obtained the precision, recall and F-score of .3057, 0.346, and .3246, which put us in first place in term of recall and second place in term of F-score.

4 Discussion

In this section, we discuss the strengths and limitations of our system and propose approaches to overcome current limitations.

The module of noun numbers, moving window and syntactic dependency for correcting errors cannot handle well some ambiguous cases. For example, in this case "*In conclusion, what I have mentioned above, we have to agree, tracking system has many benefits….*", according to the gold-standard annotations, '*system has*' is corrected to '*systems have*'.

However, this module keep the original word because of the 3rd person singular present verb, '*has*'. Before '*has*' being corrected to '*have*', there was no sufficient evidence to support that '*systems*' is a good replacement. In cases like this, it is often difficult to suggest a correction using only the sentential context and n-gram frequency and dependency relations. To correct such an error, we may need to consider the context of the discourse or combine the module of different error types such as noun numbers and verb tense, which is beyond the scope of the current system.

We handle the determiner errors with threshold λ and ε empirically derived, but it would be more effective if we could use some form of minimal error rate tuning (MERT) to set the parameters. Besides, we found that applying the dependency criteria and moving window method in parallel leads to high recall but low precision. However, the moving window method often fails because of insufficient evidence. In such case, the system can perform better in both precision and recall by favoring the dependency model output.

For our system, the performance of correcting verb form errors is severely limited by the lengths of n-gram. The failure related to verb forms correction are mostly caused by the limitation of n-gram length of Web 1T. There is a large portion of sentences where the subject (or the adverbs) and the verb are so far apart, that they are not within windows of five words. So, it is difficult to use the noun number of the subject to select the correct verb form.

Another major area of limitations of handling verb form errors has to do with rare words which lead to unseen n-grams even in a very large dataset like Web 1T. These rare words are mostly name entities that have insufficient coverage when combined other words in n-grams. Intuitively, we can generalize the n-gram matching process as in the case of handling preposition errors.

In this study, we use the preposition and object relation (POBJ) to determine whether the use of the preposition is correct. The relation is useful for generalizing the queries and in correcting preposition errors. However, many preposition errors are unrelated to POBJ. For example, in the sentence "*Surveillance technology will help to prevent the family to loss their member...*", the two words "*to loss*" should be replace with "*from losing.*" Unfortunately, the current system cannot correct such an error in the absence of POBJ relation. In order to correct this kind of error, we have to consider composed relations such as noun-preposition-verb, which is crucial to the capability of correcting such multiple consecutive errors (i.e., preposition plus verb).

5 Conclusion

In this paper, we build four modules in determiner, noun number, verb form, and preposition for error detection and correction. For different types of errors, we have developed modules independently in accordance with their features. The constructed modules rely on both moving windows and back-off model to improve grammatical error correction. Additionally, for verb form errors, we introduce point-wise mutual information for higher precision and recall.

We plan to integrate all the modules in a more flexible way than the current pipeline scheme. Yet another direction for future research is to consider the discourse context.

6 Acknowledgements

We would like to acknowledge the funding supports from Delta Electronic Corp and National Science Council, Taiwan (contract no: NSC 100-2511-S-007-005-MY3). We are also thankful for helpful comments from the anonymous reviewers.

References

Joanne Boisson, Ting-Hui Kao, Jian-Cheng Wu, Tzu-Hsi Yen and Jason S. Chang. 2013. Linggle: a Web-scale Linguistic Search Engine for Words in Context. In *proceedings of Association for Computational Linguistics demonstrations*. (*ACL 2013*)

Thorsten Brants and Alex Franz. 2006. The Google Web 1T 5-gram corpus version 1.1.LDC2006T13

Kenneth W. Church and Patrick Hanks. 1990. Word association norms, mutual information, and lexicography. Computational Linguistics 16(1) (1990) 22–29

Leacock Claudia et al. 2010. Automated grammatical error detection for language learners. *Synthesis Lectures on Human Language Technologies,* 3(1) 1–134.

Daniel Dahlmeier, Hwee Tou Ng, Siew Mei Wu. 2013. Building a Large Annotated Corpus of Learner English: The NUS Corpus of Learner English. In *Proceedings of the 8th Workshop on Innovative Use of NLP for Building Educational Applications* (*BEA 2013*).

Daniel Dahlmeier and Hwee Tou Ng. 2012. Better Evaluation for Grammatical Error Correction. In *Proceedings of the 2012 Conference of the North American Chapter of the Association for Computational Linguistics* (*NAACL 2012*). pp. 568 – 572

David Graddol. 2006. English next: Why global English may mean the end of 'English as a Foreign Language.' UK: British Council.

John Lee and Stephanie Seneff. 2006. Automatic Grammar Correction for Second-Language Learners. In *INTERSPEECH ICSLP.*

Hwee Tou Ng, Siew Mei Wu, Yuanbin Wu, Christian Hadiwinoto and Joel Tetreault. 2013. The CoNLL-2013 Shared Task on Grammatical Error Correction. In *Proceedings of the Seventeenth Conference on Computational Natural Language Learning.*

Alla Rozovskaya and Dan Roth. 2010. Generating confusion sets for context-sensitive error correction. In *Proceedings of EMNLP*, pp. 961–970.

Yoshimasa Tsuruoka et al. Developing a Robust Part-of-Speech Tagger for Biomedical Text. In *Advances in Informatics - 10th Panhellenic Conference on Informatics*, pp 382–392.

NAIST at 2013 CoNLL Grammatical Error Correction Shared Task

Ippei Yoshimoto, Tomoya Kose, Kensuke Mitsuzawa, Keisuke Sakaguchi,
Tomoya Mizumoto, Yuta Hayashibe, Mamoru Komachi, Yuji Matsumoto
Nara Institute of Science and Technology
8916-5 Takayama, Ikoma, Nara 630-0192, Japan
{ippei-y,tomoya-kos,kensuke-mi,keisuke-sa,tomoya-m,yuta-h,komachi,matsu}@is.naist.jp

Abstract

This paper describes the Nara Institute of Science and Technology (NAIST) error correction system in the CoNLL 2013 Shared Task. We constructed three systems: a system based on the Treelet Language Model for verb form and subject-verb agreement errors; a classifier trained on both learner and native corpora for noun number errors; a statistical machine translation (SMT)-based model for preposition and determiner errors. As for subject-verb agreement errors, we show that the Treelet Language Model-based approach can correct errors in which the target verb is distant from its subject. Our system ranked fourth on the official run.

1 Introduction

Grammatical error correction is the task of automatically detecting and correcting grammatical errors in text, especially text written by second language learners. Its purpose is to assist learners in writing and helps them learn languages.

Last year, HOO 2012 (Dale et al., 2012) was held as a shared task on grammatical error correction, focusing on prepositions and determiners. The CoNLL-2013 shared task (Dahlmeier et al., 2013) includes these areas and also noun number, verb form, and subject-verb agreement errors.

We divide the above 5 error types into three groups: (1) subject-verb agreement (*SVA*) and verb form (*Vform*) errors, (2) noun number (*Nn*) errors, and (3) preposition (*Prep*) and determiner (*ArtOrDet*) errors. For the subject-verb agreement and verb form errors, we used a syntactic language model, the Treelet Language Model, because syntactic information is important for verb error correction. For the noun number errors, we used a binary classifier trained on both learner and native corpora. For the preposition and determiner errors, we adopt a statistical machine translation (SMT)-based approach, aiming at correcting errors in conventional expressions. After each subsystem corrects the errors of the corresponding error types, we merge the outputs of all the subsystems.

The result shows our system achieved 21.85 in F-score on the formal run before revision and 28.14 after revision.

The rest of this paper is organized as follows. Section 2 presents an overview of related work. Section 3 describes the system architecture of each of the three subsystems. Section 4 shows experimental settings and results. Section 5 presents discussion. Section 6 concludes this paper.

2 Related Work

Lee and Seneff (2008) tried correcting English verb errors including *SVA* and *Vform*. They proposed correction candidates with template matching on parse trees and filtered candidates by utilizing *n*-gram counts. Our system suggests candidates based on the Part-Of-Speech (POS) tag of a target word and filters them by using a syntactic language model.

For the noun number errors, we improved the system proposed by Izumi et al. (2003). In Izumi et al. (2003), a noun number error detection method is a part of an automatic error detection system for transcribed spoken English by Japanese learners. They used a maximum entropy method whose features are unigrams, bigrams and trigrams of surface words, of POS tags and of the root forms. They trained a classifier on only a learner corpus. The main difference between theirs and ours is a domain of the training corpus and features we used. We trained a classifier on the mixed corpus of the leaner corpus and the native corpus. We employ a treepath feature in our system.

Our SMT system for correcting preposition and

determiner errors is based on Mizumoto et al. (2012). They constructed a translation model from the data of the language-exchange social network service Lang-8[1] and evaluated its performance for 18 error types, including preposition and determiner errors in the Konan-JIEM Learner Corpus. On preposition error correction, they showed that their SMT system outperformed a system using a maximum entropy model. The main difference with this work is that our new corpus collection here is about three times larger.

3 System Architecture

3.1 Subject-Verb Agreement and Verb Form

For *SVA* and *Vform* errors, we used the Treelet Language Model (Pauls and Klein, 2012) to capture syntactic information and lexical information simultaneously. We will first show examples of *SVA* and *Vform* errors and then describe our model used to correct them. Finally, we explain the procedure for error correction.

3.1.1 Errors

According to Lee and Seneff (2008), both *SVA* and *Vform* errors are classified as syntactic errors. Examples are as follows:

Subject-Verb Agreement (SVA) The verb is not correctly inflected in number and person with respect to its subject.

They ***has** *been to Nara many times.*

In this example, a verb "*has*" is wrongly inflected. It should be "*have*" because its subject is the pronoun "*they*".

Verb Form (Vform) This type of error mainly consists of two subtypes,[2] one of which includes auxiliary agreement errors.

They have ***be** *to Nara many times.*

Since the "*have*" in this sentence is an auxiliary verb, the "*be*" is incorrectly inflected and it should be "*been*".

The other subtype includes complementation errors like the following:

They want ***go** *to Nara this summer.*

Verbs can be a complement of another verb and preposition. The "*go*" in the above sentence is incorrect. It should be in the infinitive form, "*to go*".

3.1.2 Treelet Language Model

We used the Treelet Language Model (Pauls and Klein, 2012) for *SVA* and *Vform* error correction.

Our model assigns probability to a production rule of the form $r = P \rightarrow C_1 \cdots C_d$ in a constituent tree T, conditioned on a context h consisting of previously generated treelets,[3] where P is the parent symbol of a rule r and $C_1^d = C_1 \cdots C_d$ are its children.

$$p(r) = p(C_1^d|h)$$

The probability of a constituent tree T is given by the following equation:

$$p(T) = \prod_{r \in T} p(r)$$

The context h differs depending on whether C_1^d is a terminal symbol or a sequence of non-terminal symbols.

Terminal When C_1^d is a terminal symbol w,

$$p(C_1^d|h) = p(w|P, R, r', w_{-1}, w_{-2})$$

where P is the POS tag of w, R is the right sibling of P, r' is the production rule which yields P and its siblings, and w_{-2} and w_{-1} are the two words preceding w.

Non-Terminal When C_1^d is a sequence of non-terminal symbols,

$$p(C_1^d|h) = p(C_1^d|P, P', r')$$

where P is the parent symbol of C_1^d, P' is the parent symbol of P.

In order to capture a richer context, we apply the annotation and transformation rules below to parse trees in order. We use almost the same annotation and transformation rules as those proposed by

[1] `http://lang-8.com`

[2] In the NUCLE (Dahlmeier et al., 2013) corpus, most of semantic errors related to verbs are included in other error types such as verb tense errors, not *Vform* errors.

[3] The term *treelet* is used to refer to an arbitrary connected subgraph of a tree (Quirk et al., 2005)

Original	Candidates
am/VBP, are/VBP or is/VBZ	{am/VBP, are/VBP, is/VBZ}
was/VBD or were/VBD	{was/VBD, were/VBD}
being/VBG	{be/VB, being/VBG}
been/VBN	{be/VB, been/VBN}
be/VB	{be/VB, being/VBG, been/VBN}

Table 1: Examples of candidates in the case of *"be"*

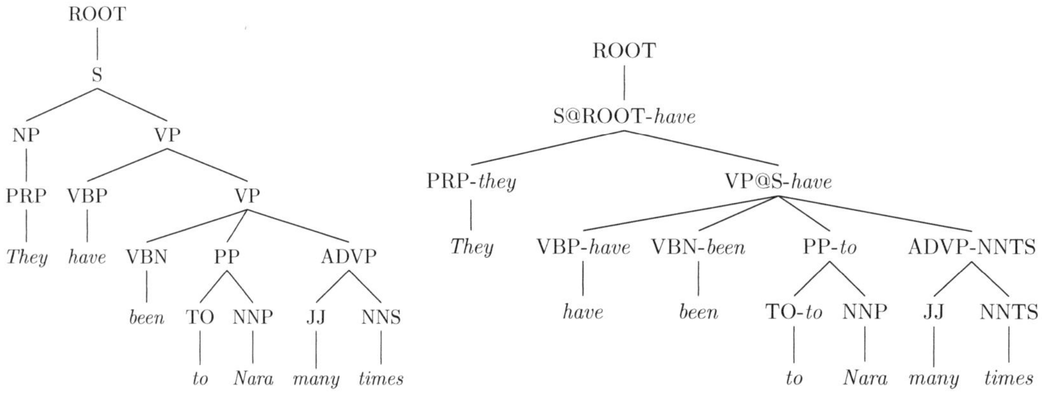

Figure 1: The tree on the left is before annotations and transformations which convert it to the tree on the right.

Pauls and Klein (2012). For instance, the common CFG tree on the left side of Figure 1 is transformed to the one on the right side.

Temporal NPs Pauls and Klein (2012) marked every noun which is the head of an NP-TMP at least once in the Penn Treebank. For example, NN → *time* is replaced with NNT → *time* and NNS → *times* is replaced with NNTS → *times*. This rule seems to be useful for correcting verb tense errors.[4]

Head Annotations We annotated every non-terminal and preterminal with its head word.[5] If the head word is not a closed class word,[6] we annotated non-terminal symbols with the head POS tag instead of the head word.

NP Flattening Pauls and Klein (2012) deleted NPs dominated by other NPs, unless the child NPs are in coordination or apposition. These NPs typically occur when nouns are modified by PPs. Our model therefore assigns probability to nouns conditioned on the head of modifying PPs with prepositions such as *"in"*, *"at"* and so on by applying simultaneously the NP Flattening and the Head Annotations. However, our model cannot assign probability to prepositions conditioned on verbs or nouns on which the prepositions depend. For this reason we did not use our model to correct prepositional errors.

Number Annotations Pauls and Klein (2012) divided numbers into five classes: CD-YR for numbers that consist of four digits, which are usually years; CD-NM for entirely numeric numbers; CD-DC for numbers that have a decimal; CD-MX for numbers that mix letters and digits; and CD-AL for numbers that are entirely alphabetic.

SBAR Flattening They removed any S nodes which are children of an SBAR.

VP Flattening They removed any VPs immediately dominated by a VP, unless it is conjoined with another VP. The chains of verbs are represented as separated VPs for each verb, such as `(VP (MD will) (VP (VB be) (VP (VBG`

[4]Verb tense (*Vt*) errors are not covered in this shared task.

[5]We identified the head with almost the same rules used in Collins (1999).

[6]We took the following to be the closed class words: all inflections of the verbs do, be, and have; and any word tagged with IN, WDT, PDT, WP, WP$, TO, WRB, RP, DT, SYM, EX, POS, PRP, AUX, MD or CC.

playing) ...))). This transformation turns the above VPs into (VP (MD will) (VB be) (VBG playing) ...). This has an effect on the correction of auxiliary agreement errors because our model can assign probability to main verbs strongly conditioned on their auxiliary verbs.

Gapped Sentence Annotation They annotated all S and SBAR nodes that have a VP before any NP.

Parent Annotation They annotated all VPs and children of the *ROOT* node with their parent symbol.

Unary Deletion All unary rules are deleted except the root and the preterminal rules. We kept only the bottom-most symbol of the unary rule chain. This brings many symbols into the context of a production rule.

3.1.3 Procedure

Our system for *SVA* and *Vform* errors tries to correct the words in a sentence from left to right. Correction proceeds in the following steps.

1. If the POS tag of the word is "*VB*", "*VBD*", "*VBG*", "*VBN*", "*VBP*" or "*VBZ*", our system generates sentences which have the word replaced with candidates. For example, if the original word is an inflection of "*be*", the system generates candidates as shown in Table 1.

2. The system parses those sentences and obtains the k-best parses for each sentence.

3. The system keeps only the one sentence to which our language model assigned the highest probability in the parses.

4. The system repeats Steps 1 to 3 with the sentence kept in Step 3 until the rightmost word of that sentence.

Note that the system uses the Berkeley Parser[7] in Step 2.

3.2 Noun Number

3.2.1 Errors

A noun number error is the mistake of using the singular form for a plural noun, and vice versa, as in the following:

*I saw many ****student*** *yesterday.*

In this example, the inflection of *"student"* is mistaken. It should be *"students"* because it is modified by *"many"*.

To correct such errors, we use a binary classification approach because the inflection of a noun is either "singular" or "plural". If the binary classifier detects an error with a sufficiently high confidence, the system changes the noun form. We adopt the adaptive regularization of weight vectors algorithm (*AROW*) (Crammer et al., 2009). *AROW* is a variant of a confidence weighted linear classification algorithm which is suitable for the classification of large scale data.

3.2.2 Binary classifier approach

The binary classifier indicates "singular" or "plural" for all nouns except proper and uncountable nouns. First, if a noun is found in the training corpus, we extract an instance with features created by the feature template in Table 2.[8] Second, we train a classifier with extracted instances and labels from the training corpus.

We use unigram, bigram, and trigram features around the target word and the path features between the target word and all the other nodes in the NPs that dominate the target word as the rightmost constituent. The path feature is commonly used in semantic role labeling tasks (Pradhan et al., 2004). For the path features, we do not use the right subtree of the NP as the path features because we assume that right subtrees do not affect the number of the target word. We limit the maximum depth of the subtree containing the NP to be *3* because nodes over this limit may be noisy. To encode the relationship between the target word and another node in the NP, we append a symbol which reflects the direction of tree traversal to the label: *'p'* for going up (parent) and *'c'* for going down (child). For example, we show extracted features in Table 2 for the phrase *"some interesting and recent topics about politics and economics"*.

In the training corpus, since the proportions of singular and plural nouns are unequal, we set different thresholds for classifying singular and plural forms. These thresholds limit the probabilities which the binary classifier uses for error detection. We have used a development set to determine the

[7] http://code.google.com/p/berkeleyparser/

[8] Target word refers to a noun whose POS tag is "NN" or "NNS" in the Penn Treebank tagset.

Feature name	Word, Pos used as features	Example
surface unigram	word±1, word±2	and, recent, about, politics
surface bigram	word±2_word±1	and_recent, about_politics
surface trigram	word±3_word±2_word±1	interesting_and_recent, about_politics_and
POS unigram	POS±1, POS±2	CC, JJ, IN, NN
POS bigram	POS±1_POS±2	CC_JJ, IN_NN
POS trigram	POS±3_POS±2_POS±1	JJ_CC_JJ, IN_NN_CONJ
lemma unigram	lemma±2, lemma±1	and, recent, about, politics
lemma bigram	lemma±2_lemma±1	and_recent, about_politics
lemma trigram	lemma±3_lemma±2_lemma±1	interesting_and_recent, about_politics_and
lemma target	lemma of target word	topic
path feature	path between the target word and the other nodes in NP	p_NP, pc_JJ, pc_recent, pp_NP, ppc_CC, ppc_and, ppc_NP, ppcc_DT, ppcc_some, ppcc_JJ, ppcc_interesting

Table 2: Features used for the detection of noun number errors and example features for the phrase "some interesting and recent topics about politics and economics".

best thresholds for singular and plural forms, respectively.

For proper and uncountable nouns, we do not change number because of the nature of those nouns. In order to determine whether to change number or not, we create a list which consists of words frequently used as singular forms in the native corpus.

3.3 Prepositions and Determiners

For preposition and determiner errors, we construct a system using a phrase-based statistical machine translation (Koehn et al., 2003) framework. The SMT-based approach functions well in corrections of conventional usage of determiners and prepositions such as "*the young*" and "*take care of*". The characteristic of the SMT-based approach is its ability to capture tendencies in learners' errors. This approach translates erroneous phrases that learners often make to correct phrases. Hence, it can handle errors in conventional expressions without over-generalization.

The phrase-based SMT framework which we used is based on the log-linear model (Och and Ney, 2002), where the decision rule is expressed as follow:

$$\underset{e}{\text{argmax}}\, P(e|f) = \underset{e}{\text{argmax}} \sum_{m=1}^{M} \lambda_m h_m(e,f)$$

Here, f is an input sentence, e are hypotheses, $h_m(e,f)$ feature functions and λ_m their weights. The hypothesis that maximizes the weighted sum of the feature functions is chosen as an output sentence.

The feature functions encode components of the phrase-based SMT, including the translation model and the language model. The translation model suggests translation hypotheses and the language model filters out ill-formed hypotheses.

For an error correction system based on SMT, the translation model is constructed from pairs of original sentences and corrected sentences, and the language model is built on a native corpus (Brockett et al., 2006).

Brockett et al. (2006) trained the translation model on a corpus where the errors are restricted to mass noun errors. In our case, we trained our model on a corpus with no restriction on error types. Consequently, the system corrects all types of errors. To focus on preposition and determiner errors, we retain proposed edits that include 48 prepositions and 25 determiners listed in Table 3.

4 Experiments

4.1 Experimental setting

4.1.1 Subject-Verb Agreement and Verb Form

We describe here the training data and tools used to train our model. Our model was trained with the Berkeley LM[9] version 1.1.3. We constructed the training data by concatenating the WSJ sections of the Penn Treebank and the AFP sections of the English Gigaword Corpus version 5.[10] Our training data consists of about 27 million sentences. Although human-annotated parses for the WSJ are available, there is no gold standard for the AFP, so we parsed the AFP automatically by using the Berkeley Parser released on October 9, 2012.

[9] http://code.google.com/p/berkeleylm/
[10] LDC2011T07

Preposition	about, across, after, against, along, among, around, as, at, before, behind, below, beside, besides, between, beyond, but, by, despite, down, during, for, from, in, inside, into, near, of, off, on, onto, opposite, outside, over, past, round, without, than, through, to, toward, towards, under, until, up, upon, with, within
Determiner	the, a, an, all, these, those, many, much, another, no, some, any, my, our, their, her, his, its, no, each, every, certain, its, this, that

Table 3: Preposition and determiner lists

4.1.2 Noun Number

We trained a binary classifier on a merged corpus of the English Gigaword and the NUCLE data. From the English Gigaword corpus, we used the New York Times (NYT) as a training corpus. In order to create the training corpus, we corrected all but noun number errors in the NUCLE data using gold annotations.

The AROW++ [11] 0.1.2 was used for the binary classification. For changing noun forms, we used the pattern.en toolkit.[12]

The maximum depth of subtrees containing an NP is set to *3* when we extracted the path features.

We built and used a list of nouns that appear in singular forms frequently in a native corpus. We counted the frequency of nouns in entire English Gigaword. If a noun appears in more than 99%[13] of occurrences in singular form, we included it in the list. The resulting list contains 836 nouns.

4.1.3 Prepositions and Determiners

We used Moses 2010-08-13 with default parameters for our decoder[14] and GIZA++ 1.0.5[15] as the alignment tool. The grow-diag-final heuristics was applied for phrase extraction. As a language modeling tool we used IRSTLM version 5.80[16] with Witten-Bell smoothing.

The translation model was trained on the NUCLE corpus and our Lang-8 corpus.[17] From the Lang-8 corpus, we filtered out noisy sentences. Out of 1,230,257 pairs of sentences, 1,217,124 pairs of sentences were used for training. As for the NUCLE corpus we used 55,151 pairs of sentences from the official data provided as training data. We used a 3-gram language model built on the entire English Gigaword corpus.

[11] `https://code.google.com/p/arowpp/`

[12] `http://www.clips.ua.ac.be/pages/pattern-en`

[13] We tested many thresholds, and set 99% as threshold.

[14] `http://sourceforge.net/projects/mosesdecoder/`

[15] `http://code.google.com/p/giza-pp/`

[16] `http://sourceforge.net/projects/irstlm/`

[17] consisting of entries through 2012.

4.2 Result

Table 4 shows the overall results of our submitted systems and the results of an additional experiment. In the additional experiment, we tried the SMT-based approach described in Section 3.3 for errors in *SVA*, *Vform* and *Nn*. While the system based on the Treelet Language Model outperformed the SMT-based system on the *SVA* errors and the *Vform* errors, the binary classifier approach did not perform as well as the SMT-based system on the *Nn* errors.

5 Discussion

5.1 Subject-Verb Agreement and Verb Form

We provide here examples of our system's output, beginning with a successful example.

source: *This is an age which most people* ****is*** *retired and* ****has*** *no sources of incomes.*

hypothesis: *This is an age which most people* ***are*** *retired and* ***have*** *no sources of incomes.*

The source sentence of this pair includes two *SVA* errors. The first is that "*be*" should agree with its subject "*people*" and must be "*are*". Our system is able to correct errors where the misinflected predicate is adjacent to its subject. The second error is also an agreement error, in this case between "*have*" and its subject "*people*". Our model can assign probability to yields related to predicates conditioned strongly on their subjects even if the distance between the predicate and its subject is long. The same can be said of *Vform* errors.

One mistake made by our system is miscorrection due to the negative effect of other errors.

source/hypothesis: *The rising life* ****expectancies*** ****are*** *like a two side sword to the modern world.*

		submitted system					additional experiments	
		ALL	Verb	Nn	Prep	ArtOrDet	Verb	Nn
original	Precision	0.2707	0.1378	0.4452	0.2649	0.3118	0.2154	0.3687
	Recall	0.1832	0.2520	0.1641	0.1286	0.2029	0.0569	0.2020
	F-score	0.2185	0.1782	0.2399	0.1732	0.2458	0.0900	0.2610
revised	Precision	0.3392	0.1814	0.5578	0.3245	0.4027	0.3846	0.4747
	Recall	0.2405	0.2867	0.1708	0.1494	0.2497	0.0880	0.2137
	F-score	0.2814	0.2222	0.2616	0.2046	0.3082	0.1433	0.2947

Table 4: Results of the submitted system for each type of error and results of additional experiments with the SMT-based system. The score is evaluated on the m2scorer (Dahlmeier and Ng, 2012). ALL is the official result of formal run, and each of the others shows the result of the corresponding error type. Since our system did not distinguish *SVA* and *Vform*, we report the combined result for them in the column Verb.

gold: *The rising life* ***expectancy is*** *like a two side sword to the modern world.*

Since the subject of "*are*" is "*expectancies*", the sentence looks correct at first. However, this example includes not only an *SVA* error but also an *Nn* error, and therefore the predicate "*are*" should be corrected along with correcting its subject "*expectancies*".

An example of a *Vform* error is shown below.

source/hypothesis: *Besides, we can try to reduce the bad effect* ****cause*** *by the new technology.*

gold: *Besides, we can try to reduce the bad effect* ***caused*** *by the new technology.*

The word "*cause*" is tagged as "*NN*" in this sentence. This error is ignored because our system makes corrections on the basis of the original POS tag. For a similar example, our system does not make modifications between the *to*-infinitive and the other forms.

5.2 Noun Number

We provide here examples of our system's output, beginning with a successful example.

source: *many of cell* ****phone*** *are equipped with GPS*

hypothesis/gold: *many of cell* ***phones*** *are equipped with GPS*

In the example, the noun *"phone"* should be in the plural form *"phones"*. This is because the phrase *"many of"* modifies the noun. In this case, the unigrams *"many"* and *"are"*, and the bigram *"many of"* are features with strong weights for the plural class as expected.

However, n-gram features sometimes work to the contrary of our expectations.

source/hypothesis: *RFID is not only used to track products for logistical and storage* ****purpose****, it is also used to track people*

gold: *RFID is not only used to track products for logistical and storage* ***purposes****, it is also used to track people*

The *"purpose"* is in the PP which is modified by *"products"*. Thus, *"purpose"* should not be affected by the following words. However, the verb *"is"*, which is immediately after *"purpose"*, has a strong influence to keep the word in singular form. Therefore, it may be better not to use a verb that the word is not immediately dependent on as a feature.

5.3 Prepositions and Determiners

While the SMT-based system can capture the statistics of learners' errors, it cannot correct phrases that are not found in the training corpus.

(1) **source:** ****with*** *economic situation*
gold: ***in*** *economic situation*

(2) **source:** ****with*** *such situation*
gold: ***in*** *such situation*

Our system was not able to correct the source phrase in (1), in spite of the fact that the similar phrase pair (2) was in the training data. To correct such errors, we should construct a system that allows a gap in source and target phrases as in Galley and Manning (2010).

6 Conclusion

This paper described the architecture of our correction system for errors in verb forms, subject verb agreement, noun number, prepositions and determiners. For verb form and subject verb agreement errors, we used the Treelet Language Model. By taking advantage of rich syntactic information, it corrects subject-verb agreement errors which need to be inflected according to a distant subject. For noun number errors, we used a binary classifier using both learner and native corpora. For preposition and determiner errors, we built an SMT-based system trained on a larger corpus than those used in prior works. We show that our subsystems are effective to each error type. On the other hand, our system cannot handle the errors strongly related to other errors well. In future work we will explore joint correction of multiple error types, especially noun number and subject-verb agreement errors, which are closely related to each other.

Acknowledgements

We would like to thank Yangyang Xi for giving us permission to use text from Lang-8 and the anonymous reviewers for helpful comments.

References

Chris Brockett, William B. Dolan, and Michael Gamon. 2006. Correcting ESL errors using phrasal smt techniques. In *Proceedings of COLING/ACL 2006*, pages 249–256.

Michael Collins. 1999. *Head-Driven Statistical Models for Natural Language Parsing*. Ph.D. thesis, University of Pennsylvania.

Koby Crammer, Alex Kulesza, and Mark Dredze. 2009. Adaptive regularization of weight vectors. In *Proceedings of NIPS 2009*, pages 414–422.

Daniel Dahlmeier and Hwee Tou Ng. 2012. Better evaluation for grammatical error correction. In *Proceedings of NAACL 2012*, pages 568–572.

Daniel Dahlmeier, Hwee Tou Ng, and Siew Mei Wu. 2013. Building a large annotated corpus of learner english: The NUS corpus of learner English. In *Proceedings of BEA 2013*, pages 313–330.

Robert Dale, Ilya Anisimoff, and George Narroway. 2012. HOO 2012: a report on the preposition and determiner error correction shared task. In *Proceedings of BEA 2012*, pages 54–62.

Michel Galley and Christopher D. Manning. 2010. Accurate non-hierarchical phrase-based translation. In *Processing of HLT/NAACL 2010*, pages 966–974.

Emi Izumi, Kiyotaka Uchimoto, Toyomi Saiga, Thepchai Supnithi, and Hitoshi Isahara. 2003. Automatic error detection in the Japanese learners' English spoken data. In *Proceedings of ACL 2003*, pages 145–148.

Philipp Koehn, Franz Josef Och, and Daniel C Marcu. 2003. Statistical phrase-based translation. In *Proceedings of HLT/NAACL 2003*, pages 48–54.

John Lee and Stephanie Seneff. 2008. Correcting misuse of verb forms. In *Proceedings of ACL 2008*, pages 174–182.

Tomoya Mizumoto, Yuta Hayashibe, Mamoru Komachi, Masaaki Nagata, and Yuji Matsumoto. 2012. The effect of learner corpus size in grammatical error correction of ESL writings. In *Proceedings of COLING 2012*, pages 863–872.

Franz Josef Och and Hermann Ney. 2002. Discriminative training and maximum entropy models for statistical machine translation. In *Proceedings of ACL 2002*, pages 295–302.

Adam Pauls and Dan Klein. 2012. Large-scale syntactic language modeling with treelets. In *Proceedings of ACL 2012*, pages 959–968.

Sameer S Pradhan, Wayne H Ward, Kadri Hacioglu, James H Martin, and Dan Jurafsky. 2004. Shallow semantic parsing using support vector machines. In *Proceedings of HLT/NAACL 2004*, pages 233–240.

Chris Quirk, Arul Menezes, and Colin Cherry. 2005. Dependency treelet translation: Syntactically informed phrasal SMT. In *Proceedings of ACL 2005*, pages 271–279.

UM-Checker: A Hybrid System for English Grammatical Error Correction

Junwen Xing, Longyue Wang, Derek F. Wong, Lidia S. Chao, Xiaodong Zeng
Natural Language Processing & Portuguese-Chinese Machine Translation Laboratory,
Department of Computer and Information Science,
University of Macau, Macau S.A.R., China
nlp2ct.{vincent, anson}@gmail.com,
{derekfw, lidiasc}@umac.mo, nlp2ct.samuel@gmail.com

Abstract

This paper describes the NLP²CT Grammatical Error Detection and Correction system for the CoNLL 2013 shared task, with a focus on the errors of article or determiner (*ArtOrDet*), noun number (*Nn*), preposition (*Prep*), verb form (*Vform*) and subject-verb agreement (*SVA*). A hybrid model is adopted for this special task. The process starts with spell-checking as a preprocessing step to correct any possible erroneous word. We used a Maximum Entropy classifier together with manually rule-based filters to detect the grammatical errors in English. A language model based on the Google *N*-gram corpus was employed to select the best correction candidate from a confusion matrix. We also explored a graph-based label propagation approach to overcome the sparsity problem in training the model. Finally, a number of deterministic rules were used to increase the precision and recall. The proposed model was evaluated on the test set consisting of 50 essays and with about 500 words in each essay. Our system achieves the 5th and 3rd F_1 scores on official test set among all 17 participating teams based on gold-standard edits before and after revision, respectively.

1 Introduction

With the increasing number of people all over the world who study English as their second language[1], grammatical errors in writing often occurs due to cultural diversity, language habits, education background, etc. Thus, there is a substantial and increasing need of using computer techniques to improve the writing ability for second language learners. Grammatical error correction is the task of automatically detecting and correction erroneous word usage and ill-formed grammatical constructions in text (Dahlmeier et al., 2012).

In recent decades, this special task has gained more attention by some organizations such as the Helping Our Own (HOO) challenge (Dale and Kilgarriff, 2010; Dale et al., 2012). Although the performance of grammatical error correction systems has been improved, it is still mostly limited to dealing with the determiner and preposition error types with a very low recall and precision. This year, the CoNLL-2013 shared task extends to include a more comprehensive list of error types, as shown in Table 1.

To take on this challenge, this paper proposes pipe-line architecture in combination with several error detection and correction models based on a hybrid approach. As a preprocessing step we firstly employ a spelling correction to correct the misspelled words. To correct the grammatical errors, a hybrid system is designed that integrated with Maximum Entropy (ME) classifier, deterministic filter and N-gram language model scorer, each of which is constructed as an individual model. According to the phenomena of the problems, we use different combinations of the models trained on specific data to tackle the corresponding types of errors. For instance, *Prep* and *Nn* have a strong inter-relation with the words (surface) that are preceding and following the active word. This can be detected and recovered by using a language model. On the other hand, *SVA* is more complicated and it is more effective to determine the mistakes by using the linguistic and grammatical rules. The correction

[1] A well-known fact is that the most popular language chosen as a first foreign language is English.

Error Type	Description	Example
Vform	Replacement	The solution can be *obtain* (obtained) by using technology.
	Insertion	However, the world has always beyond our imagination and ø (has) never let us down.
	Deletion	It also indicates that the economy has *been* (ø) dramatically grown.
SVA	Subject-verb-Agreement	My brothers *is* (are) nutritionists.
ArtOrDet	Replacement	The leakage of *these* (this) confidential information can be a sensitive issue to personal, violation of freedom and breakdown of safety.
	Insertion	The survey was done by ø (the) United Nations.
	Deletion	The air cargo of *the* (ø) Valujet plane was on fire after the plane had taken off.
Nn	Noun number	He receives two *letter* (letters).
Prep	Replacement	They work *under* (in) a conductive environment.
	Insertion	Definitely, there are point of view that agree ø (with) the technology but also the voices of objection.
	Deletion	Today, the surveillance technology has become almost manifest *to* (ø) wherever we go.

Table 1: The error types with descriptions and examples.

components are combined into a pipeline of correction steps to form an end-to-end correction system. Different types of corrections may interact with each other. Therefore, only for each focus word in a sentence will pass the filter and predict by the system.

Take the sentence for example, "*The patent applications do not need to be censored.*", if the word "*applications*" is changed to "*application*" (*Nn* error) by a correction module, then the following auxiliary verb "*do*" should be revised to "*does*" (*SVA* error) accordingly. That is, if a mistake is introduced by a component in the prior step, subsequent analyses are most likely affected negatively. To avoid the errors propagated into further components, we proposed to deploy the analytical (pipelined) components in the order of *Nn*, *ArtOrDet*, *Vform*, *SVA* and *Prep*.

For non-native language learners, over 90% usage of prepositions and articles are correctly used, which makes the errors very sparse (Rozovskaya and Roth, 2010c) in a text, and about 10% error is not "sparse" by the way. This factor severely restricts the improvement of data-driven systems. Different from the previous methods to overcome error sparsity, we explored a graph-based label propagation method that makes use of the prediction on large amount of unlabeled data. The predicted data are then used to resample our training data. This semi-supervised method may fix a skewed label distribution in the training set and is helpful to enhance the models.

The paper is organized as follows. We firstly review and discuss the related work. The data used to construct the models is described in Section 3. Section 4 discusses the proposed model based on semi-supervised learning, and the overall hybrid system is given in Section 5. The methods of grammatical error detection and correction are detailed in Section 6, followed by an evaluation, discussion and a conclusion to end the paper.

2 Related Work

The issues of grammatical error correction have been discussed from different perspectives for several decades. In this section, we briefly review some related methods.

The use of machine learning methods to tackle this problem has shown a promising performance. These methods are normally created based on a large corpus of well-formed native English texts (Tetreault and Chodorow 2008; Tetreault et al., 2010) or annotated non-native data (Gamon, 2010; Han et al., 2010). Although the manually error-tagged text is much more expensive, it has shown improvements over the models trained solely on well-formed native text (Kochmar et al., 2012). Additionally, both generative and discriminative classifiers were widely used. Among them, Maximum Entropy was generally used (Rozovskaya and Roth, 2011; Sakaguchi et al., 2012; Quan et al., 2012) and obtained a good result for preposition and article correction using a large feature set. Naive Bayes were also applied to recognize or correct the errors in speech or texts (Lynch et al., 2012). However, only using classifiers always cannot give a satisfied performance. Thus, grammar rules and probabilistic language model can be used as a simple but effective assistant for correction of spelling (Kantrowitz et al, 2003) and grammatical errors (Dahlmeier et al., 2012; Lynch et al., 2012; Quan et al., 2012; Rozovskaya et al., 2012).

3 Data Set

The training data is the NUS Corpus of Learner English (NUCLE) that provided by the National University of Singapore (Dahlmeier et al., 2013). The NUCLE contains more than one million words (1,400 essays) and has been annotated with error-tags and correction-labels. There are 27 categories of errors, with 45,106 errors in total. In this CoNLL-2013 shared task, five types of errors (around 32% of the total errors) are concerned. Figure 1 shows the statistics information of error types.

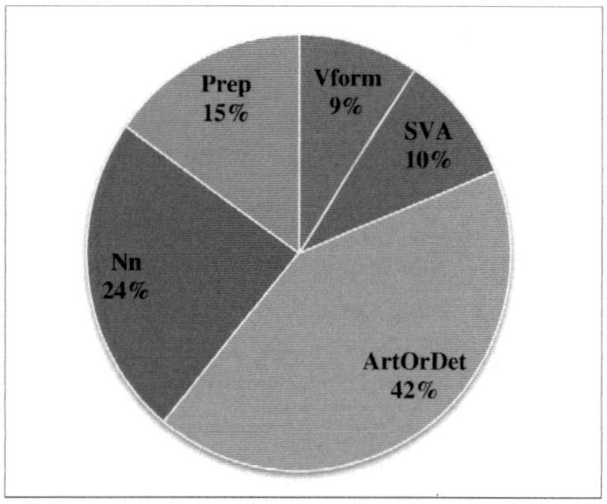

Figure 1. The distribution of different error types in the training set.

As the distribution of different errors respects the real environment, there is a serious problem hidden in it. Roughly estimated, the ratio between the *correct* and *error* classes in NUCLE is around 100:1, or even more. The imbalance problem may be heavily harmful to machine learning methods. Therefore, researchers (Rozovskaya et al., 2012; Dahlmeier et al., 2012) provided several approaches such as reducing *correct* instances to deal with error sparsity. Instead of downsampling the data, we try to upsample error instances. Different from UI system (Rozovskaya et al., 2012) which simulates learners to make mistakes artificially, we propose a semi-supervised learning method that makes use of a large amount of unlabeled data which is easy to collect. In practice, semi-supervised learning requires less human effort and gives higher accuracy in creating a model.

4 Error Examples Expansion Using Graph-Based Label Propagation

As mentioned before, the corpus contains a low amount of error examples, which results in a high sparsity in the label distribution. In reality, the balance between the error and correct data is crucial for training a robust grammar detection models. Our experiment results demonstrate that too many correct data lead to unfavorable error detection rate. In order to resolve this obstacle, this paper introduces to using external data sources, i.e., a large amount of easily accessible raw texts, to automatically achieve more labeled example for training a stronger model. This paper employs transductive graph-based semi-supervised learning approach.

4.1 Graph-Based Label Propagation

Graph-based label propagation is one of the critical subclasses of SSL. Graph-based label propagation methods have recently shown they can outperform the state-of-the-art in several natural language processing (NLP) tasks, e.g., POS tagging (Subramanya et al., 2010), knowledge acquisition (Talukdar et al., 2008), shallow semantic parsing for unknown predicate (Das and Smith, 2011). This study uses graph SSL to enrich training data, mainly the examples with incorrect tag, from raw texts.

This approach constructs a k nearest-neighbor (k-nn) similarity graph over the labeled and unlabeled data in the first step. The vertices in the constructed graph consist of all instances (feature vector) that occur in labeled and unlabeled text, and edge weights between vertices are computed using their Euclidean distance. Pairs of vertices are connected by weighted edges which encode the degree to which they are expected to have the same label (Zhu, 2003). In the second step, label propagation operates on the constructed graph. The primary objective is to propagate labels from a few labeled vertices to the unlabeled ones by optimizing a loss function based on the constraints or properties derived from the graph, e.g. smoothness (Zhu et al., 2003; Subramanya and Bilmes, 2008; Talukdar et al., 2009), or sparsity (Das and Smith, 2012). This paper uses propagation method (MAD) in (Talukdar et al., 2009).

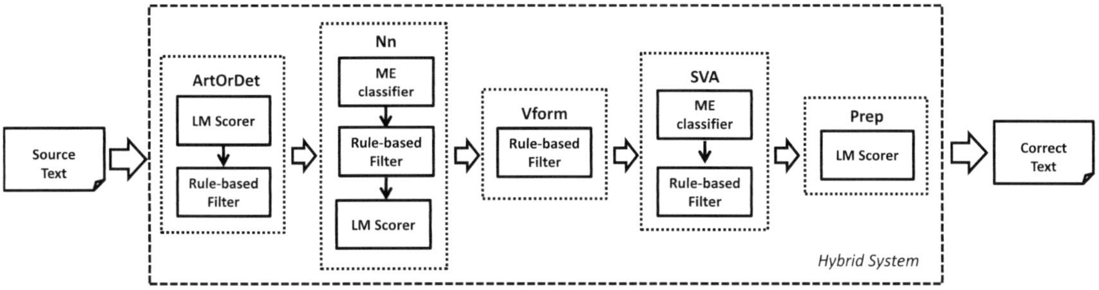

Figure 2. Workflow of our proposed system.

4.2 Implementation

In this paper, the labeled data is taken from NUCLE corpus. They are regarded as the "seed" data, including 93,000 correct and 1,200 incorrect instances. The unlabeled data is collected from the English side of news magazine corpus (LDC2005T10). Based on that, a 5-NN similarity graph is constructed. With the graph and the properties of the labeled data derived from the NUCLE, the MAD algorithm is used to propagate the error-tag (label) from labeled vertices to the unlabeled vertices. Afterwards, the unlabeled examples with incorrect tag are added into the original training data for training.

5 System Description

This section describes the details of our system, including preprocessing of training set, confusion set generating, classifier training and language models building. The grammatical error correction procedure is shown in Figure 2.

5.1 Preprocessing

As mentioned in Section 3, there is a large amount (68%) of other error types which may result in new errors or confuse the system with wrong information in correction. In order to make the best use of the corpus, it needs to filter all errors not covered by the CoNLL 2013 shared task, and then generate a separate corpus for each error type. Therefore, we recovered other irrelevant errors accordingly. For each error type, we also recover other 4 types of errors, and then we got a pure training data set which only includes one error type.

For the misspelled problem, we used an open source toolkit (JMySpell[2]) which allows us to use the dictionaries form OpenOffice. JMySpell gives a list of suggestion candidate words, and we select the first one to replace the original word.

5.2 Confusion Set Generating

Confusion sets include the correction candidates which are used to modify the wrong places of a sentence. We generated a confusion set for each type of error correction component.

The confusion set for *Nn*, *Vform* and *SVA* was built on Penn Treebank[3]. The format can be described as that each prototype word follows all possible combinations with Part-Of-Speech (POS) and variants. For instance, the format of the word "look" in confusion set should looks like "*look look#VB look#VBP looking#VBG looks#VBZ looked#VBN look#NN looks#NNS*". The prototype "look" and POS are the constraints for choosing the correct candidate. In order to quickly find the candidates according to each detected error place, we indexed the confusion set in Lucene[4] which is another open source toolkit with a high-performance, full-featured text search engine library.

For *ArtOrDet* and *Prep*, the confusion sets are manually created because the possible modifications are not so many which are discussed in Section 6.1 and 6.2.

5.3 Maximum Entropy Classifier

The machine learning algorithm we used to train the detection models is Maximum Entropy (ME), which can classify the data by giving a probability distribution. It is similar to multiclass logistic regression models, but much more profitable with sparse explanatory feature vectors. For ME classifier, the feature of text data is suitable for training the model, so we choose it as our detection classifier.

[2] Available at https://kenai.com/projects/jmyspell.

[3] Available at http://www.cis.upenn.edu/~treebank/.

[4] Available at http://lucene.apache.org/.

We employed Stanford Classifier[5] which is a Java implementation of maximum entropy (Manning & Klein, 2003).

5.4 N-gram Language Model

The probabilistic language model is constructed on Google Web 1T 5-gram corpus (Brants and Franz, 2006) by using the SRILM toolkit (Stolcke, 2002). All generated modification candidates are scored by it and only candidates that strictly increase than a threshold can be kept.

The normalized language model score is defined as

$$score_{lm} = \frac{1}{|s|} \log \Pr(s) \qquad (1)$$

in which s is the corrected sentence and $|s|$ is the sentence length in tokens (Dahlmeier et al., 2012).

6 Grammatical Error Correction

6.1 Article and Determiner

The component for *ArtOrDet* task integrates with the language model and rule-based techniques. Language models are constructed to select the best candidate from a confusion set of possible article choices {a, the, an, ø}, given the pre-corrected sentence. Each Noun Phrase (NP) in the test sentence will be pre-corrected as correction candidates. However, only using a language model to determine the best correction will often result in a low precision, because a certain amount of correct usages of *ArtOrDet* are misjudged.

In order to avoid this problem, we proposed a voting method based on multiple language models. We integrated two separate language models: one was converted from the large Google corpus (general LM) and the other one was constructed from a small in-domain corpus (in-domain LM). Additionally, the in-domain corpus involves two parts. One is the training data which has been totally corrected according to the gold answer. The other one includes the sentences which are similar to the test set. We extracted them from some well-formed native English corpora such as English News Magazine of LDC2005T10[6] using term frequency-inverse document frequency (TF-IDF) as the similarity score. Each document D_i is represented as a vector (w_{i1}, w_{i2},..., w_{in}), and n is the size of the vocabulary. So w_{ij} is calculated as follows:

$$w_{ij} = tf_{ij} \times \log(idf_j) \qquad (2)$$

where tf_{ij} is term frequency (TF) of the j-th word in the vocabulary in the document D_i, and idf_j is the is the inverse document frequency (IDF) of the j-th word calculated. The similarity between two sentences is then defined as the cosine of the angle between two vectors.

Each candidate sentence will be scored by these two LMs and compared with a threshold. Only if both of the LMs agree, the modification will be kept. We believe this method could filter a lot of wrong modification and improve the precision.

6.2 Preposition

For *Prep* error type, we used the same method as *ArtOrDet*. The only difference is confusion matrix. Our system corrects the unnecessary, missing and unwanted errors for the five most frequently prepositions which are *in*, *for*, *to*, *of* and *on*. While developing our system, we found that adding more prepositions did not increase performance in our experiments. Thus the confusion set is {in, for, to, of, on, ø}.

6.3 Noun Number

A single noun in the sentence that is hard to distinguish whether it is singular or plural, so we treat a noun phrase as a observe subject. Our strategy of correcting noun number error is to use a filter contains rule-based and machine learning method. It can filter a part of nouns that absolutely right, and the rest of nouns will be detected by the language model generated by SRILM[7].

The rule-based filter of our system contains several criteria. It can detect the noun phrase by article, i.e. it can simply find out that the noun is singular which with an article of "*a*" or "*an*". The determiner and cardinal number also will be taken into consider by the rule-based model such as "*I have three apple.*", then system can find out the "apple" should be "apples". The correct noun will keep the original one, and the incorrect noun will be replaced with a new candidate.

After the first level filtering by the rules, the rest of noun phrases are indeterminacy by system. Therefore, we use a ME classifier for further filtering. We use lexical, POS and dependency

[5] Available at http://nlp.stanford.edu/software/classifier.shtml.

[6] Available at http://www.ldc.upenn.edu/Catalog/catalogEntry.jsp?catalogId=LDC2005T10.

[7] http://www.speech.sri.com/projects/srilm/.

parse information as features. The features are listed in Table 2.

In previous steps, most of the error can be detected, but also it may give a lot of wrong suggests, in order to reduce this situation, we use N-gram language model scorer to evaluate on the candidates and choose the highest probability one.

Feature	Example
Observer word	
Word (w_0)	resource
POS (p_0)	NN
First word in NP	
Word ($w_{NP\text{-}1st}$)	a
POS ($p_{NP\text{-}1st}$)	DT
Dependency Relation	det
Previous word before observed word	
Word (w_{-1})	good
POS (p_{-1})	JJ
Word after observed word	
Word (w_1)	and
POS (p_1)	CC
Head word of observed word	
Word (w_{head})	water
POS (p_{head})	NN
Dependency relation	rcomd
Word Combination	
$w_0 + w_{NP\text{-}1st}$	resource + a
$w_0 + w_{-1}$	resource + good
$w_0 + w_1$	resource + and
$w_0 + w_{head}$	resource + water
$w_{NP\text{-}1st} + w_{head}$	a + water
POS Combination	
$p_0 + p_{NP\text{-}1st}$	NN + DT
$p_0 + p_{-1}$	NN + JJ
$p_0 + p_1$	NN + CC
$p_0 + p_{head}$	NN + NN
$p_{NP\text{-}1st} + p_{head}$	DT + NN

Table 2: Features for Nn and the example: "An example is water which is a good **resource** and is plentiful."

6.4 Verb Form

Determining the correct form of a verb in English is complex, involving a relatively wide range of choices. A verb can have many forms, such as base, gerund, preterite, past participle and so on. To detect the tense of verb error is much more related to the semantics level than syntax level. Therefore, it is hard to extract a common feature for training model. We chose to separate it into several problems and use rule-based model to do the *Vform* correction.

For auxiliary verbs, there are three categories, one is modal verbs (do, can, may, will, might, should, must, need and dare), the other is the form of "*be*" and "*have*". In a verb phrase, normally modals precede "*have*" and "*be*", and "*have*" proceed "*be*", then we can get the ordering like this: Modal, Have, Be. Auxiliary verbs can incorporate with other verbs, and have different combination. Based on the previous study of the core language engine (Alshawi, 1992), we define the rules that contain the type of verb, which tense of verbs can be used with, and their entries in the lexicon. For example:

(can (aux (modal) (vform pres) (COMPFORM bare))

This means "*can*" is a modal verb, it can be used with a verb that in the present tense, when "*can*" used alone with the main verb should as complement the base (bare) form. In here, the COMPFORM attribute is the entry condition in the grammar.

6.5 Subject-Verb Agreement

The basic principle of Subject-Verb Agreement is singular subjects need singular verbs; plural subjects need plural verbs, such as following sentences:

My **brother** *is* a nutritionist.

My **sisters** *are* dancers.

Therefore, the subject of the sentence is the key point. To decide whether the verb is singular or plural should look into the context and find out the POS of the subject. We utilize the existing information given by NUCLE to extract the subject of the verb. For example, the sentence "*Statistics show that the number are continuing to grow with the existing population explosion.*" Figure 3 shows the parse tree of this sentence.

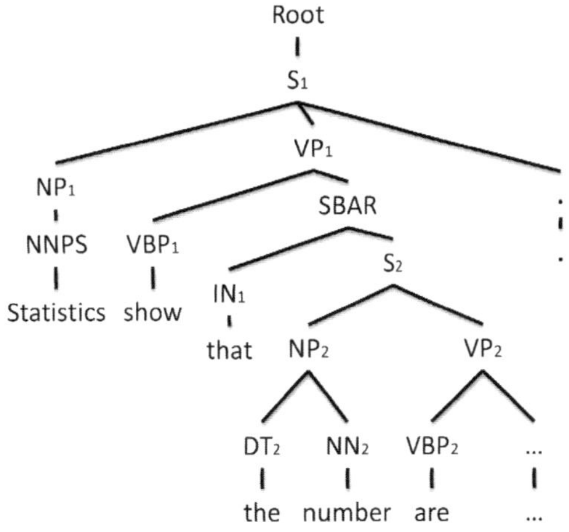

Figure 3. Parse tree of the example sentence.

Through Figure 3, the observed words are "*show*" and "*are*", the subjects are "*statistics*" and "*number*" respectively that we can conclude "*statistics*" should use plural verb and "*number*" should use singular verb "*is*" instead of "*are*". The other features extracted for training are listed in Table 3.

Feature	Example
Observer word	
Word (w_0)	are
POS (p_0)	VBP
Subject NP	
First word ($w_{NP\text{-}1st}$)	the
POS of first word ($p_{NP\text{-}1st}$)	DT
Head word ($w_{NP\text{-}head}$)	number
POS of head word ($p_{NP\text{-}head}$)	NN
Previous word before observed word	
Word (w_{-1})	number
POS (p_{-1})	NN
NP after observed word	
First word ($w_{NPa\text{-}1st}$)	the
POS of first word ($p_{NPa\text{-}1st}$)	DT
Head word ($w_{NPa\text{-}head}$)	explosion
POS of head word ($p_{NPa\text{-}head}$)	NN
Word combination	
$w_0 + w_{NP\text{-}1st}$	are + the
$w_0 + w_{NP\text{-}head}$	are + number
$w_0 + w_{-1}$	are + number
$w_0 + w_{NPa\text{-}1st}$	are + the
$w_0 + w_{NPa\text{-}head}$	are + explosion
POS combination	
$p_0 + p_{NP\text{-}1st}$	VBP + DT
$p_0 + p_{NP\text{-}head}$	VBP + NN
$p_0 + p_{-1}$	VBP + NN
$p_0 + p_{NPa\text{-}1st}$	VBP + DT
$p_0 + p_{NPa\text{-}head}$	VBP + NN

Table 3: Features for SVA and the example: "Statistics show that the number **are** continuing to grow with the existing population explosion."

The purpose of extracting the noun phrase after the observed word is in the situation of the subject is after the verb, such as "*Where are my scissors?*", "*scissors*" is the subject of this sentence.

7 Evaluation and Discussion

The evaluation is provided by the organizer and generated by M^2 scorer (Dahlmeier & Ng, 2012). The result consists of precision, recall and F-score. Our grammatical error correction system has proposed 1,011 edits. The evaluation result of our system output for the CoNLL-2013 test data is shown in Table 4.

Results	Precision	Recall	F-score
Before Revision	0.2849	0.1753	0.2170
After Revision	0.3712	0.2366	0.2890

Table 4: Evaluation result of Precision, Recall and F-score.

Error Type	Error #	Correct #	%
ArtOrDet	690	145	21.01
Nn	396	92	23.23
Vform	122	8	6.55
SVA	124	37	29.83
Prep	311	6	1.93

Table 5: Detail information of evaluation result (Before Revision).

Error Type	Error #	Correct #	%
ArtOrDet	725	177	24.42
Nn	484	132	27.27
Vform	151	16	10.60
SVA	138	47	34.06
Prep	325	9	2.77

Table 6: Detail information of evaluation result (After Revision).

The data in table 5 and 6 are the detailed information for each error type which was calculated by us, the table 5 is the data before revision, and the table 6 is that after revision. Second column is the amount of the gold edits, and the third column is the amount of our correct edits, and the last column is the percentage of correct edits. We analyzed the results in detail, and found several critical reasons of causing low recall. Firstly, the five error types are associated relatively, if one is modified, it may cause a chain reaction, such as the article will affect the noun number, and the noun number will cause the *SVA* errors. Some *Nn* errors still cannot be detected or given a wrong correction by our system, which decreases the precision and recall of *SVA*. Another reason is our system does not perform well in *Vform* and *Prep* error correction. In our output, just a few errors have been revised. This means the quantity of correction rules is not enough that cannot cover all the linguistic phenomena. For instance, the situation of missing verb or unnecessary verb cannot be detected. On the other hand, the hybrid method of our system has filtered some wrong suggestion candidates that improve the precision.

8 Conclusion

We have presented the hybrid system for English grammatical error correction. It achieves a 28.9% F_1-score on the official test set. We believe that if we find more appropriate features, our system can still be improved and achieve a better performance.

Acknowledgments

The authors are grateful to the Science and Technology Development Fund of Macau and the Research Committee of the University of Macau for the funding support for our research, under the reference No. 017/2009/A and MYRG076(Y1-L2)-FST13-WF. The authors also wish to thank the anonymous reviewers for many helpful comments as well as Liangye He, Yuchu Lin and Jiaji Zhou who give us a lot of help.

References

Hiyan Alshawi. 1992. The core language engine. *The MIT Press.*

Jon Louis Bentley. 1980. Multidimensional divide-and-conquer. *Communications of the ACM*, 23:214–229.

Alina Beygelzimer, Sham Kakade, and John Langford. 2006. Cover trees for nearest neighbor. In: *Proceedings of the 23rd International Conference on Machine Learning*, pp. 97–104.

Thorsten Brants and Alex Franz. 2006. Web 1T 5-gram Version 1. *Linguistic Data Consortium*, Philadelohia, PA.

Olivier Chapelle, Bernhard Schölkopf, Alexander Zien, and others. 2006. Semi-supervised learning. *MIT press Cambridge.*

Daniel Dahlmeier, Hwee Tou Ng, and Eric Jun Feng Ng. 2012. NUS at the HOO 2012 Shared Task. In: *Proceedings of the Seventh Workshop on Building Educational Applications Using NLP*, pp. 216–224.

Daniel Dahlmeier & Hwee Tou Ng, and Siew Mei Wu (2013). Building a Large Annotated Corpus of Learner English: The NUS Corpus of Learner English. To appear in *Proceedings of the 8th Workshop on Innovative Use of NLP for Building Educational Applications* (BEA 2013). Atlanta, Georgia, USA.

Daniel Dahlmeier, and Hwee Tou Ng (2012). Better Evaluation for Grammatical Error Correction. *Proceedings of the 2012 Conference of the North American Chapter of the Association for Computational Linguistics* (NAACL 2012), pp. 568 – 572.

Robert Dale, Ilya Anisimoff, and George Narroway. 2012. HOO 2012: A report on the preposition and determiner error correction shared task. In: *Proceedings of the Seventh Workshop on Building Educational Applications Using NLP*, pp. 54–62.

Robert Dale and Adam Kilgarriff. 2011. *Helping our own: The HOO 2011 pilot shared task.* In: *Proceedings of the 13th European Workshop on Natural Language Generation*, pp. 242–249.

Dipanjan Das and Noah A. Smith 2012. Graph-based lexicon expansion with sparsity-inducing penalties. In: *Proceedings of the 2012 Conference of the North American Chapter of the Association for Computational Linguistics: Human Language Technologies*, pp. 677-687.

Michael Gamon. 2010. Using mostly native data to correct errors in learners' writing: a meta-classifier approach. In: *Human Language Technologies: The 2010 Annual Conference of the North American Chapter of the Association for Computational Linguistics*, pp. 163–171.

Andrew B. Goldberg and Xiaojin Zhu. 2006. Seeing stars when there aren't many stars: graph-based semi-supervised learning for sentiment categorization. In: *Proceedings of the First Workshop on Graph Based Methods for Natural Language Processing*, pp. 45–52.

Na-Rae Han, Joel Tetreault, Soo-Hwa Lee, and Jin-Young Ha. 2010. Using an error-annotated learner corpus to develop an ESL/EFL error correction system. In: *Proceedings of LREC*, pp. 763–770.

Mark Kantrowitz. 2003. Method and apparatus for analyzing affect and emotion in text. *U.S. Patent* No. 6,622,140.

Ekaterina Kochmar. 2011. Identification of a writer's native language by error analysis. *Master's thesis*, University of Cambridge.

Gerard Lynch, Erwan Moreau, and Carl Vogel. 2012. A Naive Bayes classifier for automatic correction of preposition and determiner errors in ESL text. In: *Proceedings of the Seventh Workshop on Building Educational Applications Using NLP*, pp. 257–262.

Christopher Manning and Dan Klein. 2003. Optimization, Maxent Models, and Conditional Estimation without Magic. *Tutorial at HLT-NAACL 2003 and ACL 2003.*

Hwee Tou Ng, Siew Mei Wu, Yuanbin Wu, Christian Hadiwinoto, and Joel Tetreault (2013). The CoNLL-2013 Shared Task on Grammatical Error Correction. To appear in *Proceedings of the Seventeenth Conference on Computational Natural Language Learning*.

Li Quan, Oleksandr Kolomiyets, and Marie-Francine Moens. 2012. KU Leuven at HOO-2012: a hybrid approach to detection and correction of determiner and preposition errors in non-native English text. In: *Proceedings of the Seventh Workshop on Building Educational Applications Using NLP*, pp. 263–271.

Juan Ramos. 2003. Using tf-idf to determine word relevance in document queries. In: *Proceedings of the First Instructional Conference on Machine Learning*.

Alla Rozovskaya and Dan Roth. 2010. Training paradigms for correcting errors in grammar and usage. In: *Human Language Technologies: The 2010 Annual Conference of the North American Chapter of the Association for Computational Linguistics*, pp. 154–162.

Alla Rozovskaya, Mark Sammons, and Dan Roth. 2012. The UI system in the HOO 2012 shared task on error correction. In: *Proceedings of the Seventh Workshop on Building Educational Applications Using NLP*, pp. 272–280.

Keisuke Sakaguchi, Yuta Hayashibe, Shuhei Kondo, Lis Kanashiro, Tomoya Mizumoto, Mamoru Komachi, and Yuji Matsumoto. 2012. NAIST at the HOO 2012 Shared Task. In: *Proceedings of the Seventh Workshop on Building Educational Applications Using NLP*, pp. 281–288.

Andreas Stolcke and others. 2002. SRILM-an extensible language modeling toolkit. In: *Proceedings of the International Conference on Spoken Language Processing*, pp. 901–904.

Partha Pratim Talukdar and Koby Crammer. 2009. New regularized algorithms for transductive learning. In: *Machine Learning and Knowledge Discovery in Databases. Springer*, pp. 442–457.

Joel Tetreault, Jennifer Foster, and Martin Chodorow. 2010. Using parse features for preposition selection and error detection. In: *Proceedings of the Acl 2010 Conference Short Papers*, pp. 353–358.

Joel R. Tetreault and Martin Chodorow. 2008. The ups and downs of preposition error detection in ESL writing. In: *Proceedings of the 22nd International Conference on Computational Linguistics* Volume 1, pp. 865–872.

A Tree Transducer Model for Grammatical Error Correction

Jan Buys and Brink van der Merwe
MIH Media Lab and Computer Science Division
Stellenbosch University, South Africa
janbuys@ml.sun.ac.za, abvdm@cs.sun.ac.za

Abstract

We present an approach to grammatical error correction for the CoNLL 2013 shared task based on a weighted tree-to-string transducer. Rules for the transducer are extracted from the NUCLE training data. An n-gram language model is used to rerank k-best sentence lists generated by the transducer. Our system obtains a precision, recall and F1 score of 0.27, 0.1333 and 0.1785, respectively, on the official test set. On the revised annotations, the F1 score increases to 0.2505. Our system ranked 6th out of the participating teams on both the original and revised test set annotations.

1 Introduction

There has recently been an increase in research on automated grammatical error detection and correction for writing by English language learners (Leacock et al., 2010). In the most prominent line of research, statistical classifiers are trained to detect or correct specific error types. Features for these classifiers are based on word context and local syntactic information. The classifiers are combined, and a language model is often used to filter corrections. Research on this approach focusses especially on preposition and determiner errors. Most of the systems in the HOO 2011 and 2012 shared tasks (Dale and Kilgarriff, 2011; Dale et al., 2012) fall under this broad approach.

In a second class of models, a model for generating corrected sentences is formulated in the noisy-channel framework, relying strongly on a language model to distinguish between grammatical and ungrammatical candidate corrections (Lee and Seneff, 2006; Turner and Charniak, 2007; Park and Levy, 2011). Such models are often inspired by techniques developed for statistical machine translation (Brockett et al., 2006). Finally, rule-based methods are often used in commercial language processing systems such as word processors. Here large hand-crafted linguistically expressive, error-tolerant grammars are used to analyse sentences and identify where constraints have been broken.

In this paper we present our system for the CoNLL 2013 shared task in grammatical error correction (Ng et al., 2013). Our grammar correction model is based on a tree-to-string transducer that is specified by a set of rules that each rewrite a tree fragment to a string of words and variables. These rules are extracted automatically from a set of training examples. Each training example consists of an incorrect sentence, a corresponding correct sentence with its parse tree, and a word alignment between the incorrect and correct sentences. During decoding the model searches for parsed well-formed sentences that could be transformed into a given incorrect sentence with high probability. Sentences are split into linguistically plausible clauses to decrease the average sentence length, in order to improve decoding runtime. In order to discriminate more accurately between candidate sentence corrections an n-gram language model trained on a large corpus of well-formed text is used to rerank the k-best hypotheses that the transducer model generates. The tree transducer and language model scores are weighted to maximize the model F1 score on a validation set. After decoding the clauses are recombined into the original sentence structure.

The next section describes preprocessing and the resources used by our system. Section 3 defines weighted tree-to-string transducers. We present the formulation of our error correction model in section 4, and discuss decoding with it in section 5. Section 6 describes language model reranking. System results are given in section 7. Finally, section 8 draws some conclusions and discuss future work.

2 Data Pre-processing

2.1 NUCLE

We use the pre-processed version of the NUCLE corpus (Dahlmeier et al., 2013) released as training data for this shared task. The data consist of essays, subdivided into paragraphs. Using NLTK (Bird et al., 2009), paragraphs were split into sentences with NLTK *punkt* and sentences were tokenized with NLTK *word tokenize*. Though this sentence-splitting and tokenization is not error-free (for example, quotation marks are handled incorrectly in some contexts), we use it to maintain consistency in our model. An error annotation in the data consists of the start and end token offsets in a sentence, as well as the correction that should replace the text between the offsets.

We divide the corpus into 80% training data, 10% validation data and 10% development data. Splitting is performed by random selection at essay level. For each sentence with corrections, we refer to the original as the incorrect sentence, and to the version with the corrections applied to it as the correct sentence. For the purpose of training our models, all words are lowercased. As described below, we also construct an alignment between the words of each of these sentence pairs.

The 2013 shared task focusses on five error types: Article or determiner, preposition, noun number, verb form, and subject-verb agreement errors. In the training data we only apply corrections of these types to obtain the correct version of the sentences, though other error types are also included in the error annotations. An alternative would be to apply the corrections of other error types to the correct and incorrect versions of the sentences. However, we decided against that in order to keep the training data realistically close to the test data, which will also contain these other errors. We do, however, correct some of the mechanical errors, especially spelling errors, in the incorrect and correct versions of the training data, to reduce noise that these errors may introduce into the model.

In order to train a syntax-based model for grammar correction, the correct version of the sentences are parsed with the Berkeley parser (Petrov and Klein, 2007). The Berkeley parser is a state-of-the-art unlexicalized parser. Given that the correct side of our training data will still contain errors, it is unlikely that lexicalized parsing will be more accurate. Parser options are set to obtain left-binarized parse trees under Viterbi decoding.

2.2 Wikipedia language model

We train the n-gram language model used in our system on a large corpus of text extracted from the English Wikipedia. The April 2013 Wikipedia XML dump[1] is used. This is parsed with the *gwtwiki*[2] Wikipedia parser, and all sentences consisting of 6 or more words are extracted. These sentences are tokenized with NLTK and lowercased. The corpus has about 1 500 millions words. As vocabulary we use the 64 000 words with the highest frequency occurrence in the corpus. A 3-gram language model is trained from the corpus on this restricted vocabulary, to keep the size of the language model reasonable. The language model is trained and applied with the SRILM toolkit (Stolcke, 2002). Kneser-Ney smoothing is used to estimate the model weights.

2.3 Vocabulary

We set the vocabulary of the transducer model as the union of the vocabulary of our language model and the vocabulary of the words of the correct sentences in the NUCLE training data. In the transducer construction we ensure that all words in this vocabulary can be accepted. A large number of URLs occur in the training data, as citations are included in some of the essays. We replace these with a `<url>` symbol to reduce noise in the vocabulary.

In the validation, development and test data, words that do not appear in the vocabulary are replaced with an `<unk>` symbol. We record the replaced words, so that after decoding they can be replaced back to their original positions. We do not perform automatic spelling correction on the test data as a preprocessing step: The occurrence of out of vocabulary words is small enough that performing spelling correction will not have a significant impact on the performance of our system.

We use the NLTK interface to WordNet (Miller, 1995) to find pairs of singular and plural nouns and groups of verbs that have the same base form. All verbs and non-proper nouns that occur in the language model vocabulary are grouped like this. The groups are used to construct additional rules for noun number and verb form errors.

[1] http://download.wikimedia.org/enwiki/latest/enwiki-latest-pages-articles.xml.bz2

[2] http://code.google.com/p/gwtwiki/

3 Weighted Tree-to-string Transducers

Tree transducers are a class of automata-theoretic models that perform transformations on tree structures. There is a rich theory concerning these models, and tree transducers with different restrictions can compute different classes of transformations. Algorithms for weighted variants of these transducers have recently been developed (Graehl et al., 2008; May, 2010) and applied to syntax-based statistical machine translation.

Tree-to-string transducers are a class of tree transducers that generalizes synchronous context-free grammars. These transducers can be used to transform strings into trees: For a given output string, the decoding problem is to find the input tree that could be transformed into the given string with the highest probability. This decoding process is referred to as backward application. The formulation is due to the noisy-channel model often followed in statistical machine translation.

3.1 Definitions

We need a few preliminary definitions (the notation of May (2010) is generally followed): A *ranked alphabet* Σ is a finite set of symbols, each which can take a finite set of ranks. A tree $t \in T_\Sigma$ is denoted by $\sigma(t_1, \ldots, t_k)$, where $k \in \mathbb{N}$, $t_1, \ldots, t_k \in T_\Sigma$ and σ is a node of rank k. Σ_k denotes the subset of Σ of all symbols with *rank* k. $T_\Sigma(S)$ is the set of all trees in $T_{\Sigma \cup S}$ where symbols from S occur only at the leaves. We donate by $X = \{x_1, x_2, \ldots\}$ a set of *variables*, and $X_k = \{x_1, \ldots, x_k\}$. With respect to X_k, a tree $u \in T_\Sigma(X_k)$ or a sequence $u \in (\Delta \cup (Q \times X))^*$ is *linear* if each element of X_k occurs at most once in u, and *nondeleting* if each element of X_k occurs at least once in u.

Formally, a *weighted extended top-down tree-to-string transducer* M is a 5-tuple $(Q, \Sigma, \Delta, R, Q_d)$ (May, 2010, chap. 2). Q is an alphabet of states that all have rank one. Σ and Δ are the ranked input and output alphabets, respectively. Q_d is the set of initial states. R is a finite set of rules with an associated weight function $\pi : R \to \mathcal{W}$. Each rule $r \in R$ is of the form $q.t \to g$ for $q \in Q, t \in T_\Sigma(X)$ and $g \in (\Delta \cup (Q \times X))^*$. The tree t should be linear in X, and each variable in g should also be in t.

We refer to $q.t$ as the left hand side of a rule, and to g as the right hand side. M is *linear* if the right hand side of each rule is linear, and *nondeleting* if the right hand side of each rule is nondeleting with respect to X_k, the set of variables on the left hand side.

For a rule $r : q.t \to g$ and $e, f \in (\Delta \cup (Q \times T_\Sigma))^*$, a *derivation step* $e \Rightarrow^r f$ is obtained by replacing the left-most element of e of the form $q(s)$, where s matches t, by a transformation of g, where each instance of a variable is replaced with the corresponding subtree of s. The sequence $d = (r_1, \ldots, r_m)$ is a *derivation* of the pair (t, s) if $t \Rightarrow^{r_1} t_1 \Rightarrow^{r_2} \ldots \Rightarrow^{r_m} s$, where $t_i \in (\Delta \cup (Q \times T_\Sigma))^*$ for $1 \leq i < m$. The weight of d is $wt(d) = \pi(r_1) \cdot \ldots \cdot \pi(r_m)$.

The tree transducer that we use is a weighted linear, nondeleting top-down tree-to-string transducer. The expressive power of this transducer class is sufficient for the transformations that we need our model to perform. Relaxing these restrictions will increase the decoding complexity of the transducer model significantly. Since we work with binarized trees, no node will have a rank greater than 2. Our transducer only has one state, q. Look-ahead restrictions are added to restrict the variables on the left hand side to match specific constituents.

3.2 Probability model

A tree-to-string transducer can represent a conditional probability model for the output sentences given the input trees, or a joint probability model over the input trees and output strings. We will use a joint probability distribution for our model. Note that there is spurious ambiguity in the model at two levels: Firstly, it is possible that there can be different derivations for the same tree-string pair. However, during the application of the model this ambiguity occurs infrequently. Secondly, the model can generate different trees with the same yield.

Suppose c is a correct sentence in the set C of all possible correct sentences, and i is the given (possibly) incorrect sentence. Let $\tau(c)$ represent the set of all possible parse trees of c. Then we want to find sentence

$$\hat{c} = \arg\max_{c \in C} P(c, i) \tag{1}$$

$$= \arg\max_{c \in C} \Sigma_{\pi \in \tau(c)} P(\pi, i) \tag{2}$$

The rule probabilities for the joint model are conditioned on the root node of the rule left hand side (and not on the entire left hand side, as would be the case for a conditional model). The model is trained from a set of derivations constructed from the training data, as will be described below. Let $f(r)$ be the number of times that rule r occurs in all the training derivations. Then the probability estimate of a rule is

$$p(r|\text{root}(r)) = \frac{f(r)}{\sum_{r':\text{root}(r')=\text{root}(r)} f(r')} \quad (3)$$

In the construction of the transducer, some rules that do not occur in the training derivations are added. In order to give non-zero weights to these added rules, we apply Good-Turing smoothing (Katz, 1987). This method has the advantage of decreasing the counts of low-frequency rules whose rule counts may provide unreliable probability estimates. For the rules of each of the root nonterminals, the counts of rules with frequencies between 0 and 5 are re-estimated.

4 Transducer Model Formulation

4.1 Word alignment

In order to extract rules from the training data to perform transformations between incorrect and correct sentences, we need to construct an alignment between words in each pair of correct and incorrect sentences. This approach is similar to aligning words in source and target language sentences for statistical machine translation. We construct the alignments from given sequences of edit operations in the training data. Figure 1(a) gives an example of a parse tree for a correct phrase, aligned with a corresponding incorrect phrase.

Firstly, all words in a sentence that do not occur in any edits are aligned one-to-one between the correct and incorrect sentence. In the example, "that", "up" and "across" are aligned in this way. Then, for each edit annotation, we consider the incorrect and correct phrases of that edit. Note that in the NUCLE annotations the incorrect phrase will always be non-empty, but the correct phrase may be empty.

Words that occur in both the correct and incorrect edit phrases are aligned one-to-one. We restrict such alignments to prevent overlapping. In the example in Figure 1(a), there is an edit to replace "the America" with "America", so the word "America" is aligned. Adding these alignments may split a phrase into unaligned subphrases. If such a subphrase is empty on either side, then the word(s) on the other side have to be left unaligned.

(a)

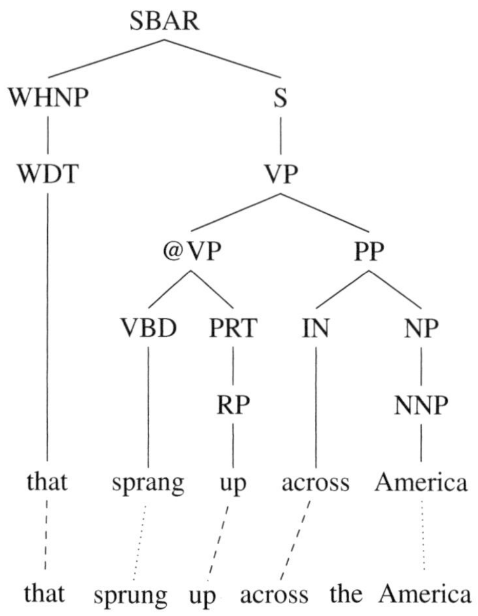

(b)

(1) q.WDT (*that*) $\rightarrow$ *that*
(2) q.VP ($x0$:@VP $x1$:PP) $\rightarrow$ $q.x0$ $q.x1$
(3) q.VBD (*sprang*) $\rightarrow$ *sprung*
(4) q.SBAR ($x0$:WHNP $x1$:S) $\rightarrow$ $q.x0$ $q.x1$
(5) q.PP ($x0$:IN $x1$:NP) $\rightarrow$ $q.x0$ *the* $q.x1$
(6) q.NNP (*America*) $\rightarrow$ *America*

Figure 1: (a) Example alignment between a correct parse tree and an incorrect clause. (b) Some rules extracted from the example.

In the example, "the" will be unaligned. But if the subphrases are non-empty on both sides, then all the words on the incorrect side are aligned to all the words on the correct side of the subphrase. In many instances, this will occur for single word replacements. In the example, "sprung" is aligned with "sprang" in this manner.

4.2 Rule extraction

We follow the GHKM transducer rule extraction algorithm described in (Galley et al., 2004) and (Galley et al., 2006). Given a training example (π, i, a), where π is the correct tree, i the incorrect sentence and a the alignment, rules are extracted for a tree-to-string derivation of (π, i) that is minimally consistent with the alignment a. Counts of how many times each rule is extracted over all the training examples are used to estimate the rule probabilities. A training example is represented as a directed graph as in Figure 1(a), with the edges going downward.

For each of the nodes in π, we compute a *span* and a *complement span* with respect to the nodes in i. The span of a node n is defined by the indexes of the first and last words in f that are reachable from n. The spans of the leaves in the tree (the words of the correct sentence) are defined by a, and the spans of the other nodes can be computed bottom-up for each node from the spans of its child nodes. The complement span of n is the union of the spans of all nodes that are neither ancestors nor descendants of n. The complement spans can be computed top-down for each node by taking the union of the complement span of its parent and the spans of its siblings. Nodes whose spans and complement spans do not overlap, are called *frontier* nodes. From each frontier node, a rule can be extracted: The left hand side of the rule is a subtree rooted at n. The subtree is extracted by traversing π top-down from n, replacing all frontier nodes reached with variables (as more rules will be extracted from there). The right hand side is formed by the words of the span of n of the incorrect side, with the span of each left hand side frontier node replaced by the corresponding variable.

Figure 1(b) gives sample rules extracted from the training example in Figure 1(a). In the example tree, all the constituent nodes are frontier nodes, as there are no complex rewrites. For constituents under which no changes are made, CFG-like rules such as (1) and (2) are extracted. In the case where a single word is substituted (in the example, "sprang" with "sprung"), a rule for this substitution will be extracted (3). If there were no alignment between these words, the algorithm would have attached the word "sprung" to the rule headed by `SBAR` (4), which would clearly not have been linguistically sensible. In the case of the deletion of a word in the incorrect sentence, that word will left be unaligned ("the" in the example). The rule for this word (5) will have as head the lowest node that spans the words in i to the left and right of the unaligned word – in the example, the `PP` node. Rewrite rules for aligned words in phrase edits are also extracted (6).

4.3 Additional rules

We add rules to the transducer that involve words in the vocabulary. Whichever of these rules have not already been extracted from the training data will be assigned a rule count of 0, otherwise their

Non-lexicalized	
q.S ($x0$:NP $x1$:VP) → $q.x0$ $q.x1$	−0.596
q.S ($x0$:VP $x1$:VP) → $q.x0$ $q.x1$	−5.781
q.VP ($x0$:VP $x1$:SBAR) → $q.x0$ $q.x1$	−3.723
Word identity	
q.NN (*work*) → *work*	−2.614
q.VBP (*work*) → *work*	−2.475
q.DT (*the*) → *the*	−0.183
Single word substitution	
q.NN (*work*) → *works*	−4.343
q.VBP (*work*) → *working*	−4.541
q.VBZ (*works*) → *work*	−4.802
q.DT (*the*) → *a*	−3.100
q.IN (*of*) → *from*	−3.901
Phrase substitution	
q.NP (DT (*the*) NN (*right*)) → *rights*	−5.109
q.VP (VBG (*being*) VP (VBN (*researched*))) → *under researching*	−6.272
Context-sensitive phrase substitution	
q.VP (TO (*to*) VP (VB (*work*) $x0$:PP)) → *working* $q.x0$	−6.272
q.PP (IN (*in*) S (VP (VBG (*generating*) $x0$:NP))) → *to generate* $q.x0$	−5.480
Context-sensitive word insertion and deletion	
q.NP (DT (*the* $x0$:NN) → $q.x0$	−2.634
q.VP (VBZ (*has*) $x0$:VP) → $q.x0$	−5.202
q.VP ($x0$:VB $x1$:NP) → $q.x0$ *into* $q.x1$	−5.203

Table 1: Example transducer rules by type, with log probability weights.

rule counts will be left unchanged.

We need to ensure that there are lexical rewrite rules for all the words in our vocabulary. For each of the words in the vocabulary we find one or two possible part-of-speech tags, using the NLTK POS tagger. We add word identity rules in the form of the examples in Table 1. An identity rule is also added for the `<unk>` symbol.

Additional rules are added for noun number and verb form errors, using the word groups extracted from the vocabulary and WordNet. These rules perform substitutions between singular and plural nouns (in both directions) and between verbs with the same base forms. Subject-verb agreement errors are also concerned with the verb form in the sentence, so added verb form rules will also be applicable to such errors. Examples of these single word substitutions are given in Table 1. Since determiner and preposition errors are restricted to a relatively small number of possible substitutions, we assume that all relevant rules involving these errors have already been extracted from the training data.

See Table 1 for rule examples categorized by the type of rewrite the rule performs. Examples of rules for all the error types under consideration are included. Log probability rule weights are also given. Phrase substitution rules can be fully lexical (without variables) or context-sensitive (when they have variables). Word insertions and deletions will always be context-sensitive.

5 Transducer Model Decoding

5.1 Sentence to clause splitting

A challenge to our transducer model on the NUCLE dataset is the length of sentences. On the training data, 46% of sentences have length greater than 20 and 13% have length greater that 30. The decoding time of our model increases sharply when the length of sentences becomes greater than 20. For lengths greater that 30 decoding is not practically feasible on our available computational resources. In order to address this problem, we perform linguistically motivated sentence splits to decrease the length of sentences passed to the decoder. Clauses that are still longer than 30 words are not decoded. Decoding was performed on a desktop computer with 8GB RAM. To keep the overall decoding time reasonable, we restrict decoding to take no more than 1 minute per sentence on average.

Sentence splitting is based on constituency parses (obtained with the Berkeley parser) of the incorrect sentences under consideration. Sentences are split at clause level, using the heuristics described below. The goal is to extracted clauses that have a form similar to that of full sentences.

We distinguish between *S-clauses*, that are indicated by `S`, `SINV` and `SQ` parse tree constituents, and *SBAR-clauses*, indicated by `SBAR` or `SBARQ` parse tree constituents. An SBAR-clause usually consists of an introductory subordinating conjunction or *wh*-word, followed by an S-clause.

We perform splits on S-clauses. A clausal split is performed between the phrase before the start position of the S-clause and the phrase after that position. If the parse tree node of the S-clause is the child of an SBAR-clause node, the split is performed between the phrase before the starting position of the SBAR-clause, and the phrase after the start of the S-clause. The introductory words in the SBAR-clause are excluded from the extracted clauses.

Splits are also performed between some phrases separated by a coordinating conjunction, which is indicated by a `CC` tag in the parse tree. Such a split is performed only if the `CC` node is a child of an S-clause node. The phrase before the conjunction is split from the phrase after the conjunction, while the conjunction itself is excluded.

After decoding and reranking has been performed, the clauses are recombined to reconstruct the original sentences. For each clause the highest-scoring correct clause is chosen. Finally, the original case of all the words in the sentence is restored, as all words were lowercased in the model.

5.2 k-Best decoding

When performing decoding with the transducer model, we need to find the highest-scoring candidate correct sentences, so that we can in turn find the best sentence according to the overall model. We found that a good trade-off between speed and accuracy is to find a list of trees of the 1000-best derivations for a given (incorrect) sentence. The weights of different derivations for which the parse trees have the same yields, are summed to find weights for each of the hypothesis sentences. Note that this is an approximation of the summation in equation (2), which is taken over all parse trees with the same yield.

In our implementation the weighted tree transducer package Tiburon (May and Knight, 2006) is used. Tiburon implements generic operations on regular tree grammars, tree-to-tree and tree-to-string transducers. We use Tiburon to perform decoding in our model, using its implementation of backwards application and k-best decoding.

The decoding algorithm implemented by Tiburon is based on a weighted version of the Earley parsing algorithm (May, 2010, chap. 4). Empirically, large rules have a detrimental impact on the decoding speed of the algorithm. To address this problem, we extract rules from binarized parse trees, which results in smaller rules than using non-binarized parse trees. In Figure 1(a), the node `@VP` indicates that a binarization has been performed on the subtree `VP (VBD PRT PP)`. All remaining rules that have more that four variables are removed.

As the search space of the model is large, we need to apply some heuristic pruning. Following practices used in parsing models such as Huang and Chiang (2005), beam search is performed. The cell limit γ, the maximum number of hypotheses that can be kept at a state in the search process, is set to 30. The beam width β is set to 10^{-4}. This means that if a hypothesis score is worse than β times the score of the best partial hypothesis found up to a specific point in the model, the hypothesis is discarded. γ and β were set to make decoding feasible on available computational resources.

The heuristic pruning may undermine some of the advantages our model might have in taking whole sentence analyses into account to generate error corrections. However, we find that despite this, the model is still able to generate hypothesis corrections that take non-local dependencies into consideration.

6 Language Model Reranking

Although the transducer model defines a joint probability distribution and is therefore sufficient to find corrections for given sentences, incorporating an n-gram language model in our system significantly increases its performance. The main reason for this is that the generative transducer model alone does not have enough discriminative power to distinguish between well-formed and ungrammatical sentences.

6.1 Evaluation

The standard evaluation metric used for grammatical error correction is precision, recall and F1 score. Changes made to a given incorrect sentence are represented by edits. For a sample sentence, the sufficient statistics for this evaluation metric is the 3-tuple (*#correct system edits*, *#system edits*, *#gold standard edits*). This can be summed over all the examples being evaluated, and the precision, recall and F1 scores can be computed from that.

The shared task uses the M^2 scorer, as described by Dahlmeier and Ng (2012). Given the original and system sentences, possible system edit sequences are represented with a lattice. The edit sequence that is the best match with the gold standard edit sequence is chosen to compute the edit scores.

6.2 Reranking

During decoding we compute the language model score for each of the hypothesis sentences generated by our transducer model for a given incorrect sentence. The log probability scores of the transducer and language models are normalized by the length of the incorrect sentence. In order to weigh these two scores, the transducer score is kept fixed, and the language model score is multiplied by a weight α. For a given incorrect sentence i and a generated set of hypothesis correct sentences $H(i)$, we want to find

$$\hat{c} = \arg\max_{c \in H(i)} [TT(c,i) + \alpha \cdot LM(c)] \quad (4)$$

where $TT(c,i)$ gives the tree transducer score and $LM(c)$ gives the language model score. The parameter α is set to maximize the F1 score of the model on a validation set. Let I be the set of incorrect sentences in this set. Then we want to find

$$\hat{\alpha} = \arg\max_{\alpha} \text{F1}[\Sigma_{i \in I} edits(\hat{c}, i, g(i))] \quad (5)$$

where $\hat{c}$ is given by (4) and *edits* is the sufficient statistics for the F1 score of $\hat{c}$ for the incorrect sentence i and gold standard edits $g(i)$.

Data set	Precision	Recall	F1 score
Validation	0.065	0.153	0.092
Development	0.079	0.149	0.103
Test (original)	0.2700	0.1333	0.1785
Test (revised)	0.3712	0.1891	0.2505

Table 2: Model results

7 Results

We now present results of the model on our validation and development sets, as well as on the official test set. A useful measure to analyze the performance of our model is to perform *oracle* reranking on the hypothesis sets generated by the transducer model. For each sentence, the oracle picks the hypothesis that will contribute to the best possible F1 score. We are especially interested in how frequently the correct sentence is among the hypothesis sentences – this is called the *hypothesis coverage*.

7.1 Development sets

On the development set, only 21% of clauses are annotated with corrections. For clauses that have no annotations, the hypothesis coverage is 99%, while for clauses that have annotations the hypothesis coverage is 49%. The oracle obtains a 0.64 F1 score.

We tune the value of α on the validation set to maximize the F1 score. The best F1 score is obtained with $\alpha = 1.6949$. The system results on the validation set and the development set with this α are given in Table 2. It was found that a strong

Error type	Development recall	Test recall
Noun number	0.2231	0.1818
Verb form	0.1839	0.1475
Article or determiner	0.1564	0.1261
Preposition	0.1655	0.0932
Subject-verb agreement	0.0957	0.1048

Table 3: Recall for each error type, on the development set and original test set.

weight on the language model (a relatively large α) increases the recall of the model.

A breakdown of the recall for each error type is given in Table 3. On the development set, the best recall is obtained for noun number errors, and the worst for subject-verb agreement errors. A reason for the relatively low performance on agreement errors may be due to the constituency parse tree representation used. In a clause, the subject noun phrase and the predicate verb phrase, whose head verb must agree with the subject, are in different subtrees. This increases the difficulty in modelling the dependency between the subject and the verb.

7.2 Test set

The test set released for this shared task consists of 1381 sentences, which we split into 2247 clauses using the heuristic described above. The distribution of sentence lengths is very similar to that of the training data. The number of out of vocabulary words is quite small at 0.03%. The set does not include any URLs, and the general impression was that it is less noisy than the training data.

The system result on the test set is given in Table 2. Scores for both the original and revised test data annotations are given. We submitted plausible corrections suggested by our system for the gold standard revision. This contributed to a significant increase in our model score on the revised annotations. The model recall on the test set is similar to that of the development on most error types, though the preposition error recall is significantly lower and the subject-verb agreement recall is slightly higher. This may indicate that preposition error correction rules in the model does not generalize well enough.

The precision of our model is significantly better on the test set than on the development set. This can be explained by differences in the characteristics of the test set. The relative occurrence of annotated errors is much higher in the test set than in the development set: 46% of clauses have corrections. It has been found previously that a low frequency of errors increase the difficulty of the correction task (Dahlmeier and Ng, 2011). This is caused especially by an increase in the number of system edits suggested for sentences that should not be changed. Our oracle found that for sentences that should not be changed, 100% of the correct unchanged hypotheses were generated by the tree transducer, while for sentences that should be changed, 50% of hypothesis sets contained the correct result. The oracle obtains a 0.75 F1 score. The precision of the oracle model increases significantly, from 0.65 to 0.95. Varying the choice of α controls the trade-off between precision and recall better on the test set than on the validation set. These results indicate that our model is more suited for data with the characteristics of the test set than for data similar to the development sets.

8 Conclusion

We presented a novel approach to grammatical error correction based on tree transducers, obtaining promising results. One of the weaknesses of our model is handling insertions and deletions. The model performs too many unnecessary deletions, especially removing content words or non-article determiners. It also has difficulty in finding edits where insertions such as article insertions should be performed.

For future work, ways of constructing better rule sets for the transducer should be investigated to take more dependencies into consideration and to improve probability estimates. Techniques to improve the runtime of the decoding algorithm while minimizing the loss in accuracy caused by heuristic pruning should be considered. Alternative approaches to reranking could also be investigated. Including additional features may increase the ability of the model to discriminate between grammatical and ungrammatical sentences.

Acknowledgement

The financial support of MIH is acknowledged.

References

Steven Bird, Ewan Klein, and Edward Loper. 2009. *Natural Language Processing with Python*. O'Reilly Media.

Chris Brockett, William B. Dolan, and Michael Gamon. 2006. Correcting ESL errors using phrasal SMT techniques. In *Proceedings of ACL*, pages 249–256.

Daniel Dahlmeier and Hwee Tou Ng. 2011. Grammatical error correction with alternating structure optimization. In *Proceedings of ACL*, pages 915–923.

Daniel Dahlmeier and Hwee Tou Ng. 2012. Better evaluation for grammatical error correction. In *Proceedings of HTL-NAACL*, pages 568–572.

Daniel Dahlmeier, Hwee Tou Ng, and Siew Mei Wu. 2013. Building a large annotated corpus of learner English: The NUS corpus of learner English. In *Proceedings of the 8th Workshop on Innovative Use of NLP for Building Educational Applications*, Atlanta, Georgia, USA.

Robert Dale and Adam Kilgarriff. 2011. Helping our own: The HOO 2011 pilot shared task. In *Proceedings of the 13th European Workshop on Natural Language Generation*, pages 242–249, Nancy, France.

Robert Dale, Ilya Anisimoff, and George Narroway. 2012. HOO 2012: A report on the preposition and determiner error correction shared task. In *Proceedings of the 7th Workshop on the Innovative Use of NLP for Building Educational Applications*, pages 54–62, Montreal, Canada.

Michel Galley, Mark Hopkins, Kevin Knight, and Daniel Marcu. 2004. What's in a translation rule? In *Proceedings of HLT-NAACL*, pages 273–280.

Michel Galley, Jonathan Graehl, Kevin Knight, Daniel Marcu, Steve DeNeefe, Wei Wang, and Ignacio Thayer. 2006. Scalable inference and training of context-rich syntactic translation models. In *Proceedings of ACL*, pages 961–968.

Jonathan Graehl, Kevin Knight, and Jonathan May. 2008. Training tree transducers. *Computational Linguistics*, 34(3):391–427.

Liang Huang and David Chiang. 2005. Better k-best parsing. In *Proceedings of the Ninth International Workshop on Parsing Technologies*, pages 53–64.

Slava M. Katz. 1987. Estimation of probabilities from sparse data for the language model of a speech recognizer. *IEEE Transactions on Acoustics, Speech, and Signal Processing*, 35(3):400–401.

Claudia Leacock, Martin Chodorow, Michael Gamon, and Joel R. Tetreault. 2010. *Automated Grammatical Error Detection for Language Learners*. Synthesis Lectures on Human Language Technologies. Morgan & Claypool Publishers.

John Lee and Stephanie Seneff. 2006. Automatic grammar correction for second-language learners. In *Proceedings of Interspeech*, pages 1978–1981.

Jonathan May and Kevin Knight. 2006. Tiburon: A weighted tree automata toolkit. In *CIAA*, volume 4094 of *Lecture Notes in Computer Science*, pages 102–113. Springer.

Jonathan May. 2010. *Weighted Tree Automata and Transducers for Syntactic Natural Language Processing*. Ph.D. thesis, University of Southern California.

George A. Miller. 1995. WordNet: A lexical database for English. *Communications of the ACM*, 38(11):39–41.

Hwee Tou Ng, Siew Mei Wu, Yuanbin Wu, Christian Hadiwinoto, and Joel Tetreault. 2013. The CoNLL-2013 shared task on grammatical error correction. In *Proceedings of CoNLL*.

Y. Albert Park and Roger Levy. 2011. Automated whole sentence grammar correction using a noisy channel model. In *Proceedings of ACL*, pages 934–944.

Slav Petrov and Dan Klein. 2007. Improved inference for unlexicalized parsing. In *Proceedings of HLT-NAACL*, pages 404–411.

Andreas Stolcke. 2002. SRILM: An extensible language modeling toolkit. In *Proceedings of ICSLP*, pages 901–904.

Jenine Turner and Eugene Charniak. 2007. Language modeling for determiner selection. In *Proceedings of HTL-NAACL*, pages 177–180.

Constrained grammatical error correction using Statistical Machine Translation

Zheng Yuan
Computer Laboratory
University of Cambridge
United Kingdom
zy249@cam.ac.uk

Mariano Felice
Computer Laboratory
University of Cambridge
United Kingdom
mf501@cam.ac.uk

Abstract

This paper describes our use of phrase-based statistical machine translation (PB-SMT) for the automatic correction of errors in learner text in our submission to the CoNLL 2013 Shared Task on Grammatical Error Correction. Since the limited training data provided for the task was insufficient for training an effective SMT system, we also explored alternative ways of generating pairs of incorrect and correct sentences automatically from other existing learner corpora. Our approach does not yield particularly high performance but reveals many problems that require careful attention when building SMT systems for error correction.

1 Introduction

Most approaches to error correction for non-native text are based on machine learning classifiers for specific error types (Leacock et al., 2010; Dale et al., 2012). Thus, for correcting determiner or preposition errors, for example, a multiclass model is built that uses a set of *features* from the local context around the target and predicts the expected article or preposition. If the output of the classifier is the same as the original sentence, the sentence is not corrected. Otherwise, a correction is made based on the predicted class. This is the de facto approach to error correction and is widely adopted in previous work.

Building effective classifiers requires identification of features types from the text that discriminate well correcting each specific error type, such as part-of-speech tags of neighbouring words, n-gram statistics, etc., which in turn require additional linguistic resources. Classifiers designed to correct only one type of error do not perform well on nested or sequential errors. Correcting more than one type of error requires building and combining multiple classifiers. These factors make the solution highly dependent on engineering decisions (e.g. as regards features and algorithms) as well as complex and laborious to extend to new types.

An attractive and simpler alternative is to think of error correction as a translation task. The underlying idea is that a statistical machine translation (SMT) system should be able to translate text written in 'bad' (incorrect) English into 'good' (correct) English. An advantage of using this approach is that there is no need for an explicit encoding of the contexts that surround each error (i.e. features) since SMT systems learn contextually-appropriate source-target mappings from the training data. Likewise, they do not require any special modification for correcting multiple error types sequentially, since they generate an overall corrected version of the sentence fixing as much as possible from what they have learnt. Provided the system is trained using a sufficiently large parallel corpus of incorrect-to-correct sentences, the model should handle all the observed errors without any further explicit information like previously detected error types, context or error boundaries, and so forth.

The increasing performance of state-of-the-art SMT systems also suggests they could prove successful for other applications, such as error correction. In fact, SMT systems have been successfully used in a few such experiments, as we report below. The work presented here builds upon these initial experiments and explores the factors that may affect the performance of such systems.

The remainder of this paper is organised as follows: Section 2 gives a summary of previous research using SMT for error correction, Section 3 describes our approach and resources, and Section 4 reports our experiments and results. Section 5 discusses a number of issues related to the performance of our system and reports some attempts at improving it while Section 6 includes our official performance in the shared task. Finally, Section 7 provides conclusions and ideas for future work.

2 Related Work

Brockett et al. (2006) describe the use of an SMT system for correcting a set of 14 countable/uncountable nouns which are often confusing for learners of English as a second language. Their training data consists of a large corpus of sentences extracted from news articles which were deliberately modified to include typical countability errors involving the target words as observed in a Chinese learner corpus. Artificial errors are introduced in a deterministic manner using hand-coded rules including operations such as changing quantifiers (*much* → *many*), generating plurals (*advice* → *advices*) or inserting unnecessary determiners. Experiments show their SMT system was generally able to beat the standard Microsoft Word 2003 grammar checker, although it produced a relatively higher rate of erroneous corrections.

Similar experiments were carried out by Mizumoto et al. (2011) for correcting Japanese as a second language. However, their training corpus comprised authentic learner sentences together with corrections made by native speakers on a social learning network website. Because the original data has no explicit annotation of error types, the resulting SMT system is not type-constrained. Their results show that the approach is a viable way of obtaining very high performance at a relatively low cost provided a large amount of training data is available. These claims were later supported by similar experiments using English texts written by Japanese students (Mizumoto et al., 2012)

Ehsan and Faili (2013) trained SMT systems for correcting grammatical errors and context-sensitive spelling mistakes in English and Farsi. Datasets are obtained by injecting artificial errors into well-formed treebank sentences using predefined error templates. Whenever an original sentence from the corpus matches one of these templates, a pair of correct and incorrect sentences is generated. This process is repeated multiple times if a single sentence matches more than one error template, thereby generating many pairs for the same original sentence. A comparison between the proposed systems and rule-based grammar checkers show they are complementary, with a hybrid system achieving the best performance.

Other approaches using machine translation for error correction are not aimed at training SMT systems but rather at using them as auxiliary tools for producing *round-trip* translations (i.e. translations into a pivot foreign language and back into English) which are used for subsequent post-editing of the original sentence (Hermet and Désilets, 2009; Madnani et al., 2012). This differs from our work in that we focus on training and adapting SMT systems to make all the targeted corrections sequentially rather than using them as 'black boxes' on top of which other systems are built.

3 Method

We approach error correction as a translation task from incorrect into correct English. Several SMT systems are built using different training data and the best one is selected for further refinement. Given the CoNLL-2013 shared task specification, systems are required to correct five specific error types involving articles and determiners (ArtOrDet), noun number (Nn), prepositions (Prep), subject-verb agreement (SVA) and verb forms (Vform) and must ignore other errors in order to achieve a good score.

3.1 Data

The training data provided for the task is a subset of the NUCLE v2.3 corpus (Dahlmeier et al., 2013), which comprises essays written in English by students at the National University of Singapore. The original corpus contains around 1,400 essays, which amount to 1,220,257 tokens, but since a portion of this data (25 essays of about 500 words each) was included in the test set, we estimate the remaining 1,375 essays in the training set contain around 1,207,757 tokens. All the sentences were manually annotated by human experts using a set of 27 error types, although we used a filtered version containing only the five types selected for the shared task.

Because the size of the supplied training data is too small to train an effective SMT system, we used additional data from the Cambridge Learner Corpus[1] (CLC). In particular, we derived new pairs of incorrect and correct sentences using the

[1] http://www.cup.cam.ac.uk/gb/elt/catalogue/subject/custom/item3646603/Cambridge-International-Corpus-Cambridge-Learner-Corpus/

publicly available scripts from the First Certificate in English (FCE) (Yannakoudakis et al., 2011) and others from the International English Language Testing System (IELTS) examinations, which include mainly academic writing. These corpora include about 16,068 sentences (532,033 tokens) and 64,628 sentences (1,361,841 tokens) respectively. Given that the error annotation scheme used in the CLC is more detailed than the one used in NUCLE, a mapping had to be defined so that we could produce corrections only for the five target error types (Table 1).

3.2 Generating Artificial Errors

Following previous approaches, we decided to increase the size of our training set by introducing new sentences containing artificial errors. This has many potential advantages. First, it is an economic and efficient way of generating error-tagged data, which otherwise requires manual annotation and is difficult to obtain. Second, it allows us to introduce only the types of errors we want, thus giving us the ability to imitate the original NUCLE data and circumvent annotation incompatibility. Finally, we can choose our initial sentences so that they match specific requirements, such as topic, length, linguistic phenomena, etc.

Again, we use a publicly available portion of the CLC formed by all the corrected samples featured on the English Vocabulary Profile[2] (EVP) website. These sentences come from a variety of examinations at different levels and amount to 18,830 sentences and approximately 351,517 tokens.

In order to replicate NUCLE errors in EVP sentences as accurately as possible, we applied the following procedure:

1. We extract all the possible correction patterns from the NUCLE v2.3 gold standard and rewrite them as *correct-fragment → incorrect-fragment*. Two types of patterns are extracted, one in terms of lexical items (i.e. surface forms/words) and another using part-of-speech (PoS) tags. Table 2 shows some sample patterns.

2. For each correct sentence in the EVP (target), we generate a pseudo-source sentence by applying zero or more of extracted rules.

   Our approach is very naive and assumes all error-injection rules have equal probability. The injection of errors is incremental and non-overlapping. Figure 1 illustrates this procedure.

3. Lexical patterns take precedence over PoS patterns. However, because the application of a rule is decided randomly, a sentence might end up being distorted by both types of patterns, only one, or none at all (i.e. no errors are introduced). In the last case, both the source and target sentences contain correct versions.

4. A parallel corpus is built using the error-injected sentences on the source side and their original (correct) versions on the target side.

[2] http://www.englishprofile.org/index.php?option=com_content&view=article&id=4&Itemid=5

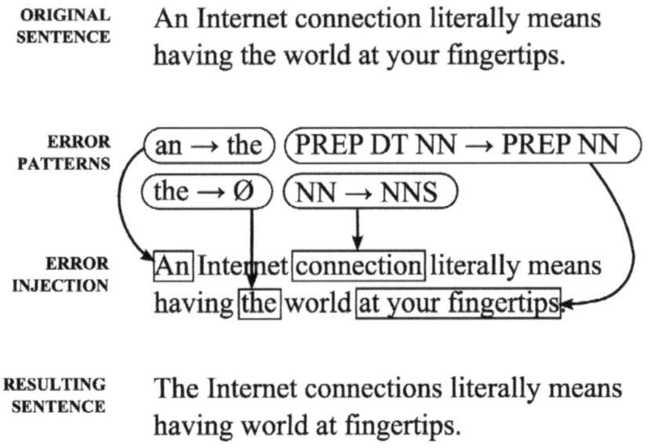

Figure 1: An example of the artificial error injection process.

As we explain in Section 4, this corpus is combined with other training data in order to build different SMT systems.

3.3 Tools

All our systems were built using the Moses SMT system (Koehn et al., 2007), together with Giza++ (Och and Ney, 2003) for word alignment and the IRSTLM Toolkit (Federico et al., 2008) for language modelling. For training *factored models* (Koehn, 2010, Chapter 10) which use PoS information, we use RASP's PoS tagger (Briscoe et al., 2006). Sentence segmentation, tokenisation and PoS tagging for artificial error generation were carried out using NLTK (Bird et al., 2009).

NUCLE v2.3		CLC	
Error Category	**Tag**	**Error Category**	**Tag**
Article or determiner	ArtOrDet	Incorrect determiner inflection	DI
		Determiner agreement error	AGD
		Wrong determiner because of noun countability	CD
		Derivation of determiner error	DD
		Incorrect determiner form	FD
		Missing determiner	MD
		Replace determiner	RD
		Unnecessary determiner	UD
Noun number	Nn	Countability of noun error	CN
		Wrong noun form	FN
		Incorrect noun inflection	IN
		Noun agreement error	AGN
Preposition	Prep	Derivation of preposition error	DT
		Wrong preposition form	FT
		Missing preposition	MT
		Replace preposition	RT
		Unnecessary preposition	UT
Subject-verb agreement	SVA	Verb agreement error	AGV
		Determiner agreement error	AGD
Verb form	Vform	Wrong verb form	FV
		Incorrect verb inflection	IV
		Derivation of verb error	DV
		Incorrect tense of verb	TV
		Missing verb	MV

Table 1: Mapping of error tags between NUCLE v2.3 and the CLC.

Lexical		PoS	
Pattern	**Example**	**Pattern**	**Example**
has → have	*temperature **has** risen → temperature **have** risen*	NN → NNS	*information → informations*
to be used → to be use	*technology to be **used** → technology to be **use***	DT NNP → NNP	*the US → US*
during → for	***during** the early 60s → **for** the early 60s*	NN VBZ VBN → NN VBP VBN	*expenditure **is** reduced → expenditure **are** reduced*

Table 2: Sample error injection patterns extracted from the NUCLE v2.3 corpus.

4 Experiments and Results

We first built a baseline SMT system using only the NUCLE v2.3 corpus and compared it to other systems trained on incremental additions of the remaining corpora. All our systems were trained using 4-fold cross-validation where the training set for each run always included the full FCE, IELTS and EVP corpora but only 3/4 of the NUCLE data, leaving the remaining fourth chunk for testing. This training method allowed us to concentrate on how the system performed on NUCLE data.

Performance was evaluated in terms of precision, recall and F_1 as computed by the M^2 Scorer (Dahlmeier and Ng, 2012), with the maximum number of unchanged words per edit set to 3 (an initial suggestion by the shared task organisers which was eventually changed for the official evaluation). The average performance of each system is reported in Table 3.

In general, results show that precision tends to drop as we add more training data whereas recall and F_1 slightly increase. This suggests that our additional corpora do not resemble NUCLE very much, although they allow the system to correct some further errors. Contrary to our expectations, the biggest difference between precision and recall is observed when we add the EVP-derived data, which was deliberately engineered to replicate NUCLE errors. Although it has been reported that artificial errors often cause drops in performance (Sjöbergh and Knutsson, 2005; Foster and Andersen, 2009), in our case this may also be due to differences in form (e.g. sentence length, grammatical structures covered, error coding) and content (i.e. topics) between our source (EVP) and target (NUCLE) corpora as well as poor control over the artificial error generation process. In fact, our method does not explicitly consider error contexts, error type distribution or other factors that

Model	P	R	F_1	σ
NUCLE	0.1505	0.1530	0.1517	0.0201
NUCLE+FCE	**0.1547**	0.1518	0.1532	0.0216
NUCLE+FCE+IELTS	0.1217	0.2068	0.1532	0.0151
NUCLE+FCE+IELTS+EVP	0.1187	**0.2183**	**0.1538**	0.0206

Table 3: Performance of our lexical SMT models. The best results are marked in bold. Standard deviation (σ) indicates how stable/homogeneous each dataset is (lower values are better).

Model	P	R	F_1	σ
NUCLE	0.1989	0.1013	0.1342	0.0165
NUCLE+FCE	**0.2248**	0.0933	0.1319	0.0151
NUCLE+FCE+IELTS	0.1706	0.1392	0.1533	0.0163
NUCLE+FCE+IELTS+EVP	0.1696	**0.1480**	**0.1581**	0.0148

Table 4: Performance of our PoS factored SMT models. The best results are marked in bold. Standard deviation (σ) indicates how stable/homogeneous each dataset is (lower values are better).

certainly have an impact on the quality of the generated sentences and may introduce noise if not controlled. Nevertheless, the system trained on all four corpora yields the best F_1 performance.

We also tested factored models which include PoS information. Results are shown in Table 4. The same behaviour is observed for the metrics, although values for precision are now generally higher while values for recall are lower. Again, the best system in terms of F_1 is the one trained on all our corpora, slightly outperforming our previous best system.

5 Error Analysis and Further Improvements

When building error correction systems, minimising the number of cases where correct language is flagged as incorrect is often regarded as more important than covering a large number of errors. Technically, this means high precision is often preferred over high recall, especially when it is difficult to achieve both (as is the case for our systems). A closer observation of the training data, translation tables and system output reveals a series of issues that are affecting performance, which are summarised below.

In order to test some solutions to these problems, we used our best system as a baseline and retrained it to include each proposed modification individually. Results are included in Table 5 and referenced accordingly.

5.1 Size of training corpus

With slightly over a million tokens, the NUCLE corpus seems too small to train an efficient SMT system. However, the additional data we were able to use differs from the NUCLE corpus in terms of learner-level, native language, and the tasks being attempted.

5.2 Word reordering

In many cases, our system made corrections by reordering words. Since the five error types in the shared task rarely implied reordering, this caused unnecessary edits that harmed precision, as in the following example.

Original sentence

High Temperture Behaviour Of Candidate...

System hypothesis

High Behaviour Of Temperture Candidate...

Gold standard

High Temperture Behaviour Of Candidate... (unchanged)

Disabling word reordering in our system helped to avoid this problem and increased precision without harming recall (Table 5 #1).

5.3 Limited translation model

Because of the relatively small size of our training corpus, the resulting phrase tables used by our SMT systems contain very general alignments (i.e. corrections) with high probability, which are often applied in inappropriate contexts and result in a large number of miscorrections.
In order to minimise this effect, we forced our SMT system to output the alignments that were used for correcting each sentence in our development sets and deleted from the phrase table those which consistently caused deviations from the gold standard. This was done by manually comparing our systems' hypotheses to their gold-standard versions and identifying common patterns in the alignments that led to miscorrections, such as *to* $\rightarrow$ *to the*, *have* $\rightarrow$ *have a*, *people* $\rightarrow$ *people to*, etc. 1,120 out of the total 11,421,886 alignments in the original translation table were removed ($\sim$0,01%). Removing such alignments re-

sults in higher precision but lower recall, as shown in Table 5 #2.

We also observed that the system was biased towards making unnecessary insertions of the definite article before some specific nouns. This means that the system would almost always change words like *cost*, *elderly* or *government* for *the cost*, *the elderly* or *the government*, regardless of whether this fits the context or not. We believe this is due to the lack of sufficient training samples where these words remained unaltered on the source and target side, so we decided to augment the NUCLE corpus by adding a copy of all the corrected versions of the sentences on both sides. Then, the system should learn that these words can also remain unchanged in corrections. Table 5 #3 shows this improves precision but harms recall.

Out-of-vocabulary words (i.e. words not seen during training) are a also common problem in SMT systems, and this is directly related to the amount of data available for training. In our systems, all out-of-vocabulary words were directly transferred from source to target. That is, whenever our system encounters a word it has not seen previously, it keeps it unchanged. Because of the way our SMT system works, there is no explicit generation of verb or noun forms so unless the system has learnt this from appropriate contexts (for example, that a progressive tense is consistently being used after a preposition), it is unable to make such corrections.

5.4 Inability to distinguish between prepositions

We also observed that our systems did not often correct prepositions. We believed this was due to the PoS language model using the same tag for all prepositions and therefore being unable to distinguish when each preposition must be used. In fact, when using an ordinary PoS language model, the original PoS patterns match those of the expected corrections (i.e. the expected correction has a preposition and the hypothesis has one too) so no change is proposed. The following example illustrates this problem.

Original sentence

...	*the*	*need*	*toward*	*energy*	...
	DT	NN	PREP	NN	

System hypothesis

...	*the*	*need*	*toward*	*energy*	...
	DT	NN	PREP	NN	

(unchanged)

Expected output (not in gold standard)

...	*the*	*need*	*for*	*energy*	...
	DT	NN	PREP	NN	

However, when the PoS language model is modified to use preposition-specific tags, the difference between the original sentence and the expected output should be detected and fixed by the system, as shown below.

Original sentence

...	*the*	*need*	*toward*	*energy*	...
	DT	NN	PREP_TOWARD	NN	

System hypothesis

...	*the*	*need*	*for*	*energy*	...
	DT	NN	PREP_FOR	NN	

(unchanged)

Expected output (not in gold standard)

...	*the*	*need*	*for*	*energy*	...
	DT	NN	PREP_FOR	NN	

We expected this change to improve system performance. Although it increased recall, it lowered precision (Table 5 #4).

5.5 Unnecessary edits

In many cases, our system makes good corrections which are not considered to belong to any of the target error types, as illustrated in the following example.

Original sentence

Thus, we should not compare now with the past but we need to worried about the future problems that caused by this situation.

System hypothesis

Thus, we should not compare now with the past but we need to ***worry*** *about the future problems that* ***are*** *caused by this situation.*

Gold standard

Thus, we should not compare now with the past but we need to ***worry*** *about the future problems that caused by this situation.*

We believe this can be traced to two main causes. First, there is no clear-cut definition of each error type, so it is not possible to know the annotation criteria or scope of each error type. Therefore, inferring this information from the annotated examples may result in poor error mapping between the CLC and NUCLE, making the system learn corrections that are not part of our target set and miss others which are actually useful. For example, it is not clear if 'verb form' errors (Vform) include change of tense or the addition of missing verbs. Second, because SMT systems learn from all parts of a parallel corpus and maximise fluency using a general language model, it is hard to limit the corrections to a predefined set of error types. Using a larger language model based on the corrected version of the CLC confirms this: precision drops while recall improves (Table 5 #5).

5.6 Gold-standard annotation

The original NUCLE corpus contains corrections for 27 error types. However, the version used for the shared task only includes 5 error types and discards all the remaining corrections. Because nested and context-dependent errors are very frequent, the systematic removal of annotations which do not belong to these five types often generates mutilated or partly-corrected sentences, a deficiency that has also been reported in other shared tasks (Kochmar et al., 2012). Here is a typical example.

Original sentence

These approaches may not produce effect soon, but it is sustainable for the future generation.

Corrected sentence

These approaches may not produce [immediate effects]$_{Wci}$, but [they]$_{Pref}$ [are]$_{SVA}$ [useful]$_{Wci}$ for the future [generations]$_{Nn}$.

Type-constrained sentence

These approaches may not produce effect soon, but it [are]$_{SVA}$ sustainable for the future [generations]$_{Nn}$.

These ill-formed sentences are particularly harmful for SMT systems which, unlike classifiers, work at a global rather than local level. As a result, many corrections proposed by our system are considered incorrect because they do not match the gold-standard version, as shown below.

Original sentence

Although it is essential for all the fields, ...

System hypothesis

Although it is essential for all the fields, ... (unchanged)

#	System settings	P	R	F_1
0	*NUCLE+FCE+IELTS+EVP*	*0.1696*	*0.1480*	*0.1581*
1	Disabled reordering	**0.1702**	0.1480	**0.1583**
2	Removal of incorrect alignments	**0.1861**	0.1399	**0.1598**
3	Double NUCLE data	**0.1792**	0.1229	0.1458
4	Detailed Prep PoS tags	0.1632	**0.1504**	0.1565
5	Bigger LMs	0.1532	**0.1676**	**0.1601**
6	Final system (0+1+2+3+5)	**0.1844**	0.1375	0.1575

Table 5: Performance of the baseline system plus different individual settings. Bold values indicate an improvement over the original baseline system.

Gold standard

Although it [are]$_{SVA}$ essential for all the fields, ...

This raises the question of how to design an effective and challenging shared task.

5.7 Scoring criteria

The official evaluation using the M^2 scorer is sensitive to capitalisation and white space, although these error types were not part of the task. Both this fact and the lack of alternative corrections for each gold-standard edit leave out many other valid corrections, which in turn means true system performance is underestimated.

5.8 Other factors

Differences between the training and test data can also affect performance, such as changes in the writers' native language, their level of language proficiency or the topic of their compositions.

The final system submitted to the shared task is a combination of our best factored model (i.e. baseline) plus a selection of improvements (Table 5 #6).

6 Official Evaluation Results

Systems were evaluated using a set of 50 essays containing about 500 words each (~25,000 words in total) which were written in response to two different prompts. One of these prompts had been used for a subset of the training data while the other was new. No error annotations were initially available for this set. As we mentioned above, the M^2 scorer was set to be sensitive to capitalisation and white space as well as limit the maximum number of unchanged tokens per edit to 2.

Initially, each participating team received their official system results individually. After the gold-standard annotations of the test set were released,

Evaluation round	Corr. edits	Prop. edits	Gold edits	P	R	F_1
First (pre-revision)	166	424	1643	0.3915	0.1010	0.1606
Second (post-revision)	222	426	1565	0.5211	0.1419	0.2230

Table 6: Official results of our system before and after revision of the test set annotations. The number of correct, proposed and gold edits are also included for comparison.

many participants raised concerns about their accuracy so they were given the opportunity to submit alternative annotations. These suggestions were manually revised by a human annotator and merged into a new test set which was used to rescore all the submitted systems in a second official evaluation round. Evaluation results of our system in both rounds (before and after revision of the test set annotations) are included in Table 6. Although this measure helped overcome some of the problems described in Section 5.6, other problems such as whitespace and case sensitivity were not addressed.

In both evaluation rounds, our system scores third in terms of precision, which is particularly encouraging for error correction environments where precision is preferred over recall. However, these values should be considerably higher in order to prove useful in applications like self-assessment and tutoring systems (Andersen et al., 2013).

Results also reveal precision on the test set is considerably higher than in our cross-validation experiments. This may be partly a result of the larger amount of training data in our final system and/or greater grammatical or thematic similarity between the test and training sets.

Table 7 shows the distribution of system edits by error type. The results suggest that lexical heterogeneity in the contexts surrounding errors is a factor in performance, which might be improved through larger training sets.

7 Conclusions and Future Work

In this paper we have described the use of SMT techniques for building an error correction system. We trained lexical and factored phrase-based systems using incremental combinations of training data and observed that, in general, recall increases at the expense of precision. However, this might be due to structural and thematic differences in the corpora we used. We also tried a relatively simple mechanism for injecting artificial errors into new data, which caused a drop in precision but increased recall and F_1.

Error Type	Pre-revision			Post-revision		
	Corr.	Missed	Unnec.	Corr.	Missed	Unnec.
ArtOrDet	104	586	161	134	548	132
Nn	30	366	25	38	362	20
Prep	11	301	18	13	246	15
SVA	7	116	0	8	103	0
Vform	14	108	41	29	84	25
Other	0	0	13	0	0	12
TOTAL	166	1477	258	222	1343	204

Table 7: Distribution of system edits by error type for the two official evaluation rounds (before and after revision of the test annotations). 'Corr.' stands for correct edits, 'Missed' for missed edits and 'Unnec.' for unnecessary edits. The category 'Other' includes changes made by our system which do not belong to any of the other categories.

Cross-validation experiments show that our systems were unable to achieve particularly high performance (with precision, recall and F_1 consistently below 0.20). A careful analysis revealed many factors that affect system performance, such as annotation criteria, training parameters and corpus size and heterogeneity. Our final system submitted to the CoNLL 2013 shared task was designed to circumvent some of these problems and maximise precision.

Plans for future work include more detailed error analysis and the implementation of new solutions to avoid drops in performance. We would also like to test our approach in an unrestricted scenario (i.e. using corpora which are not limited to a fixed number of error types) and use more flexible evaluation schemes. We believe further study of the methods used for generating artificial errors is also vital to help SMT systems become a useful approach to error correction.

Acknowledgements

We would like to thank Ted Briscoe and Ekaterina Kochmar for their valuable comments and suggestions. We are also grateful to Øistein Andersen from iLexIR Ltd. for giving us additional feedback, providing us with corrected data to build our language models and granting access to paired samples of the CLC for training our systems. Our gratitude goes also to Cambridge English Language Assessment, a division of Cambridge Assessment, for supporting this research.

References

Øistein E. Andersen, Helen Yannakoudakis, Fiona Barker, and Tim Parish. 2013. Developing and testing a self-assessment and tutoring system. In *Proceedings of the Eighth Workshop on Innovative Use of NLP for Building Educational Applications*, BEA 2013, pages 32–41, Atlanta, GA, USA, June. Association for Computational Linguistics.

Steven Bird, Edward Loper, and Ewan Klein. 2009. *Natural Language Processing with Python*. O'Reilly Media Inc.

Ted Briscoe, John Carroll, and Rebecca Watson. 2006. The second release of the RASP system. In *Proceedings of the COLING/ACL on Interactive presentation sessions*, COLING-ACL '06, pages 77–80, Sydney, Australia. Association for Computational Linguistics.

Chris Brockett, William B. Dolan, and Michael Gamon. 2006. Correcting ESL Errors Using Phrasal SMT Techniques. In *Proceedings of the 21st International Conference on Computational Linguistics and 44th Annual Meeting of the Association for Computational Linguistics*, pages 249–256, Sydney, Australia, July. Association for Computational Linguistics.

Daniel Dahlmeier and Hwee Tou Ng. 2012. Better evaluation for grammatical error correction. In *Proceedings of the 2012 Conference of the North American Chapter of the Association for Computational Linguistics: Human Language Technologies*, NAACL 2012, pages 568 – 572, Montreal, Canada.

Daniel Dahlmeier, Hwee Tou Ng, and Siew Mei Wu. 2013. Building a Large Annotated Corpus of Learner English: The NUS Corpus of Learner English. In *Proceedings of the 8th Workshop on Innovative Use of NLP for Building Educational Applications*, BEA 2013, Atlanta, Georgia, USA. To appear.

Robert Dale, Ilya Anisimoff, and George Narroway. 2012. Hoo 2012: A report on the preposition and determiner error correction shared task. In *Proceedings of the Seventh Workshop on Building Educational Applications Using NLP*, pages 54–62, Montréal, Canada, June. Association for Computational Linguistics.

Nava Ehsan and Heshaam Faili. 2013. Grammatical and context-sensitive error correction using a statistical machine translation framework. *Software: Practice and Experience*, 43(2):187–206.

Marcello Federico, Nicola Bertoldi, and Mauro Cettolo. 2008. IRSTLM: an open source toolkit for handling large scale language models. In *Proceedings of the 9th Annual Conference of the International Speech Communication Association*, INTERSPEECH 2008, pages 1618–1621, Brisbane, Australia, September. ISCA.

Jennifer Foster and Øistein Andersen. 2009. Generrate: Generating errors for use in grammatical error detection. In *Proceedings of the Fourth Workshop on Innovative Use of NLP for Building Educational Applications*, pages 82–90, Boulder, Colorado, June. Association for Computational Linguistics.

Matthieu Hermet and Alain Désilets. 2009. Using first and second language models to correct preposition errors in second language authoring. In *Proceedings of the Fourth Workshop on Innovative Use of NLP for Building Educational Applications*, EdAppsNLP '09, pages 64–72, Boulder, Colorado. Association for Computational Linguistics.

Ekaterina Kochmar, Øistein Andersen, and Ted Briscoe. 2012. Hoo 2012 error recognition and correction shared task: Cambridge university submission report. In *Proceedings of the Seventh Workshop on Building Educational Applications Using NLP*, pages 242–250, Montreal, Canada. Association for Computational Linguistics.

Philipp Koehn, Hieu Hoang, Alexandra Birch, Chris Callison-Burch, Marcello Federico, Nicola Bertoldi, Brooke Cowan, Wade Shen, Christine Moran, Richard Zens, Chris Dyer, Ondřej Bojar, Alexandra Constantin, and Evan Herbst. 2007. Moses: open source toolkit for statistical machine translation. In *Proceedings of the 45th Annual Meeting of the ACL on Interactive Poster and Demonstration Sessions*, ACL '07, pages 177–180, Prague, Czech Republic. Association for Computational Linguistics.

Philipp Koehn. 2010. *Statistical Machine Translation*. Cambridge University Press, New York, NY, USA, 1st edition.

Claudia Leacock, Martin Chodorow, Michael Gamon, and Joel Tetreault. 2010. *Automated Grammatical Error Detection for Language Learners*. Morgan and Claypool Publishers.

Nitin Madnani, Joel Tetreault, and Martin Chodorow. 2012. Exploring grammatical error correction with not-so-crummy machine translation. In *Proceedings of the Seventh Workshop on Building Educational Applications Using NLP*, pages 44–53, Montreal, Canada. Association for Computational Linguistics.

Tomoya Mizumoto, Mamoru Komachi, Masaaki Nagata, and Yuji Matsumoto. 2011. Mining Revision Log of Language Learning SNS for Automated Japanese Error Correction of Second Language Learners. In *Proceedings of 5th International Joint Conference on Natural Language Processing*, pages 147–155, Chiang Mai, Thailand, November. Asian Federation of Natural Language Processing.

Tomoya Mizumoto, Yuta Hayashibe, Mamoru Komachi, Masaaki Nagata, and Yuji Matsumoto. 2012. The effect of learner corpus size in grammatical error correction of ESL writings. In *Proceedings of COLING 2012: Posters*, pages 863–872, Mumbai,

India, December. The COLING 2012 Organizing Committee.

Franz Josef Och and Hermann Ney. 2003. A systematic comparison of various statistical alignment models. *Comput. Linguist.*, 29(1):19–51, March.

Jonas Sjöbergh and Ola Knutsson. 2005. Faking errors to avoid making errors: Very weakly supervised learning for error detection in writing. In *Proceedings of RANLP 2005*, pages 506–512, Borovets, Bulgaria, September.

Helen Yannakoudakis, Ted Briscoe, and Ben Medlock. 2011. A new dataset and method for automatically grading esol texts. In *Proceedings of the 49th Annual Meeting of the Association for Computational Linguistics: Human Language Technologies*, pages 180–189, Portland, Oregon, USA, June. Association for Computational Linguistics.

LFG-based Features for Noun Number and Article Grammatical Errors

Gábor Berend[1], Veronika Vincze[2], Sina Zarriess[3], Richárd Farkas[1]
[1]University of Szeged
Department of Informatics
{berendg, rfarkas}@inf.u-szeged.hu
[2]Research Group on Artificial Intelligence
Hungarian Academy of Sciences
vinczev@inf.u-szeged.hu
[3]University of Stuttgart
Institute for Natural Language Processing
zarriesa@ims.uni-stuttgart.de

Abstract

We introduce here a participating system of the CoNLL-2013 Shared Task "Grammatical Error Correction". We focused on the noun number and article error categories and constructed a supervised learning system for solving these tasks. We carried out feature engineering and we found that (among others) the f-structure of an LFG parser can provide very informative features for the machine learning system.

1 Introduction

The CoNLL-2013 Shared Task aimed at identifying and correcting grammatical errors in the NUCLE learner corpus of English (Dahlmeier et al., 2013). This task has become popular in the natural language processing (NLP) community in the last few years (Dale and Kilgariff, 2010), which manifested in the organization of shared tasks. In 2011, the task Helping Our Own (HOO 2011) was held (Dale and Kilgariff, 2011), which targeted the promotion of NLP tools and techniques in improving the textual quality of papers written by non-native speakers of English within the field of NLP. The next year, HOO 2012 (Dale et al., 2012) specifically focused on the correction of determiner and preposition errors in a collection of essays written by candidates sitting for the Cambridge ESOL First Certificate in English (FCE) examination. In 2013, the CoNLL-2013 Shared Task has continued this direction of research.

The CoNLL-2013 Shared Task is based on the NUCLE corpus, which consists of about 1,400 student essays from undergraduate university students at The National University of Singapore (Dahlmeier et al., 2013). The corpus contains over one million words and it is completely annotated with grammatical errors and corrections. Among the 28 error categories, this year's shared task focused on the automatic detection and correction of five specific error categories.

In this paper, we introduce our contribution of the CoNLL-2013 Shared Task. We propose a supervised learning-based approach. The main contribution of this work is the exploration of several feature templates for grammatical error categories. We focused on the two "nominal" error categories:

1.1 Article and Determiner Errors

This error type involved all kinds of errors which were related to determiners and articles (`ArtOrDet`). It required multiple correction strategies. On the one hand, superfluous articles or determiners should be deleted from the text. On the other hand, missing articles or determiners should be inserted and at the same time it was sometimes also necessary to replace a certain type of article or determiner to an other type. Here is an example:

> For nations like Iran and North Korea, the development of nuclear power is mainly determined by **the** political forces. → For nations like Iran and North Korea, the development of nuclear power is mainly determined by political forces.

1.2 Wrong Number of the Noun

The wrong number of nouns (`Nn`) meant that either a singular noun should occur in the plural form or a plural noun should occur in the singular form. A special case of such errors was that sometimes uncountable nouns were used in the plural, which is ungrammatical. The correction involved here the change of the number. Below we provide an example:

> All these measures are implemented to meet the safety expectation of the operation of nuclear power **plant**. → All these measures are implemented to meet the safety expectation of the operation of nuclear power **plants**.

2 System Description

Our approach for grammatical error detection was to construct supervised classifiers for each candidate of grammatical error locations. In general, our candidate extraction and features are based on the output of the preprocessing step provided by the organizers which contained both the POS-tag sequences and the constituency phrase structure outputs for every sentence in the training and test sets determined by Stanford libraries. We employed the Maximum Entropy based supervised classification model using the MALLET API (McCallum, 2002), which was responsible for suggesting the various corrections.

The most closely related approach to ours is probably the work of De Felice and Pulman (2008). We also employ a Maximum Entropy classifier and a syntax-motivated feature set. However, we investigate deeper linguistic features (based on the f-structure of an LFG parser).

In the following subsections we introduce our correction candidate recognition procedure and the features used for training and prediction of the machine learning classifier. We employed the same feature set for each classification task.

2.1 Candidate Locations

We used the following heuristics for the recognition of the possible locations of grammatical errors. We also describe the task of various classifiers at these candidate locations.

Article and Determiner Error category We handled the beginning of each noun phrase (NP) as a possible location for errors related to articles or determiners. The NP was checked if it started with any definite or indefinite article. If it did, we asked our three-class classifier whether to leave it unmodified, change its type (i.e. an indefinite to a definite one or vice versa) or simply delete it. However, when there was no article at all at the beginning of a noun phrase, the decision made by a different three-class classifier was whether to leave that position empty or to put a definite or indefinite article in that place.

Wrong Number of the Noun Error category Every token tagged as a noun (either in plural or singular) was taken into consideration at this subtask. We constructed two – i.e. one for the word forms originally written in plural and singular – binary classifiers whether the number (i.e. plural or singular) of the noun should be changed or left unchanged.

2.2 LFG parse-based features

We looked for the minimal governing NP for each candidate location. We reparsed this NP without context by a Lexical Functional Grammar (LFG) parser and we acquired features from its f-structure. In the following paragraph, LFG is introduced briefly while Table 1 summarizes the features extracted from the LFG parse.

Lexical Functional Grammar (LFG) (Bresnan, 2000) is a constraint-based theory of grammar. It posits two levels of representation, c(onstituent)-structure and f(unctional)-structure.

C-structure is represented by context free phrase-structure trees, and captures surface grammatical configurations. F-structures approximate basic predicate-argument and adjunct structures.

The experiments reported in this paper use the English LFG grammar constructed as part of the ParGram project (Butt et al., 2002). The grammar is implemented in XLE, a grammar development environment, which includes a very efficient LFG parser. Within the spectrum of approaches to natural language parsing, XLE can be considered a hybrid system combining a hand-crafted grammar with a number of automatic ambiguity management techniques:
(i) c-structure pruning where, based on information from statistically obtained parses, some trees are ruled out before f-structure unification (Cahill et al., 2007)

COORD	NP/PP is coordinated +/-
COORD-LEVEL	syntactic category of coordinated phrase
DEG-DIM	dimension for comparitive NPs, ("equative"/"pos"/"neg")
DEGREE	semantic type of adjectival modifier ("positive"/"comparative"/"superlative")
DET-TYPE	type of determiner ("def"/"indef"/"demon")
LOCATION-TYPE	marks locative NPs
NAME-TYPE	"first_name"/"last_name"
NSYN	syntactic noun type ("common"/"proper"/"pronoun")
PRON-TYPE	syntactic pronoun type (e.g. "pers", "refl", "poss")
PROPER-TYPE	type of proper noun (e.g. "company", "location", "name")

Table 1: Short characterization of the LFG features incorporated in our models designed to correct noun phrase-related grammatical errors

(ii) an Optimality Theory-style constraint mechanism for filtering and ranking competing analyses (Frank et al., 2001),
and (iii) a stochastic disambiguation component which is based on a log-linear probability model (Riezler et al., 2002) and works on the packed representations.

Although we use a deep, hand-crafted LFG grammar for processing the data, our approach is substantially different from other grammar-based approaches to CALL. For instance, Fortmann and Forst (2004) supplement a German LFG developed for newspaper text with so-called malrules that accept marked or ungrammatical input of some predefined types. In our work, we apply an LFG parser developed for standard texts to get a rich feature representation that can be exploited by a classifier. While malrules would certainly be useful for finding other error types, such as agreement errors, the NP- and PP-errors are often analyzed as grammatical by the parser (e.g. "the political forces" vs. "political forces"). Thus, the grammaticality of a phrase predicted by the grammar is not necessarily a good indicator for correction in our case.

2.3 Phrase-based contextual features

Besides the LFG features describing the internal structure of the minimal NP that dominates a candidate location, we defined features describing its context as well. Phrase-based contextual features searched for those minimal prepositional and noun phrases that governed a token at a certain candidate location of the sentence where a decision was about to be taken. Then features encoding the types of the phrases that preceded and succeeded a given minimal governing noun or prepositional phrase were extracted.

The length of those minimal governing noun and prepositional phrases as well as those of the preceding and succeeding ones were taken into account as numeric features. The motivation behind using the span size of the minimal governing and neighboring noun and prepositional phrases is that it was assumed that grammatical errors in the sentence result in unusual constituency subtree patterns that could manifest in minimal governing phrases having too long spans for instance. The relative position of the candidate position inside the smallest dominating noun and prepositional phrases was also incorporated as a feature since this information might carry some information for noun errors.

	Final results	Corrected output
P	0.0552	0.1260
R	0.0316	0.0292
F	0.0402	0.0474

Table 2: Overall results aggregated over the five error types

2.4 Token-based contextual features

A third group of features described the context of the candidate location at the token level. Here, two sets of binary features were introduced to mark the fact if the token was present in the four token-sized window to its left or right. Dedicated nominal features were introduced to store the word form of the token immediately preceding a decision point within a sentence and the POS-tags at the preceding and actual token positions.

Two lists were manually created which consisted of entirely uncountable nouns (e.g. `blood`) and nouns that are uncountable most of the times (e.g. `aid` or `dessert`). When generating features for those classifiers that can modify the plurality of a noun, we marked the fact in a binary feature if they were present in any of these lists. Another binary feature indicated if the actual noun to be classified could be found at an earlier point of the document.

	Only erroneous	All sentences
P	0.1260	0.1061
R	0.0292	0.0085
F	0.0474	0.0158

Table 3: Overall results aggregated over the five error types

	Only erroneous	All sentences
P	0.2500	0.0167
R	0.0006	0.0006
F	0.0012	0.0012

Table 4: Overall results aggregated over the five error types, not using the LFG parser based features

3 Results

It is important to note that our officially submitted architecture included an unintended step which meant that whenever our system predicted that at a certain point an indefinite article should be inserted or (re-)written, the indefinite article `an` was put at that place erroneously when the succeeding token started with a consonant (e.g. outputting `an serious` instead of `a serious`).

Since the output that contained this kind of error served as the basis of the official ranking we include in Table 2 the results achieved with the output affected by this unintended behavior, however, in the following we present our results in such a manner where this kind of error is eliminated from the output of our system.

Upon training our systems we followed two strategies. For the first approach we used all the sentences regardless if they had any error in them at all. However, in an alternative approach we utilized only those sentences from the training corpus that had at least one error in them from the five error categories to be dealt with in the shared task. The different results achieved on the test set according to the two approaches are detailed in Table 3. Turning off the LFG features ended up in the results detailed in Table 4.

Since our framework in its present state only aims at the correction of errors explicitly related to noun phrases, no error categories besides `ArtOrDet` and `Nn` (for more details see Sections 1.1 and 1.2, respectively) could be possibly corrected by our system. Note that these two error categories covered 66.1% of the corrections on the test set, so with our approach this was the highest possibly achievable score in recall.

In order to get a clearer picture on the effectiveness of our proposed methodology on the two error types that we aimed at, we present results focusing on those two error classes.

	`Nn`	`ArtOrDet`
P	0.4783 (44/92)	0.0151 (4/263)
R	0.1111 (44/396)	0.0058 (4/690)
F	0.1803	0.0084

Table 5: The scores achieved and the number of true positive, suggestions, real errors for the Noun Number (`Nn`) and Article and Determiner Errors (`ArtOrDet`) categories.

4 Error Analysis

In order to analyze the performance of our system in more detail, we carried out an error analysis. As our system was optimized for errors related to nouns (i.e. `Nn` and `ArtOrDet` errors), we focus on these error categories in our discussion and neglect verbal and prepositional errors.

Some errors in our system's output were due to pronouns, which are conventionally tagged as nouns (e.g. *something*), but were incorrectly put in the plural, resulting in the erroneous correction *somethings*. These errors would have been avoided by including a list of pronouns which could not be used in the plural (even if they are tagged as nouns).

Another common source of errors was that countable and uncountable uses of nouns which can have both features in different senses or metonymic usage (e.g. *coffee* as a substance is uncountable but *coffee* meaning "a cup of coffee" is countable) were hard to separate. Performance on this class of nouns could be ameliorated by applying word sense disambiguation/discrimination or a metonymy detector would also prove useful for e.g. mass nouns.

A great number of nominal errors involved cases where a singular noun occurred in the text without any article or determiner. In English, this is only grammatical in the case of uncountable nouns which occur in generic sentences, for instance:

> **Radio-frequency identification** is a technology which uses a wireless non-contact system to scan and transfer the data [...]

The above sentence offers a definition of radio-frequency identification, hence it is a generic statement and should be left as it is. In other cases, two possible strategies are available for correction. First, the noun gets an article or a determiner. The actual choice among the articles or determiners depends on the context: if the noun has been mentioned previously and thus is already known (definite) in the context, it usually gets a definite article (or a possessive determiner). If it is mentioned for the first time, it gets an indefinite article (unless it is a unique thing such as *the sun*). The difficulty of the problem lies in the fact that in order to adequately assign an article or determiner to the noun, it is not sufficient to rely only on the sentence. Thus, is also necessary to go beyond the sentence and move on the level of text or discourse, which requires natural language processing techniques that we currently lack but are highly needed. With the application of such techniques, we would have probably achieved better results but this remains now for future work.

Second, the noun could be put in the plural. This strategy is usually applied when either there are more than one of the thing mentioned or it is a generic sentence (i.e. things are discussed in general and no specific instances of things are spoken of). In this case, the detection of generic sentences/events would be helpful, which again requires deep semantic processing of the discourse and is also a possible direction for future work.

To conclude, the successful identification of noun number and article errors would require a much deeper semantic (and even pragmatic) analysis and representation of the texts in question.

5 Discussion and further work

Comparing the columns of Table 3 we can conclude that restricting the training sentences to only those which had some kind of grammatical error in them had a useful effect on the overall effectiveness of our system.

In a similar way, it can be stated based on the results in Table 4 that composing features from the output of an LFG parser is essentially beneficial for the determination of `Nn`-type errors. Table 5 reveals, however, that those features which work relatively well on the correction of `Nn` type errors are less useful on `ArtOrDet`-type errors without any modification.

As our only target at this point was to suggest error corrections related to noun phrases, our obvious future plans include the extension of our system to deal with error categories of different types. Simultaneously, we are planning to utilize large scale corpus statistics, such as the Google N-gram Corpus to build a more effective system.

Acknowledgements

This work was supported in part by the European Union and the European Social Fund through the project FuturICT.hu (grant no.: TÁMOP-4.2.2.C-11/1/KONV-2012-0013).

References

Joan Bresnan. 2000. *Lexical-Functional Syntax*. Blackwell, Oxford.

Miriam Butt, Helge Dyvik, Tracy Holloway King, Hiroshi Masuichi, and Christian Rohrer. 2002. The Parallel Grammar Project. In *Proceedings of COLING-2002 Workshop on Grammar Engineering and Evaluation, Taipei, Taiwan.*

Aoife Cahill, John T. Maxwell III, Paul Meurer, Christian Rohrer, and Victoria Rosén. 2007. Speeding up LFG Parsing using C-Structure Pruning. In *Coling 2008: Proceedings of the workshop on Grammar Engineering Across Frameworks*, pages 33 – 40.

Daniel Dahlmeier, Hwee Tou Ng, and Siew Mei Wu. 2013. Building a Large Annotated Corpus of Learner English: The NUS Corpus of Learner English. In *Proceedings of the 8th Workshop on Innovative Use of NLP for Building Educational Applications (BEA 2013)*, Atlanta, Georgia, USA. Association for Computational Linguistics.

Robert Dale and Adam Kilgariff. 2010. Helping Our Own: Text massaging for computational linguistics as a new shared task. In *Proceedings of the 6th International Natural Language Generation Conference*, pages 261–265, Dublin, Ireland.

Robert Dale and Adam Kilgariff. 2011. Helping Our Own: The HOO 2011 Pilot Shared Task. In *Proceedings of the 13th European Workshop on Natural Language Generation*, Nancy, France.

Robert Dale, Ilya Anisimoff, and George Narroway. 2012. HOO 2012: A Report on the Preposition and Determiner Error Correction Shared Task. In *Proceedings of the Seventh Workshop on Building Educational Applications Using NLP*, pages 54–62, Montréal, Canada, June. Association for Computational Linguistics.

Rachele De Felice and Stephen G. Pulman. 2008. A Classifier-Based Approach to Preposition and Determiner Error Correction in L2 English. In *Proceedings of the 22nd International Conference on Com-*

putational Linguistics (Coling 2008), pages 169–176.

Christian Fortmann and Martin Forst. 2004. An LFG Grammar Checker for CALL. In *Proceedings of ICALL 2004*.

Anette Frank, Tracy Holloway King, Jonas Kuhn, and John T. Maxwell. 2001. Optimality Theory Style Constraint Ranking in Large-Scale LFG Grammars. In Peter Sells, editor, *Formal and Empirical Issues in Optimality Theoretic Syntax*, pages 367–397. CSLI Publications.

Andrew Kachites McCallum. 2002. MALLET: A Machine Learning for Language Toolkit. http://mallet.cs.umass.edu.

Stefan Riezler, Tracy Holloway King, Ronald M. Kaplan, Richard Crouch, John T. Maxwell, and Mark Johnson. 2002. Parsing the Wall Street Journal using a Lexical-Functional Grammar and Discriminative Estimation Techniques. In *Proceedings of ACL 2002*.

Toward More Precision in Correction of Grammatical Errors

Dan Flickinger
Center for the Study of
Language and Information
Stanford University
danf@stanford.edu

Jiye Yu
Center for the Study of
Language and Information
Stanford University
jyu2009@stanford.edu

Abstract

We describe a system for detecting and correcting instances of a small class of frequently occurring grammatical error types in a corpus of essays which have been manually annotated for these errors. Our system employs a precise broad-coverage grammar of English which has been augmented with a set of *mal-rules* and *mal-entries* to explicitly license certain types of erroneous expressions. The derivation tree produced by a parser using this grammar identifies the location and type of an error in an ill-formed sentence, enabling a post-processing script to use the tree and the inventory of error types to delete and/or insert tokens in order to produce a corrected version of the original sentence.

1 Overview

As a participating group in the 2013 CoNLL Shared Task on Grammatical Error Correction, we adapted an existing system for error detection in a simpler closed-vocabulary domain to meet the additional demands of accommodating an open vocabulary and producing corrections for the errors identified. The training and test data for this shared task are from the NUCLE corpus (Dahlmeier et al., 2013), which consists of about one million words of short essays written by relatively competent English language learners. Each sentence has been manually annotated to identify and correct a wide range of grammatical and stylistic error types, though the shared task focused only on correcting instances of five of these types. Following standard procedure for such shared tasks, the organizers supplied most of the annotated data as a development corpus, and held out a 1381-sentence test corpus which was used for the evaluation of system output.

2 Resources and Method

The system developed for this task is an extension of an existing language-processing engine used to identify grammatical errors in short sentences and paragraphs written by elementary school students as part of the automated Language Arts and Writing course included in the EPGY (Education Program for Gifted Youth) course offerings (Suppes et al., 2012). This error detection engine consists of a grammar, a parser, and a post-processing script that interprets the error codes in the derivation tree for each parsed sentence. Both the grammar and the parser are open-source resources developed and distributed as part of the DELPH-IN consortium (*www.delph-in.net*). We use the English Resource Grammar, described below, which we have augmented with both rules and lexical entries that license instances of certain error types, using the *mal-rule* approach of (Schneider and McCoy, 1998), adapted and extended for the ERG as described in (Bender et al., 2004). For parsing each sentence with this grammar, we use the relatively efficient PET parser (Callmeier, 2002), along with a parse-ranking method based on a model trained on a manually disambiguated treebank, so far consisting only of parses of well-formed sentences. In addition to using the manually constructed 37,000-word lexicon included in the ERG, we accommodate unknown words by mapping POS tags produced by TnT (Brants, 2000) to generic lexical entry types on the fly. The bottom-up chart parser then exhaustively applies the rules of the grammar to the lexical entries introduced by the tokens in the input sentence, producing a packed forest of analyses (derivations) ranked by likelihood, and then presents the most likely derivation for post-processing. The post-processor is a script which uses the derivation tree to identify the type and location of each error, and then takes appropriate action, which in the course is an instructional message to the student, and in this shared task is a corrected version of the original sentence.

2.1 English Resource Grammar

The English Resource Grammar used for this task (ERG: (Flickinger, 2000), (Flickinger, 2011)) is a broad-coverage grammar implementation which has been under continuous development since the mid-1990s at Stanford. As an implementation within the theoretical framework of Head-driven Phrase Structure Grammar (HPSG: (Pollard and Sag, 1994)), the ERG has since its inception encoded both morphosyntactic and semantic properties of English, in a declarative representation that enables both parsing and generation. While development has always taken place in the context of specific applications, primary emphasis in the ERG has consistently been on the linguistic accuracy of the resulting analyses, at some expense to robustness. Its initial use was for generation within the German-English machine translation prototype developed in the Verbmobil project (Wahlster, 2000), so constraining the grammar to avoid overgeneration was a necessary design requirement that fit well with the broader aims of its developers. Applications using the grammar since then have included automatic processing of e-commerce customer support email messages, a second machine translation system (LOGON: (Lnning et al., 2004)), and information extraction over the full English Wikipedia (Flickinger et al., 2010).

At present, the ERG consists of a rich hierarchy of types encoding regularities both in the lexicon and in the syntactic constructions of English. The lexicon contains 40,000 manually constructed lexeme entries, each assigned to one of 975 lexical types at the leaves of this hierarchy, where the types encode idiosyncracies of subcategorization, modification targets, exceptional behavior with respect to lexical rules, etc. The grammar also includes 70 derivational and inflectional rules which apply to these lexemes (or to each other's outputs) to produce the words as they appear in text. The grammar provides 225 syntactic rules which admit either unary or binary phrases; these include a relatively small number of highly schematic rules which license ordinary combinations of heads with their arguments and their modifiers, and a rather larger number of construction-specific rules both for frequently occurring phrase types such as coordinate structures or appositives, and for phrase types that occur with markedly differing frequencies in verious corpus domains, such as questions or vocatives. Statistical models trained on manually annotated treebanks are used both in parsing (Toutanova et al., 2005) and in generation (Velldal, 2008) to rank the relative likelihoods of the outputs, in order to address the issue of disambiguation which is central to the use of any broad-coverage grammar for almost any task.

2.2 Mal-rule example

Each of the hand-coded mal-rules added to the standard ERG is a variant of a rule needed to analyse well-formed English input. A simple example of a mal-rule is given below, expressed in the attribute-value representation for an HPSG rule; this unary rule licenses a noun phrase headed by a singular count noun but lacking its normally obligatory article, as for the NP *black cet* in *That dog chased black cat*. Here the single daughter in this noun phrase (the HD-DTR) is a nominal phrase still seeking an obligatory specifier (the article or determiner in a well formed noun phrase), where the head noun is a singular count noun (non-divisible). The SYNSEM value in the rule discharges that obligatory specifier requirement just as the normal unary rule for bare plural noun phrases does, and supplies the necessary implicit quantifier in the semantics of the phrase.

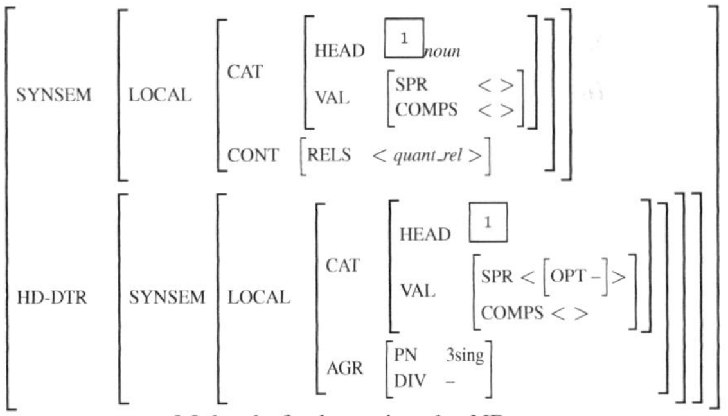

Mal-rule for bare singular NP

2.3 Error types in the task

Of the five error types used in the shared task, four were already included in the grammar as used in the EPGY course, involving errors with articles/determiners, number on nouns, subject-verb agreement, and verb form. For the task, we added mal-rules and mal-entries to analyze a subset of errors of the fifth type, which involve incorrect use of prepositions. Within the ERG, each of the five error types is associated with multiple mal-rules or mal-entries, each licensing one specific error configuration, such as a mal-rule to accommodate the omission of an obligatory determiner for a noun phrase headed by a singular count noun, or a mal-entry for the unwanted use of *the* with a proper name.

Most of these grammar-internal error identifiers correspond to a simple adjustment for correction in the original sentence, such as the insertion or deletion of a particular token, or a change to the inflection of a particular noun or verb. However, for some errors, several candidate corrections are triggered by the error identifier, so the post-processing script must select the most suitable of these correction candidates. The most frequent correction illustrating this ambiguity is for singular count noun phrases missing the determiner, such as *black cat* in *we admired black cat.*, where the correction might be *the black cat*, *a black cat*, or *black cats*. Lacking a rich discourse representation of the context surrounding the error, we employ an N-gram based ranking approach to choose among the three alternatives, where the post-processor currently calls the Microsoft N-gram online resource (Wang et al., 2011).

Since the development and test data is presented as pre-tokenized input with one token per line in familiar CoNLL format, we also employ an offline script which converts a file of this format into one which has a single sentence per line, preserving the tokenization of the CoNLL file, and it is this one-sentence-per-line file which is processed by the correction script, which in turn calls the parser and applies the post-processing steps to its output.

3 An example

We illustrate our method with a simple example sentence, to show each step of the process. Consider the analysis in Figure 1 of the following sentence taken from the test corpus:

In supermarkets monitors is needed because we have to track thieves .

The parser is called with this sentence as input, constructs a packed forest of all candidate analyses licensed by the grammar, and identifies the most likely analysis as determined by a general-purpose statistical model trained only on analyses of well-formed sentences. A more detailed view of the parse tree in Figure 1 is the bracketed derivation tree given in (2). Each line of the derivation identifies the syntactic construction, lexical rule, or lexical entry used to build each constituent, and shows its token span, and for the leaf nodes, the lexical entry, its type (after the slash), and the surface form of that word in the input sentence. The boldface identifier on the first line of the derivation tree shows that this analysis contains at least one erroneous constituent, which a perusal of the tree locates as the other boldface identifier, *be_c_is_rbst*, for the mal-entry for *is* that licenses a mismatch in subject-verb agreement.

(2) Derivation tree view of Fig. 1:

```
hd-aj_scp_c 0 11 [ root_robust_s ]
 flr-hd_nwh-nc-pp_c 0 5
  hd-cmp_u_c 0 2
   in/p_np_i-reg 0 1 "in"
   hdn_bnp_c 1 2
    n_pl_olr 1 2
     supermarket_n1/n_-_c 1 2
      "supermarkets"
  sb-hd_nmc_c 2 5
   hdn_bnp_c 2 3
    n_pl_olr 2 3
     monitor_n1/n_-_c 2 3 "monitors"
   hd-cmp_u_c 3 5
    be_c_is_rbst 3 4  "is"
    hd_xaj-int-vp_c 4 5
     hd_optcmp_c 4 5
      v_pas_odlr 4 5
       need_v1/v_np 4 5 "needed"
 hd-cmp_u_c 5 11
  because/p_cp_s 5 6 "because"
  sb-hd_nmc_c 6 11
   hdn_bnp-qnt_c 6 7
    we/n_-_pr-we 6 7 "we"
   hd-cmp_u_c 7 11
    v_n3s-bse_ilr 7 8
     have_to1/v_vp_ssr 7 8 "have"
    hd-cmp_u_c 8 11
     to_c_prop/cm_vp_to 8 9 "to"
     hd-cmp_u_c 9 11
      v_n3s-bse_ilr 9 10
       track_v1/v_np* 9 10 "track"
      hdn_bnp_c 10 11
       period_plr 10 11
        n_pl_olr 10 11
         thief_n1/n_-_c 10 11 "thieves."
```

The correction script finds this mal-entry identifier in the derivation tree, notes its token position, and determines from the identifier that the required correction consists of a simple token substitution, replacing the surface token *is* with *are*. Since no other errors are present in the derivation tree, the script then records in the corpus output file the corrected sentence with only the one alteration from its original form.

Of course, a derivation tree will often identify multiple errors, and for some error types may require that multiple tokens be modified for a sin-

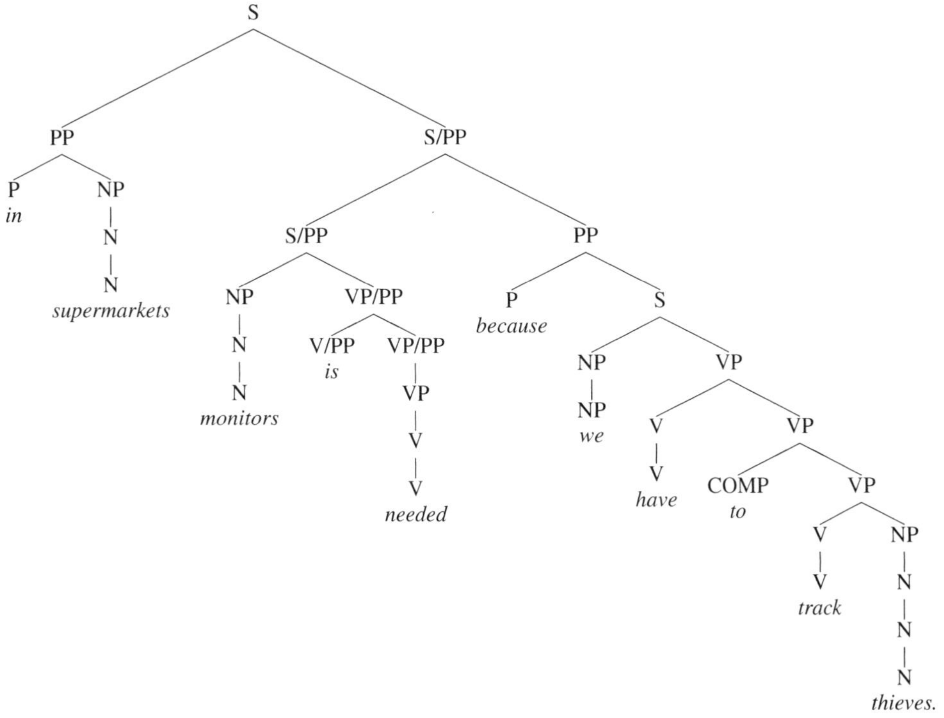

Figure 1: Sample parse tree produced with ERG

gle error, such as in the correction of *the equipments have arrived* to *the equipment has arrived.* Each mal-rule or mal-entry identifier is associated with a specific correction procedure defined in the correction script, and the script carries out these changes in a pre-determined order, for the relatively infrequent instances where the order of application matters. For simple alterations such as a change of number on nouns or verbs, we could have used the grammar-internal inflectional rule machinery, but found it more convenient to use existing Perl and Python modules for English word inflection.

4 Results and Discussion

During the development phase of the shared task, we adapted and refined our method using the first 5000 NUCLE sentences from the roughly 50,000-sentence development corpus. Since our focus in this task is on precision more than on recall, we carried out repeated detailed examinations of the correction procedure's outputs on the first 500 sentences. In comparing our system's proposed corrections with the 'gold' human annotations of errors for these 500, we found the following frequencies of mismatches between system and gold:

(3) Comparison of System and Gold on Dev-500

Alteration	# of Sentences
Both match	34
Missing gold	26
Differing correction	25
Wrong alteration	28

Examples of the missing gold annotations include (a) "ArtOrDet" errors such as the missing article for *habitable environment* in sentence 829-4-0 and for *password* in sentence 830-1-1; (b) "SVA" errors such as for the verb *increase* in sentence 831-3-8, and the verb *are* in sentence 840-4-2; and (c) "Nn" errors such as for the noun *equipments* appearing in sentence 836-1-0, or *evidences* in sentence 837-2-11.

These varying sources of mismatches made the automated scoring script used in the evaluation phase of the shared task (Dahlmeier and Ng, 2012) not so helpful during development, since it reported our system's precision as 28%, whereas the system is actually correct in more than 50% of the alterations it makes for these first 500 sentences of the development corpus.

This inconsistency in the gold annotations was less of an issue, but still present, in our system's precision measure in the evaluation phase of the shared task, as we found in studying the gold annotations distributed for the test data after the evaluation phase ended. The official scored results for the system output that we submitted are given in the table in (4).

(4) Official scoring of system output on test data

Precision	29.93%
Recall	5.86 %
F1	9.81 %

In examining the gold annotations for the 1381 sentences comprising the test corpus, we found 47 instances of genuine errors that were missing gold annotation, but that our system correctly identified and repaired. While this led to a somewhat lower precision measure, we acknowledge that compared with the total number of more than 1600 annotated corrections, this level of imperfection in the annotations was not seriously problematic for evaluation, and we view the official results in (4) as a reasonable measure of the system output we submitted for scoring.

While comparing our system results with the gold test annotations after the evaluation phase ended, we have found and repaired several sources of undesirable behavior in the grammar and in our correction script, with the most significant being the revision of lexical entries for two compound nouns appearing with high frequency in the test corpus: *life expectancy* (91 occurrences) and *population aging/ageing* (40 occurrences). Our lexicon had erroneously identified *life expectancy* as countable, and the parser had wrongly analyzed *population aging* as a noun modified by a participle, analogous to *the person speaking*. A third frequently occurring error in the corpus was not so simple to correct in our grammar, namely the word *society* (95 occurrences), which is used consistently in the test corpus as an abstract noun often wrongly appearing with *the*. Since this noun can be used in a different sense (as an organization) where the article is appropriate, as in *the society of wealthy patrons*, we would need to find some other knowledge source to determine that in the domain of the test corpus, this sense is not used. Hence our system still fails to identify and correct the frequent and spurious *the* in *the society*.

With the small number of corrections made to our system's lexicon, and some minor improvements to the post-processing script, our system now produces output on the test corpus with an improved precision measure of 47.5%, and a more modest improvement in recall to 13.2%, for an F1 of 20.7%. Given the inconsistency of annotation in the development corpus, it is as yet difficult to evaluate whether these changes to our correction script will result in corresponding improvements in precision on unseen data.

5 Next steps

We see prospects for significant improvement using the method we are developing for the kind of automatic correction studied in this shared task. Many of the missteps that our correction procedure makes can be traced to imperfect parse selection from among the candidate analyses produced by the parser, and this could well be improved by creating a Redwoods-style treebank that includes both well-formed and ill-formed sentences for annotation, so the mal-rules and mal-entries get included in the ranking model trained on such a treebank. While our primary focus will continue to be on increased precision in the corrections the system proposes, we welcome the attention to recall that this task brings, and expect to work with hybrid systems that do more with large-scale corpora such as the English Wikipedia.

References

Emily M. Bender, Dan Flickinger, Stephan Oepen, Annemarie Walsh, and Timothy Baldwin. 2004. Arboretum. Using a precision grammar for grammar checking in CALL. In *Proceedings of the InSTIL Symposium on NLP and Speech Technologies in Advanced Language Learning Systems*, Venice, Italy, June.

Thorsten Brants. 2000. TnT - A statistical part-of-speech tagger. In *Proceedings of the 6th ACL Conference on Applied Natural Language Processing*, Seattle, WA.

Ulrich Callmeier. 2002. Preprocessing and encoding techniques in PET. In Stephan Oepen, Daniel Flickinger, J. Tsujii, and Hans Uszkoreit, editors, *Collaborative Language Engineering. A Case Study in Efficient Grammar-based Processing*. CSLI Publications, Stanford, CA.

Daniel Dahlmeier and Hwee Tou Ng. 2012. Better evaluation for grammatical error correction. In *Proceedings of the 2012 Conference of the North American Chapter of the Association for Computational Linguistics: Human Language Technologies*, pages 568 – 572, Montreal, Canada.

Daniel Dahlmeier, Hwee Tou Ng, and Siew Mei Wu. 2013. Building a large annotated corpus of learner english: The NUS Corpus of Learner English. In *To appear in Proceedings of the 8th Workshop on Innovative Use of NLP for Building Educational Applications*, Atlanta, Georgia.

Dan Flickinger, Stephan Oepen, and Gisle Ytrestøl. 2010. WikiWoods. Syntacto-semantic annotation for English Wikipedia. In *Proceedings of the 6th International Conference on Language Resources and Evaluation*, Valletta, Malta.

Dan Flickinger. 2000. On building a more efficient grammar by exploiting types. *Natural Language Engineering*, 6 (1) (Special Issue on Efficient Processing with HPSG):15 – 28.

Dan Flickinger. 2011. Accuracy vs. robustness in grammar engineering. In Emily M. Bender and Jennifer E. Arnold, editors, *Language from a Cognitive Perspective: Grammar, Usage, and Processing*, pages 31–50. Stanford: CSLI Publications.

Jan Tore Lnning, Stephan Oepen, Dorothee Beermann, Lars Hellan, John Carroll, Helge Dyvik, Dan Flickinger, Janne Bondi Johannessen, Paul Meurer, Torbjrn Nordgrd, Victoria Rosn, and Erik Velldal. 2004. LOGON. A Norwegian MT effort. In *Proceedings of the Workshop in Recent Advances in Scandinavian Machine Translation*, Uppsala, Sweden.

Carl Pollard and Ivan A. Sag. 1994. *Head-Driven Phrase Structure Grammar*. Studies in Contemporary Linguistics. The University of Chicago Press and CSLI Publications, Chicago, IL, and Stanford, CA.

David Schneider and Kathleen McCoy. 1998. Recognizing syntactic errors in the writing of second language learners. In *Proceedings of Coling-ACL 1998*, pages 1198 – 1204, Montreal.

Patrick Suppes, Dan Flickinger, Elizabeth Macken, Jeanette Cook, and L. Liang. 2012. Description of the EPGY Stanford University online courses for Mathematics and the Language Arts. In *Proceedings of the International Society for Technology in Education*, San Diego, California.

Kristina Toutanova, Christoper D. Manning, Dan Flickinger, and Stephan Oepen. 2005. Stochastic HPSG parse selection using the Redwoods corpus. *Journal of Research on Language and Computation*, 3(1):83 – 105.

Erik Velldal. 2008. *Empirical Realization Ranking*. Ph.D. thesis, University of Oslo, Department of Informatics.

Wolfgang Wahlster, editor. 2000. *Verbmobil. Foundations of Speech-to-Speech Translation*. Springer, Berlin, Germany.

Kuansan Wang, Christopher Thrasher, Evelyne Viegas, Xiaolong Li, , and Paul Hsu. 2011. An overview of Microsoft Web N-gram corpus and applications. In *Proceedings of the 2011 Conference of the North American Chapter of the Association for Computational Linguistics: Human Language Technologies*, Portland, Oregon.

Grammatical Error Correction as Multiclass Classification with Single Model*

Zhongye Jia, Peilu Wang and Hai Zhao†
MOE-Microsoft Key Laboratory for Intelligent Computing and Intelligent Systems,
Center for Brain-Like Computing and Machine Intelligence
Department of Computer Science and Engineering, Shanghai Jiao Tong University
800 Dongchuan Road, Shanghai 200240, China
{jia.zhongye,plwang1990}@gmail.com, zhaohai@cs.sjtu.edu.cn

Abstract

This paper describes our system in the shared task of CoNLL-2013. We illustrate that grammatical error detection and correction can be transformed into a multiclass classification task and implemented as a single-model system regardless of various error types with the aid of maximum entropy modeling. Our system achieves the F1 score of 17.13% on the standard test set.

1 Introduction and Task Description

Grammatical error correction is the task of automatically detecting and correcting erroneous word usage and ill-formed grammatical constructions in text (Dahlmeier et al., 2012). This task could be helpful for hundreds of millions of people around the world that are learning English as a second language. Although there have been much of work on grammatical error correction, the current approaches mainly focus on very limited error types and the result is far from satisfactory.

The CoNLL-2013 shared task, compared with the previous Help Our Own (HOO) tasks focusing on only determiner and preposition errors, considers a more comprehensive list of error types, including determiner, preposition, noun number, verb form, and subject-verb agreement errors. The evaluation metric used in CoNLL-2013 is Max-Matching (M^2) (Dahlmeier and Ng, 2012) precision, recall and F1 between the system edits and a manually created set of gold-standard edits. The corpus used in CoNLL-2013 is NUS Corpus of Learner English (NUCLE) of which the details are described in (Dahlmeier et al., 2013).

In this paper, we describe the system submission from the team 1 of Shanghai Jiao Tong University (SJT1). Grammatical error detection and correction problem is treated as multiclass classification task. Unlike previous works (Dahlmeier et al., 2012; Rozovskaya et al., 2012; Kochmar et al., 2012) that train a model upon each error type, we use one single model for all error types. Instead of the original error type, a more detailed version of error types is used as class labels. A rule based system generates labels from the golden edits utilizing an extended version of Levenshtein edit distance. We use maximum entropy (ME) model as classifier to obtain the error types and use rules to do the correction. Corrections are made using rules. Finally, the corrections are filtered using language model (LM).

2 System Architecture

Our system is a pipeline of grammatical error detection and correction. We treats grammatical error detection as a classification task. First all the tokens are relabeled according to the golden annotation and a sequence of modified version of error types is generated. This relabeling task is rule based using an extended version of Levenshtein edit distance which will be discussed in the following section. Then with the modified error types as the class labels, a classifier using ME model is trained. The grammatical error correction is also rule based, which is basically the reverse of the relabeling phase. The modefied version of error types that we used is much more detailed than the original five types so that it enables us to use one rule to do the correction for each modified error type. After all, the corrections are filtered by LM, to remove those corrections that seem much worse than the original sentence.

As typical classification task, we have a training step and a test step. The training step consists three phases:

- Error types relabeling.
- Training data refinement.
- ME training.

The test step includes three phases:

- ME classification.

*This work was partially supported by the National Natural Science Foundation of China (Grant No.60903119, Grant No.61170114, and Grant No.61272248), and the National Basic Research Program of China (Grant No.2009CB320901 and Grant No.2013CB329401).

†Corresponding author

- Error correction according to lebels.
- LM filtering.

2.1 Rebeling by Levenshtein Edit Distance with Inflection

In CoNLL-2013 there are 5 error types but they cannot be used directly as class labels, since they are too general for error correction. For example, the verb form error includes all verb form inflections such as converting a verb to its infinitive form, gerund form, paste tense, paste participle, passive voice and so on. Previous approaches (Dahlmeier et al., 2012; Rozovskaya et al., 2012; Kochmar et al., 2012) manually decompose each error types to more detailed ones. For example, in (Dahlmeier et al., 2012), the determinater error is decomposed into:

- replacement determiner (RD): { *a* → *the* }
- missing determiner (MD): { ϵ → *a* }
- unwanted determiner (UD): { *a* → ϵ }

For limited error types such as merely determinatives error and preposition error in HOO 2012, manually decomposition may be sufficient. But for CoNLL-2013 with 5 error types including complicated verb inflection, an automatic method to decompose error types is needed. We present an extended version of Levenshtein edit distance to decompose error types into more detailed class labels and relabel the input with the labels generated.

The original Levenshtein edit distance has 4 edit types: unchange ($\mathcal{U}$), addition ($\mathcal{A}$), deletion ($\mathcal{D}$) and substitution ($\mathcal{S}$). We extend the "substitution" edit into two types of edits: inflection ($\mathcal{I}$) and the orignal substitution ($\mathcal{S}$). To judge whether two words can be inflected from each other, the extended algorithm needs lemmas as input. If the two words have the same lemma, they can be inflected from each other. The extended Levenshtein edit distance with inflection is shown in Algorithm 1. It takes the source tokens tok_{src}, destination tokens tok_{dst} and their lemmas lem_{src}, lem_{dst} as input and returns the edits $\mathbb{E}$ and the parameters of edits $\mathbb{P}$. For example, for the golden edit {*look* → *have been looking at*}, the edits $\mathbb{E}$ returned by DISTANCE will be $\{\mathcal{A}, \mathcal{A}, \mathcal{U}, \mathcal{A}\}$, and the parameters $\mathbb{P}$ of edits returned by DISTANCE will be {*have, been, looking, at*}.

Then with the output of DISTANCE, the labels can be generated by calculating the edits between original text and golden edits. For those tokens without errors, we directly assign a special label "$\odot$" to them. The tricky part of the relabeling algorithm is the problem of the edit "addition", $\mathcal{A}$. A new token can only be added before or after an existing token. Thus for labels with addition, we must find some token that the label can be assigned to. That sort of token is defined as *pivot*. A pivot can be a token that is not changed in an edit, such as the "*apple*" in edit {*apple* → *an apple*}, or some other types of edit such as the inflection of "*look*" to "*looking*" in edit {*look* → *have been look-*

Algorithm 1 Levenshtein edit distance with inflection

```
function DISTANCE(tok_src, tok_dst, lem_src, lem_dst)
    (l_src, l_dst) ← (len(tok_src), len(tok_dst))
    D[0...l_src][0...l_dst] ← 0
    B[0...l_src][0...l_dst] ← (0, 0)
    E[0...l_src][0...l_dst] ← φ
    for i ← 1...l_src do
        D[i][0] ← i
        B[i][0] ← (i − 1, 0)
        E[i][0] ← 𝒟
    end for
    for j ← 1...l_dst do
        D[0][j] ← j
        B[0][j] ← (0, j − 1)
        E[0][j] ← 𝒜
    end for
    for i ← 1...l_src; j ← 1...l_dst do
        if tok_src[i − 1] = tok_dst[j − 1] then
            D[i][j] ← D[i − 1][j − 1]
            B[i][j] ← (i − 1, j − 1)
            E[i][j] ← 𝒰
        else
            m ← min(D[i − 1][j − 1], D[i − 1][j], D[i][j − 1])
            if m = D[i − 1][j − 1] then
                D[i][j] ← D[i − 1][j − 1] + 1
                B[i][j] ← (i − 1, j − 1)
                if lem_src[i − 1] = lem_dst[j − 1] then
                    E[i][j] ← 𝒮
                else
                    E[i][j] ← ℐ
                end if
            else if m = D[i − 1][j] then
                D[i][j] ← D[i − 1][j] + 1
                B[i][j] ← (i − 1, j)
                E[i][j] ← 𝒟
            else if m = D[i][j − 1] then
                D[i][j] ← D[i][j − 1] + 1
                B[i][j] ← (i, j − 1)
                E[i][j] ← 𝒜
            end if
        end if
    end for
    (i, j) ← (l_src, l_dst)
    while i > 0 ∨ j > 0 do
        insert E[i][j] into head of 𝔼
        insert tok_dst[j − 1] into head of ℙ
        (i, j) ← B[i][j]
    end while
    return (𝔼, ℙ)
end function
```

ing at}. In the CoNLL-2013 task, the addition edits are mostly adding articles or determinaters, so when generating the label, adding before the pivot is preferred and only those trailing edits are added after the last pivot. At last, the label is normalized to upper case.

The BNF syntax of labels is defined in Figure 1. The the non-terminal ⟨*inflection-rules*⟩ can be substituted by terminals of inflection rules that are used for correcting the error types of noun number, verb form, and subject-verb agreement errors. All the inflection rules are listed in Table 1. The ⟨*stop-word*⟩ can be subsituted by terminals of stop words which contains all articles, determinnaters and prepositions for error types of determiner and preposition, and a small set of other common stop words. All the stop words are listed in Table 2.

⟨*label*⟩ ::= ⟨*simple-label*⟩ | ⟨*compound-label*⟩

⟨*simple-label*⟩ ::= ⟨*pivot*⟩ | ⟨*add-before*⟩ | ⟨*add-after*⟩

⟨*compound-label*⟩ ::= ⟨*add-before*⟩ ⟨*pivot*⟩
  | ⟨*pivot*⟩ ⟨*add-after*⟩
  | ⟨*add-before*⟩ ⟨*pivot*⟩ ⟨*add-after*⟩

⟨*pivot*⟩ ::= ⟨*inflection*⟩ | ⟨*unchange*⟩ | ⟨*substitution*⟩
  | ⟨*deletion*⟩

⟨*add-before*⟩ ::= ⟨*stop-word*⟩⊕
  | ⟨*stop-word*⟩⊕⟨*add-before*⟩

⟨*add-after*⟩ ::= ⊕⟨*stop-word*⟩
  | ⊕⟨*stop-word*⟩⟨*add-after*⟩

⟨*substitution*⟩ ::= ⟨*stop-word*⟩

⟨*inflection*⟩ ::= ⟨*inflection-rules*⟩

⟨*unchange*⟩ ::= ⊙

⟨*deletion*⟩ ::= ⊖

Figure 1: BNF syntax of label

Algorithm 2 is used to generate the label from the extended Levenshtein edits according to the syntax defined in Figure 1. It takes the original tokens, tok_{orig} and golden edit tokens, tok_{gold} in an annotation and their lemmas, lem_{orig}, lem_{gold} as input and returns thc generated label $\mathbb{L}$. For our previous example of edit {*looked* → *have been looking at*}, the $\mathbb{L}$ returned by RELABEL is {HAVE⊕BEEN⊕GERUND⊕AT}. Some other examples of relabeling are demonstrated in Table 3.

The correction step is done by rules according to the labels. The labels are parsed with a simple LL(1) parser and edits are made according to labels. A bit of extra work has to be taken to handle the upper/lower case problem. For additions and substitutions, the words added or substituted are normalized to lowercase. For inflections, original case of words are reserved. Then a bunch of regular expressions are applied to correct upper/lower case for sentence head.

Catalog	Rules
Noun Number	LEMMA, NPLURAL
Verb Number	VSINGULAR, LEMMA
Verb Tense	LEMMA, GERUND, PAST, PART

Table 1: Inflection rules

Catalog	Words
Determinater	a an the my your his her its our their this that these those
Preposition	about along among around as at beside besides between by down during except for from in inside into of off on onto outside over through to toward towards under underneath until up upon with within without
Modal Verb	can could will would shall should must may might
BE	be am is are was were been
HAVE	have has had
Other	many much

Table 2: Stop words

Tokens	Edit	Label
to reveal	{*to reveal*→*revealing*}	⊖ GERUND
a woman	{*a woman*→*women*}	⊖ NPLURAL
developing wold	{*developing world* →*the developing world*}	THE⊕ ⊙
a	{*a*→ ϵ}	⊖
in	{*in*→*on*}	ON
apple	{*apple*→*an apple*}	AN⊕

Table 3: Examples of relabeling

2.2 Training Corpus Refinement

The corpus used to train the grammatical error recognition model is highly imbalanced. The original training corpus has 57,151 sentences and only 3,716 of them contain at least one grammatical error, and only 5,049 of the total 1,161K words are needed to be corrected. This characteristic makes it hard to get a well-performed machine learning model, since the samples to be recognized are so sparse and those large amount of correct data will severely affect the machine learning process as it is an optimization on the global training data. While developing our system, we found that only using sentences containing grammatical errors will lead to a notable improvement of the result.

Algorithm 2 Relabeling using the extended Levenshtein edit distance

```
function RELABEL(tok_orig, tok_gold, lem_orig, lem_gold)
    (𝔼, ℙ) ← DISTANCE(tok_orig, tok_gold, lem_orig, lem_gold)
    pivot ← number of edits in 𝔼 that are not 𝒜
    𝕃 ← ϕ
    L ← ''
    while i < length of 𝔼 do
        if 𝔼[i] = 𝒜 then
            L ← L+ label of edit 𝔼[i] with ℙ[i]
            i ← i + 1
        else
            l ← L+ label of edit 𝔼[i] with ℙ[i]
            pivot ← pivot − 1
            if pivot = 0 then
                i ← i + 1
                while i < length of 𝔼 do
                    l ← l + ⊕ + ℙ[i]
                    i ← i + 1
                end while
            end if
            push l into 𝕃
            L ← ''
        end if
    end while
    𝕃 ← upper case of 𝕃
    return 𝕃
end function
```

Algorithm 3 Training Corpus Refine Algorithm

```
function CORPUSREFINE(sentence, c, n)
    context ← ϕ
    if sentence contains no error then
        return ϕ
    end if
    build the syntax tree T of sentence
    enode ← the node with error in T
    e ← enode
    while True do
        pnode ← parent node of e in T
        cnodes ← all the children nodes of pnode in T
        if len(cnodes) > c then
            context ← cnodes
            break
        end if
        e ← pnode
    end while
    i ← the position of enode in context
    l ← size of context
    if i < n then
        add (n-i) words before context at the head of context
    end if
    if l-i<n then
        append (l-i) words after context in context
    end if
    return context
end function
```

Inspired by this phenomenon, we propose a method to refine the training corpus which will reduce the error sparsity of the training data and notably improve the recall rate.

The refined training corpus is composed of contexts containing grammatical errors. To keep the information which may have effects on the error identification and classification, those contexts are selected based on both syntax tree and n-gram, of which the process is shown in Algorithm 3. For a word with error, its *syntax context* of size c is those words in the minimal subtree in the syntax tree with no less than c leaf nodes; and its *n-gram context* of size n is $n-1$ words before and after itself. In the CORPUSREFINE algorithm, the input c gives the size of syntax context and n provides the size of the n-gram context. These two parameters decide the amount of information that may affect the recognition of errors. To obtain the context, given a $sentence$ containing a grammatical error, we first get a minimum syntax tree whose number of terminal nodes exceed the c threshold, then check whether the achieved context containing the error word's n-gram, if not, add the n-gram to the context. At last the $context$ is returned by CORPUSREFINE.

An example illustrating this process is presented in Figure 2. In this example, n and c are both set to 5, the minimal syntax tree and the context decided by it are colored in green. Since the syntax context in the green frame does not contain the error word's 5-gram, therefore, the 5-gram context in the blue frame is added to the syntax context and the final achieved context of this sentence is "*have to stop all works for the development*".

2.3 LM Filter

All corrections are filtered using a large LM. Only those corrections that are not too much worse than the original sentences are accepted. Perplexity (PPL) of the n-gram is used to judge whether a sentence is good:

$$PPL = 2^{-\sum_{w \in n\text{-gram}} p(w) \log p(w)},$$

We use r_{PPL}, the ratio between the PPL before and after correction, as a metric of information gain.

$$r_{PPL} = \frac{PPL_{corrected}}{PPL_{original}},$$

Only those corrections with an r_{PPL} lower than a certain threshold are accepted.

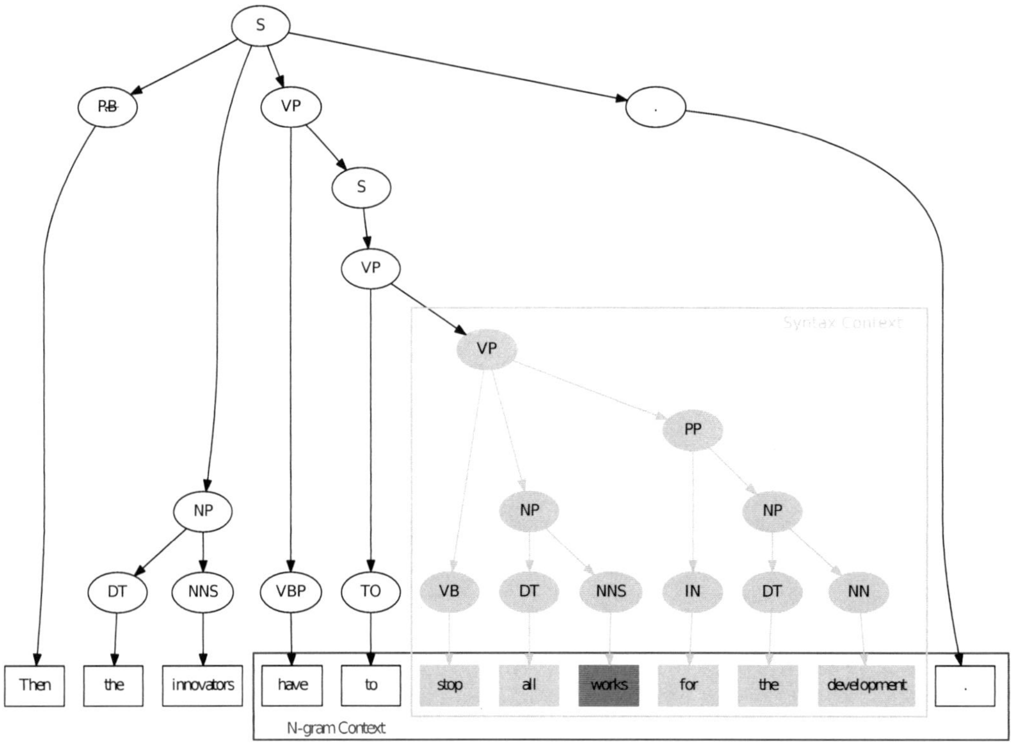

Figure 2: Example of training corpus refinement

3 Features

The single model approach enables us only to optimize one feature set for all error type in the task, which can drastically reduce the computational cost in feature selection.

As many previous works have proposed various of features, we first collected features from different previous works including (Dahlmeier et al., 2012; Rozovskaya et al., 2012; HAN et al., 2006; Rozovskaya et al., 2011; Tetreault, Joel R and Chodorow, Martin, 2008). Then experiments with different features were built to test these features' effectiveness and only those have positive contribution to the final performance were preserved. The features we used are presented in Table 4, where $word_0$ is the word that we are generating features for, and $word$ and POS is the word itself and it's POS tag for various components. **NPHead** denotes the head of the minimum Noun Phrase (**NP**) in syntax tree. $word_{NP-1}$ represents the word appearing before **NP** in the sentence. **NC** stands for noun compound and is composed of the last n words ($n \geq 2$) in **NP** which are tagged as a noun. **Verb** feature is the $word$ that is tagged as a verb whose direct object is the **NP** containing current word. **Adj** feature represents the first $word$ in the **NP** whose POS is adjective. **Prep** feature denotes the preposition $word$ if it immediately precedes the **NP**. **DPHead** is the parent of the current word in the dependency tree, and **DPRel** is the dependency relation with parent.

4 Experiments

4.1 Data Sets

The CoNLL-2013 training data consist of 1,397 articles together with gold-standard annotation. The documents are a subset of the NUS Corpus of Learner English (NUCLE) (Dahlmeier et al., 2013). The official test data consists of 50 new essays which are also from NUCLE. The first 25 essays were written in response to one prompt. The remaining 25 essays were written in response to a second prompt. One of the prompts had been used for the training data, while the other prompt is new. More details of the data set are described in (Ng et al., 2013).

We split the the entire training corpus ALL by article. For our training step, we randomly pick 90% articles of ALL and build a training corpus TRAIN of 1,258 articles. The rest 10% of ALL with 139 articles are for developing corpus DEV .

For the final submission, we use the entire corpus ALL for relabeling and training.

Feature	**Example**
Lexical features	
$word_0$ (current word)	*the*
$word_i, (i = \pm1, \pm2, \pm3)$	*man, stared, at, old, oak, tree*
n words before $word_0$, (n=2, 3, 4)	*stared+at, man+stared+at...*
n words after $word_0$, (n=2, 3, 4)	*old+oak, old+oak+tree ...*
$word_i + POS_i, (i = \pm1, \pm2, \pm3)$	*stared+VBD, at+IN...*
First word in **NP**	*the*
ith word before/after **NP**, $(i = \pm1, \pm2, \pm3)$	*man, stared, at, period ...*
$word_{NP-1}$ + **NP**	*at + (the + old + oak + tree)*
Bag of $words$ in **NP**	*old+oak+the+tree*
NC	*oak tree*
Adj + **NC**	*old oak tree*
Adj_POS + **NC**	*JJ+oak tree*
POS features	
POS_0 (current word POS)	*NNS*
$POS_i, (i = \pm1, \pm2, \pm3)$	*NN, VBD, IN ...*
$POS_{-n} + POS_{-(n-1)} + \cdots + POS_{-1}, (n = 2, 3, 4)$	*VBD + IN, NN + VBD + IN ...*
$POS_1 + POS_2 + \cdots + POS_n, (n = 2, 3, 4)$	*JJ + NN, JJ + NN + NNS ...*
Bag of POS in **NP**	*DT+JJ+NN+NN*
Head word features	
NPHead of **NP**	*tree*
NPHead_POS	*NN*
NPHead + **NPHead**_POS	*tree+NN*
Bag of POS in **NP** + **NPHead**	*DT JJ NN NN+tree*
$word_{NP-1}$ + **NPHead**	*at+tree*
Adj + **NPHead**	*old+tree*
Adj_POS + **NPHead**	*JJ+tree*
$word_{NP-1}$ + **Adj** + **NPHead**	*at+old+tree*
$word_{NP-1}$ + **Adj**_POS + **NPHead**	*at+JJ+tree*
Preposition features	
Prep	*at*
Prep + **NPHead**	*at+tree*
Prep + **Adj** + **NPHead**	*at+old+tree*
Prep + **Adj**_POS + **NPHead**	*at+JJ+tree*
Prep + **NC**	*at+(oak+tree)*
Prep + **NP**	*at + (the + old + oak + tree)*
Prep + **NPHead**_POS	*at+NN*
Prep + **Adj** + **NPHead**_POS	*at+old+NN*
Prep + **Adj**_POS + **NPHead**_POS	*at + JJ + NN*
Prep + Bag of **NP**_POS	*at + (DT + JJ + NN)*
Prep + **NPHead**_POS + **NPHead**	*at + NN + tree*
Lemma features	
Lemma	the
Dependency features	
DPHead $word$	tree
DPHead POS	NN
DPRel	det

Table 4: Features for grammatical error recognition. The example sentence is:"*That man stared at the old oak tree.*" and the current word is "*the*" .

Feature	**Example**
Verb features	
Verb	stared
Verb POS	VBD
Verb + **NPHead**	stared+tree
Verb + **Adj** + **NPHead**	stared+old+tree
Verb + **Adj**_POS + **NPHead**	stared+JJ+tree
Verb + **NP**	stared+(the+old+oak+tree)
Verb + Bag of **NP**_POS	stared+(DT+JJ+NN)

Table 5: Features Continued

Count	Label
1146000	⊙
3369	⊖
3088	NPLURAL
2766	THE⊕
1470	LEMMA
706	A⊕
200~300	IN AN⊕ THE ARE FOR TO OF
100 ~200	ON A IS GERUND PAST VSINGULAR
50~100	WITH ⊕THE AT AN BY THIS INTO
5~50	FROM TO⊕ WAS ABOUT WERE ⊕A THESE TO⊕LEMMA OF⊕ ⊕OF ARE⊕ ⊕TO THROUGH BE⊕PAST AS AMONG IN⊕ BE⊕ THEIR THE⊕LEMMA OVER ⊕ON HAVE⊕ DURING FOR⊕ ⊕WITH PART ⊕IN HAVE WITHIN BE MANY ⊕AN THE⊕NPLURAL MUCH IS⊕ WITH⊕ TOWARDS ⊕FOR HAVE⊕PART ⊕ABOUT WILL ⊕UPON THEIR⊕ HAVE⊕PAST HAS⊕PART HAS⊕ HAS BY⊕ BEEN⊕ BE⊕⊙ AN⊕LEMMA THAT⊕ ITS HAD FROM⊕ BETWEEN A⊕LEMMA
4	WERE⊕ UPON THOSE ON⊕ MANY⊕ IS⊕⊙ ⊕FROM CAN AS⊕
3	WILL⊕LEMMA WILL⊕ TOWARD THIS⊕ THAT ITS⊕ HAVE⊕⊙ ⊕BE AT⊕ ⊕AS ABOUT⊕
2	WOULD WAS⊕ TO⊕BE⊕ THE⊕⊙ ONTO IS⊕PAST IS⊕GERUND INSIDE HAVE⊕BEEN⊕ CAN⊕LEMMA ⊕BEEN ⊕AT
1	WOULD⊕LEMMA WITHOUT UNDER TO⊕THE TO⊕THAT⊕OF TO⊕HAVE THIS⊕WILL⊕ THIS⊕MAY THIS⊕HAS⊕ THESE⊕ THE⊕⊙⊕OF THEIR⊕LEMMA THE⊕GERUND THE⊕A⊕ THAT⊕HAS⊕BEEN⊕ THAT⊕HAS⊕ SHOULD⊕ ⊕OVER OF⊕THE⊕ OF⊕THE OF⊕GERUND OFF OF⊕A⊕ MAY⊕ MAY IS⊕TO IS⊕LEMMA INTO⊕ ⊕INTO IN⊕THE⊕ HIS HAVE⊕AN HAS⊕PAST HAS⊕BEEN⊕GERUND HAS⊕BEEN⊕ HAD⊕⊙ HAD⊕ DURING⊕ COULD CAN⊕BE⊕ CAN⊕ BY⊕GERUND ⊕BY ⊕BETWEEN BESIDES BEEN⊕PART BEEN AT⊕AN AT⊕A AS⊕THE AS⊕HAS AROUND ARE⊕PAST ARE⊕A ARE⊕⊙ A⊕⊙⊕OF AM⊕

Table 6: All labels after relabeling

4.2 Resources

We use the following NLP resources in our system. For relabeling and correction, perl module Lingua::EN::Inflect[1] (Conway, 1998) is used for determining noun and verb number and Lingua::EN::VerbTense[2] is used for determining verb tense. A revised and extended version of maximum entropy model[3] is used for ME modeling. For lemmatization, the Stanford CoreNLP lemma annotator (Toutanova et al., 2003; Toutanova and Manning, 2000) is used. The language model is built by the SRILM toolkit (Stolcke and others, 2002). The corpus for building LM is the EuroParl corpus (Koehn, 2005). The English part of the German-English parallel corpus is actually used. We use such a corpus to build LM for the following reasons: 1. LM for grammatical error correction should be trained from corpus that itself is grammatically correct, and the EuroParl corpus has very good quality of writing; 2. the NUCLE corpus mainly contains essays on subjects such as environment, economics, society, politics and so on, which are in the same dormain as those of the EuroParl corpus.

4.3 Relabeling the Corpus

There are some complicated edits in the annotations that can not be represented by our rules, for example substitution of non-stopwords such as $\{$*human* $\rightarrow$ *people*$\}$ or $\{$*are not short of* $\rightarrow$ *do not lack*$\}$. The relabeling phase will ignore those ones thus it may not cover all the edits. After all, we get 174 labels after relabeling on the entire corpus as shown in Table 6. These labels are generated following the syntax defined in Figure1 and terminals defined in Table 1 and Table 2. Directly applying these labels for correction receives an M^2 score of Precission $= 91.43\%$, Recall $= 86.92\%$ and F1 $= 89.12\%$. If the non-stopwords non-inflection edits are included, of course the labels will cover all the golden annotations and directly applying labels for correction can receive a score up to almost F1 $= 100\%$. But that will get nearly 1,000 labels which is too computationally expensive for a classification task. Cut out labels with very low frequency such as those exists only once reduces the training time, but does not give significant performance improvement, since it hurts the coverage of error detection. So we use all the labels for training.

4.4 LM Filter Threshold

To choose the threshold for r_{PPL}, we run a series of tests on the DEV set with different thresholds. From our empirical observation on those right corrections and those wrong ones, we find the right ones seldomly have $r_{PPL} > 2$, so we test thresholds ranging from 1.5 to 3. The curves are shown in Figure 3.

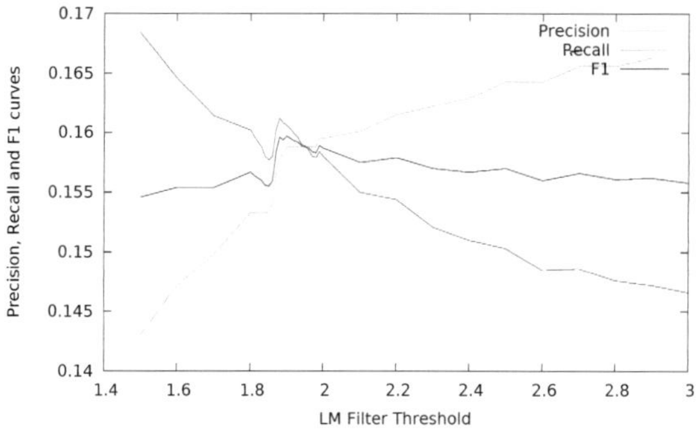

Figure 3: Different thresholds of LM filters

With higher threshold, more correction with lower information gain will be obtained. Thus the recall grows higher but the precission grows lower. We can observe a peak of F1 arround 1.8 to 2.0, and the threshold chosen for final submission is 1.91.

4.5 Evaluation and Result

The evaluation is done by calculating the M^2 precission, recall and F1 score between the system output and golden annotation. All the error types are evaluated jointly. Only one run of a team is permitted to be submitted. Table 7 shows our result on our DEV data set and the official test data set.

Data Set	Precission	Recall	F1
DEV	16.03%	15.88%	15.95%
Official	40.04%	10.89%	17.13%

Table 7: Evaluation Results

5 Conclusion

In this paper, we presented the system from team 1 of Shanghai Jiao Tong University that participated in the HOO 2012 shared task. Our system achieves an F1 score of 17.13% on the official test set based on gold-standard edits.

References

DM Conway. 1998. An algorithmic approach to english pluralization. In *Proceedings of the Second Annual Perl Conference. C. Salzenberg. San Jose, CA, O'Reilly.*

Daniel Dahlmeier and Hwee Tou Ng. 2012. Better Evaluation for Grammatical Error Correction. In *Proceedings of the 2012 Conference of the North American Chapter of the Association for Computational Linguistics: Human Language Technologies*, pages 568–572, Montréal, Canada, June. Association for Computational Linguistics.

[1] http://search.cpan.org/~dconway/Lingua-EN-Inflect-1.89/

[2] http://search.cpan.org/~jjnapiork/Lingua-EN-VerbTense-3.003/

[3] http://www.nactem.ac.uk/tsuruoka/maxent/

Daniel Dahlmeier, Hwee Tou Ng, and Eric Jun Feng Ng. 2012. NUS at the HOO 2012 Shared Task. In *Proceedings of the Seventh Workshop on Building Educational Applications Using NLP*, pages 216–224, Montréal, Canada, June. Association for Computational Linguistics.

Daniel Dahlmeier, Hwee Tou Ng, and Siew Mei Wu. 2013. Building a Large Annotated Corpus of Learner English: The NUS Corpus of Learner English. In *Proceedings of the 8th Workshop on Innovative Use of NLP for Building Educational Applications*, Atlanta, Georgia, USA.

NA-RAE HAN, MARTIN CHODOROW, and CLAUDIA LEACOCK. 2006. Detecting Errors in English Article Usage by Non-Native Speakers. *Natural Language Engineering*, 12:115–129, 5.

Ekaterina Kochmar, Øistein Andersen, and Ted Briscoe. 2012. HOO 2012 Error Recognition and Correction Shared Task: Cambridge University Submission Report. In *Proceedings of the Seventh Workshop on Building Educational Applications Using NLP*, pages 242–250, Montréal, Canada, June. Association for Computational Linguistics.

Philipp Koehn. 2005. Europarl: A Parallel Corpus For Statistical Machine Translation. In *MT summit*, volume 5.

Hwee Tou Ng, Siew Mei Wu, Yuanbin Wu, Christian Hadiwinoto, and Joel Tetreault. 2013. The conll-2013 shared task on grammatical error correction. In *Proceedings of the Seventeenth Conference on Computational Natural Language Learning*.

Alla Rozovskaya, Mark Sammons, Joshua Gioja, and Dan Roth. 2011. University of Illinois System in HOO Text Correction Shared Task. In *Proceedings of the 13th European Workshop on Natural Language Generation*, pages 263–266. Association for Computational Linguistics.

Alla Rozovskaya, Mark Sammons, and Dan Roth. 2012. The UI System in the HOO 2012 Shared Task on Error Correction. In *Proceedings of the Seventh Workshop on Building Educational Applications Using NLP*, pages 272–280, Montréal, Canada, June. Association for Computational Linguistics.

Andreas Stolcke et al. 2002. SRILM-An Extensible Language Modeling Toolkit. In *Proceedings of the international conference on spoken language processing*, volume 2, pages 901–904.

Tetreault, Joel R and Chodorow, Martin. 2008. The Ups and Downs of Preposition Error Detection in ESL Writing. In *Proceedings of the 22nd International Conference on Computational Linguistics-Volume 1*, pages 865–872. Association for Computational Linguistics.

Kristina Toutanova and Christopher D Manning. 2000. Enriching the Knowledge Sources Used in a Maximum Entropy Part-of-Speech Tagger. In *Proceedings of the 2000 Joint SIGDAT conference on Empirical methods in natural language processing and very large corpora: held in conjunction with the 38th Annual Meeting of the Association for Computational Linguistics-Volume 13*, pages 63–70. Association for Computational Linguistics.

Kristina Toutanova, Dan Klein, Christopher D Manning, and Yoram Singer. 2003. Feature-rich Part-of-speech tagging with a cyclic dependency network. In *Proceedings of the 2003 Conference of the North American Chapter of the Association for Computational Linguistics on Human Language Technology-Volume 1*, pages 173–180. Association for Computational Linguistics.

IITB System for CoNLL 2013 Shared Task: A Hybrid Approach to Grammatical Error Correction

Anoop Kunchukuttan **Ritesh Shah** **Pushpak Bhattacharyya**
Department of Computer Science and Engineering, IIT Bombay
{anoopk,ritesh,pb}@cse.iitb.ac.in

Abstract

We describe our grammar correction system for the CoNLL-2013 shared task. Our system corrects three of the five error types specified for the shared task - noun-number, determiner and subject-verb agreement errors. For noun-number and determiner correction, we apply a classification approach using rich lexical and syntactic features. For subject-verb agreement correction, we propose a new rule-based system which utilizes dependency parse information and a set of conditional rules to ensure agreement of the verb group with its subject. Our system obtained an F-score of 11.03 on the official test set using the M^2 evaluation method (the official evaluation method).

1 Introduction

Grammatical Error Correction (GEC) is an interesting and challenging problem and the existing methods that attempt to solve this problem take recourse to deep linguistic and statistical analysis. In general, GEC may partly assist in solving natural language processing (NLP) tasks like Machine Translation, Natural Language Generation *etc*. However, a more evident application of GEC is in building automated grammar checkers thereby benefiting non-native speakers of a language. The CoNLL-2013 shared task (Ng et al., 2013) looks at improving the current approaches for GEC and for inviting novel perspectives towards solving the same. The shared task makes the NUCLE corpus (Dahlmeier et al., 2013) available in the public domain and participants have been asked to correct grammatical errors belonging to the following categories: noun-number, determiner, subject-verb agreement (SVA), verb form and preposition. The key challenges are handling interaction between different error groups and handling potential mistakes made by off-the-shelf NLP components run on erroneous text.

For the shared task, we have addressed the following problems: noun-number, determiner and subject-verb agreement correction. For noun-number and determiner correction, we use a classification based approach to predict corrections - which is a widely used approach (Knight and Chander, 1994; Rozovskaya and Roth, 2010). For subject-verb agreement correction, we propose a new rule-based approach which applies a set of conditional rules to correct the verb group to ensure its agreement with its subject. Our system obtained a score of 11.03 on the official test set using the M^2 method. Our SVA correction system performs very well with a F-score of 28.45 on the official test set.

Section 2 outlines our approach to solving the grammar correction problem. Sections 3, 4 and 5 describe the details of the noun-number, determiner and SVA correction components of our system. Section 6 explains our experimental setup. Section 7 discusses the results of the experiments and Section 8 concludes the report.

2 Problem Formulation

In this work, we focus on correction of three error categories related to nouns: noun-number, determiner and subject-verb agreement. The number of the noun, the choice of determiner and verb's agreement in number with the subject are clearly inter-related. Therefore, a coordinated approach is necessary to correct these errors. If these problems are solved independently of each other, wrong corrections may be generated. The following are some examples:

Erroneous sentence

A good workmen does not blame his tools

Good corrections

A good workman does not blame his tools

Good workmen do not blame his tools

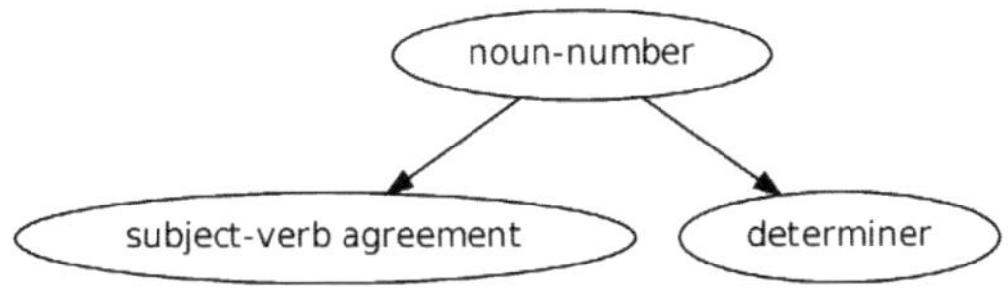

Figure 1: Dependencies between the noun-number, determiner and subject-verb agreement errors

Bad corrections
A good workman do not blame his tools
Good workman does not blame his tools

The choice of noun-number is determined by the discourse and meaning of the text. The choice of determiner is partly determined by the noun-number, whereas the verb's agreement depends completely on the number of its subject. Figure 1 shows the proposed dependencies between the number of a noun, its determiner and number agreement with the verb for which the noun is the subject. Assuming these dependencies, we first correct the noun-number. The corrections to the determiner and the verb's agreement with the subject are done taking into consideration the corrected noun. The noun-number and determiner are corrected using a classification based approach, whereas the SVA errors are corrected using a rule-based system; these are described in the following sections.

3 Noun Number Correction

The major factors which determine the number of the noun are: (i) the intended meaning of the text, (ii) reference to the noun earlier in the discourse, and (iii) stylistic considerations. Grammatical knowledge is insufficient for determining the noun-number, which requires a higher level of natural language processing. For instance, consider the following examples:
(1) I bought all the recommended books. These books are costly.
(2) Books are the best friends of man.

In Example (1), the choice of plural noun in the second sentence is determined by a reference to the entity in the previous sentence. Example (2) is a general statement about a class of entities, where the noun is generally a plural. Such phenomena make noun-number correction a difficult task. As information at semantic and discourse levels is difficult to encode, we explored lexical and syntactic information to obtain cues about the number of the noun. The following is a summary of the cues we have investigated:

Noun properties: Is the noun a mass noun, a *pluralia tantum*, a named entity or an acronym?
Lexical context: The presence of a plurality indicating word in the context of the noun (e.g. the ancient *scriptures* **such as** the Vedas, Upanishads, etc.)
Syntactic constraints:

- Nouns linked by a conjunction agree with each other (e.g. *The pens, pencils and books*).
- Presence/value of the determiner in the noun group. However, this is only a secondary cue, since it is not possible to determine if it is the determiner or the noun-number that is incorrect (e.g. *A books*).
- Agreement with the verb of which the noun is the subject. This is also a secondary feature.

Tokens, POS and chunk tags in ± 2 word-window around the noun
Is the noun capitalized ?
Is the noun an acronym ?
Is the noun a named entity?
Is the noun a mass noun, *pluralia tantum*?
Does the noun group have an article/ demonstrative/quantifier?
What article/demonstrative/quantifier does the noun phrase have ?
Are there words indicating plurality in the context of the noun?
The first two words of the sentence and their POS tags
The number of the verb for which this noun is the subject
Grammatical Number of majority of nouns in noun phrase conjunction

Table 1: Feature set for noun-number correction

Given that we are dealing with erroneous text, these cues could themselves be wrong. The problem of noun-number correction is one of making a prediction based on multiple cues in the face of such uncertainty. We model the problem as a binary classification problem, the task being to predict if the observed noun-number of every noun in the text needs correction (labels: *requires_correction/no_correction*). Alternatively, we could formulate the problem as a *singular/plural* number prediction problem, which would not require annotated learner corpora text. However, we prefer the former approach since we can learn corrections from learner corpora text (as opposed to native speaker text) and use knowledge of the observed number for prediction. Use of observed values has been shown to be beneficial for grammar correction (Rozovskaya and Roth, 2010; Dahlmeier and Ng, 2011).

If the model predicts *requires_correction*, then the observed number is toggled to obtain the corrected noun-number. In order to bias the system towards improved precision, we apply the correction only if classifier's confidence score for the *requires_correction* prediction exceeds its score for the *no_correction* prediction by at least a threshold value. This threshold value is determined empirically. The feature set designed for the classifier is shown in Table 1.

4 Determiner Correction

Determiners in English consist of articles, demonstratives and quantifiers. The choice of determiners, especially articles, depends on many factors including lexical, syntactic, semantic and discourse phenomena (Han et al., 2006). Therefore, the correct usage of determiners is difficult to master for second language learners, who may (i) insert a determiner where it is not required, (ii) omit a required determiner, or (iii) use the wrong determiner. We pose the determiner correction problem as a classification problem, which is a well explored method (Han et al., 2006; Dahlmeier and Ng, 2011). Every noun group is a training instance, with the determiner as the class label. Absence of a determiner is indicated by a special class label *NO_DET*. However, since the number of determiners is large, a single multi-class classifier will result in ambiguity. This ambiguity can be reduced by utilizing of the fact that a particular observed determiner is replaced by one of a small subset of all possible determiners (which we call its *confusion set*). For instance, the confusion set for *a* is {*a, an, the, NO_DET*}. It is unlikely that *a* is replaced by any other determiner like *this, that, etc.* Rozovskaya and Roth (2010) have used this method for training preposition correction systems, which we adopt for training a determiner correction system. For each observed determiner, we build a classifier whose prediction is

	Description	**Path**
1	Direct subject	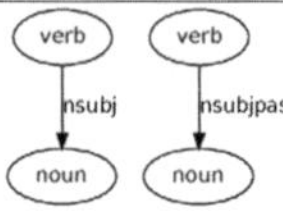
2	Path through Wh-determiner	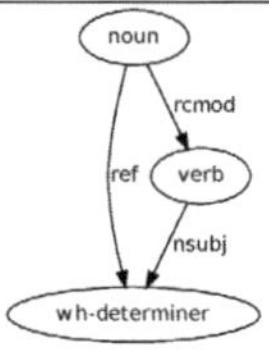
3	Clausal subject	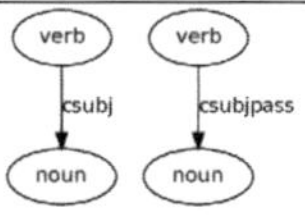
4	External subject	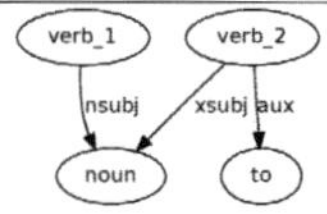
5	Path through copula	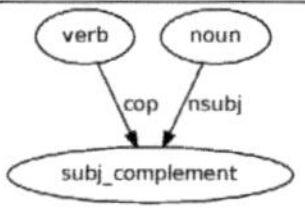
6	Subject in a different clause	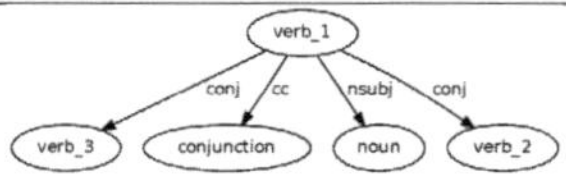
7	Multiple subjects	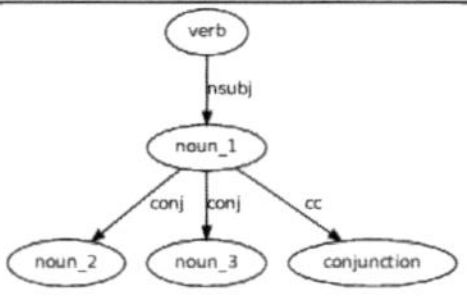

Table 2: Some rules from the *singularize_verb_group* rule-set

limited to the confusion set of the observed determiner. The confusion sets were obtained from the training corpus. The feature set is almost the same as the one for noun-number correction. The only difference is that context window features (token, POS and chunk tags) are taken around the determiner instead of the noun.

5 Subject-Verb Agreement

The task in subject-verb agreement correction is to correct the verb group components so that it agrees with its subject. The correction could be made either to the verb inflection (*He run* $\rightarrow$ *He runs*) or to the auxiliary verbs in the verb group (*He are running* $\rightarrow$ *He is running*). We assume that noun-number and verb form errors (tense, aspect, modality) do not exist or have already been corrected. We built a rule-based system for performing SVA correction, whose major components are (i) a system for detecting the subject of a verb, and

(ii) a set of conditional rules to correct the verb group.

We use a POS tagger, constituency parser and dependency parser for obtaining linguistic information (noun-number, noun/verb groups, dependency paths) required for SVA correction. Our assumption is that these NLP tools are reasonably robust and do a good analysis when presented with erroneous text. We have used the Stanford suite of tools for the shared task and found that it makes few mistakes on the NUCLE corpus text.

The following is our proposed algorithm for SVA correction:

1. Identify noun groups in a sentence and the information associated with each noun group: (i) number of the head noun of the noun group, (ii) associated noun groups, if the noun group is part of a noun phrase conjunction, and (iii) head and modifier in each noun group pair related by the *if* relation.

2. Identify the verb groups in a sentence.

3. For every verb group, identify its subject as described in Section 5.1.

4. If the verb group does not agree in number with its subject, correct each verb group by applying the conditional rules described in Section 5.2.

5.1 Identifying the subject of the verb

We utilize dependency relations (uncollapsed) obtained from the Stanford dependency parser to identify the subject of a verb. From analysis of dependency graphs of sentences in the NUCLE corpus, we identified different types of dependency paths between a verb and its subject, which are shown in Table 2. Given these possible dependency path types, we identify the subject of a verb using the following procedure:

- First, check if the subject can be reached using a direct dependency path (paths (1), (2), (3) and (4))

- If a direct relation is not found, then look for a subject via path (5)

- If the subject has not been found in the previous step, then look for a subject via path (6)

A verb can have multiple subjects, which can be identified via dependency path (7).

Rule	Condition	Action
1	$\exists w \in vg, \text{pos\_tag}(w) = \text{MD}$	Do nothing
2	$\exists w \in vg, \text{pos\_tag}(w) = \text{TO}$	Do nothing
3	$\text{subject}(vg) \neq \text{I}$	Replace *are* by *is*
4	$\text{subject}(vg) = \text{I}$	Replace *are* by *am*
5	$\text{do, does} \notin vg \wedge \text{subject}(vg) \neq \text{I}$	Replace *have* by *has*
6	$\text{do, does} \notin vg \wedge \text{subject}(vg) = \text{I}$	Replace *has* by *have*

Table 3: Some rules from the *singularize_verb_group* rule-set
w is a word, vg is a verb group, POS tags are from the Penn tagset

5.2 Correcting the verb group

For correcting the verb group, we have two sets of conditional rules (*singularize_verb_group* and *pluralize_verb_group*). The *singularize_verb_group* rule-set is applied if the subject is singular, whereas the *pluralize_verb_group* rule-set is applied if the subject is plural or if there are multiple subjects (path (7) in Table 2). For verbs which have subjects related via dependency paths (3) and (4) no correction is done.

The conditional rules utilize POS tags and lemmas in the verb group to check if the verb group needs to be corrected and appropriate rules are applied for each condition. Some rules in the *singularize_verb_group* rule-set are shown in Table 3. The rules for the *pluralize_verb_group* rule-set are analogous.

6 Experimental Setup

Our training data came from the NUCLE corpus provided for the shared task. The corpus was split into three parts: training set (55151 sentences), threshold tuning set (1000 sentences) and development test set (1000 sentences). In addition, evaluation was done on the official test set (1381 sentences). Maximum Entropy classifiers were trained for noun-number and determiner correction systems. In the training set, the number of instances with no corrections far exceeds the number of instances with corrections. Therefore, a balanced training set was created by including all the instances with corrections and sampling α instances with no corrections from the training set. By trial and error, α was determined to be 10000 for the noun-number and determiner correction systems. The confidence score threshold which maximizes the F-score was calibrated on the tuning set. We determined $threshold = 0$

Task	Development test set			Official test set		
	P	R	F-1	P	R	F-1
Noun Number	31.43	40	35.2	28.47	9.84	14.66
Determiner	35.59	17.5	23.46	21.43	1.3	2.46
SVA	16.67	23.42	19.78	29.57	27.42	28.45
Integrated	**29.59**	**17.24**	**21.79**	**28.18**	**4.99**	**11.03**

Table 4: M^2 scores for IIT Bombay correction system: component-wise and integrated

for the noun-number and the determiner correction systems.

The following tools were used in the development of the system for the shared task: (i) NLTK (MaxEntClassifier, Wordnet lemmatizer), (ii) Stanford tools - POS Tagger, Parser and NER and Python interface to the Stanford NER, (iii) Lingua::EN::Inflect module for noun and verb pluralization, and (iv) Wiktionary list of mass nouns, *pluralia tantum*.

7 Results and Discussion

Table 4 shows the results on the test set (development and official) for each component of the correction system and the integrated system. The evaluation was done using the M^2 method (Dahlmeier and Ng, 2012). This involves computing F1 measure between a set of proposed system edits and a set of human-annotated gold-standard edits. However, evaluation is complicated by the fact that there may be multiple edits which generate the same correction. The following example illustrates this behaviour:

Source: I ate mango
Hypothesis: I ate **a** mango

The system edit is $\epsilon \rightarrow a$, whereas the gold standard edit is *mango→a mango*. Though both the edits result in the same corrected sentence, they do not match. The M^2 algorithm resolves this problem by providing an efficient method to detect the sequence of phrase-level edits between a source sentence and a system hypothesis that achieves the highest overlap with the gold-standard annotation.

It is clear that the low recall of the noun-number and determiner correction components have resulted in a low overall score for the system. This underscores the difficulty of the two problems. The feature sets seem to have been unable to capture the patterns determining the noun-number and determiner. Consider a few examples, where the evidence for correction look strong:

1. products such as RFID tracking **system** have become real

2. With the installing of the **surveillances** for every corner of Singapore

A cursory inspection of the corpus indicates that in the absence of a determiner (example (1)), the noun tends to be plural. This pattern has not been captured by the correction system. The coverage of the *Wiktionary* mass noun and *pluralia tantum* dictionaries is low, hence this feature has not had the desired impact (example(2)).

The SVA correction component has a reasonably good precision and recall - performing best amongst all the correction components. Since most errors affecting agreement (noun-number, verb form, etc.) were not corrected, the SVA agreement component could not correct the agreement errors. If these errors had been corrected, the accuracy of the standalone SVA correction component would have been higher than that indicated by the official score. To verify this, we manually analyzed the output from the SVA correction component and found that 58% of the missed corrections and 43% of the erroneous corrections would not have occurred if some of the other related errors had been fixed. If it is assumed that all these errors are corrected, the effective accuracy of SVA correction increases substantially as shown in Table 5. A few errors in the gold standard for SVA agreement were also considered for computing the effective scores. The standalone SVA correction module therefore has a good accuracy.

A major reason for SVA errors ($\sim$18%) is wrong output from NLP modules like the POS tagger, chunker and parser. The following are a few examples:

- The verb group is incorrectly identified if there is an adverb between the main and auxiliary verbs.

  It [do ***not only*** *restrict] their freedom in all*

SVA Score	Development test set			Official test set		
	P	**R**	**F-1**	**P**	**R**	**F-1**
Official	16.67	23.42	19.78	29.57	27.42	28.45
Effective	51.02	55.55	53.18	65.32	66.94	66.12

Table 5: M^2 scores (original and modified) for SVA correction

aspects , but also causes leakage of personal information .

- Two adjacent verb groups are not distinguished as separate chunks by the chunker when the second verb group is non-finite involving an infinitive.

  The police arrested all of them before they [starts ***to*** *harm] the poor victim.*

- The dependency parser makes errors in identifying the subject of a verb. The noun *problems* is not identified as the subject of *is* by the dependency parser.

  Although rising of life expectancies is an challenge to the entire human nation , the detailed ***problems*** *each country that will encounter* ***is*** *different.*

Some phenomena have not been handled by our rules. Our system does not handle the case where the subject is a gerund phrase. Consider the example,

Collecting coupons from individuals are the first step.

The verb-number should be singular when a gerund phrase is the subject. In the absence of rules to handle this case, *coupons* is identified as the subject of *are* by the dependency parser and consequently, no correction is done.

Our rules do not handle interrogative sentences and interrogative pronouns. Hence the following sentence is not corrected,

People do not know who are tracking them.

Table 6 provides an analysis of the error type distribution for SVA errors on the official test set.

8 Conclusion

In this paper, we presented a hybrid grammatical correction system which incorporates both machine learning and rule-based components. We proposed a new rule-based method for subject-verb agreement correction. As future work, we plan to explore richer features for noun-number and determiner errors.

Error types	% distribution
Noun-number errors	58.02 %
Wrong tagging, chunking, parsing	18.52 %
Wrong gold annotations	7.40%
Rules not designed	6.1%
Others	9.88 %

Table 6: Causes for missed SVA corrections and their distribution in the official test set

References

Daniel Dahlmeier and Hwee Tou Ng. 2011. Grammatical error correction with alternating structure optimization. In *Proceedings of the 49th Annual Meeting of the Association for Computational Linguistics: Human Language Technologies-Volume 1.*

Daniel Dahlmeier and Hwee Tou Ng. 2012. Better evaluation for grammatical error correction. In *Proceedings of the 2012 Conference of the North American Chapter of the Association for Computational Linguistics.*

Daniel Dahlmeier, Hwee Tou Ng, and Siew Mei Wu. 2013. Building a large annotated corpus of learner english: The NUS Corpus of Learner English. In *To appear in Proceedings of the 8th Workshop on Innovative Use of NLP for Building Educational Applications.*

Na-Rae Han, Martin Chodorow, and Claudia Leacock. 2006. Detecting errors in english article usage by non-native speakers. *Natural Language Engineering.*

Kevin Knight and Ishwar Chander. 1994. Automated postediting of documents. In *AAAI.*

Hwee Tou Ng, Siew Mei Wu, Yuanbin Wu, Christian Hadiwinoto, and Joel Tetreault. 2013. The CoNLL-2013 Shared Task on Grammatical Error Correction. In *To appear in Proceedings of the Seventeenth Conference on Computational Natural Language Learning.*

Alla Rozovskaya and Dan Roth. 2010. Generating confusion sets for context-sensitive error correction. In *Proceedings of the 2010 Conference on Empirical Methods in Natural Language Processing.*

UdS at the CoNLL 2013 Shared Task

Desmond Darma Putra, Lili Szabó
Saarland University
Faculty of Computational Linguistics and Phonetics
{ddputra, lilis}@coli.uni-saarland.de

Abstract

This paper describes our submission for the CoNLL 2013 Shared Task, which aims to to improve the detection and correction of the five most common grammatical error types in English text written by non-native speakers. Our system concentrates only on two of them; it employs machine learning classifiers for the *ArtOrDet*-, and a fully deterministic rule based workflow for the *SVA* error type.

1 Introduction

Grammatical error correction is not a new task in Natural Language Processing field. Many previous research was done to solve the problem. Most of these works focus on article and preposition correction.

In this paper we present our implementation of our system that participated in the CoNLL 2013 Shared Task for grammatical error correction. Out of the 28 annotated error types in the training data, this year's task focuses on 5 error types: article or determiner (*ArtOrDet*), preposition (*Prep*), noun number (*Nn*), verb form (*Vform*) and subject-verb agreement (*SVA*). This error proportion can be seen in Table 1.

From these error types we focused on *ArtOrDet* and *SVA* mistakes only.

Error type	Counts
ArtOrDet	6658
Nn	3779
Prep	2404
Vform	1453
SVA	1527

Table 1: Error types in NUCLE corpus

The remaining part of this paper is organized as follows. Chapters refcorp and 3 describe the data and system architecture. Chapter 4.2 explains the *ArtOrDet* classification task. Our experimental setup for *ArtOrDet* error is presented in Section 4.3. Chapter 4.4 describes the results from our experiments and some analysis regarding the results. Chapters 5.1 and 5.1.1 describe the task and issues respectively, Chapter 5.2 explains the how the subject-verb pairs are extracted, Chapter 5.3 is about the evaluation of the pairs. Lastly, Chapter 8 will conclude our work.

2 Corpora and Tools

The training corpus (Dahlmeier, 2013) consists of approx. 1400, 40-sentence long essays (summing up to overall 1161567 tokens), written by non-native speakers, and annotated by professional English language instructors for error tags and corrections.

The tokenized, POS-tagged and dependency and constituency parsed version of the corpus was also provided, along with the tools (tokenization - NLTK, POS-tagging and parsing - Stanford parser (Marie-Catherine de Marneffe, 2011)).

The other NLP-tools used in our implementation (described in the relevant sections) are the LIBLINEAR classifier and NodeBox.

For evaluation of the system results the M2 Scorer (Dahlmeier, 2012) was used.

3 System and Pipeline

Our system consists of two independent subsystems, which are combined serially. The parsed version of the input text first goes through the *ArtOrDet* subsystem whose output is re-parsed, and serves as the input for the *SVA* subsystem:

1. Article and determiner correction
2. Re-parsing of the data
3. Subject-verb agreement correction

In the following 2 Chapters we present the workflows for the *ArtOrDet* and *SVA* mistake types separately.

4 ArtOrDet Correction

4.1 *ArtOrDet* Mistake Type

The *ArtOrDet* error type is the most common mistake. We pose this *ArtOrDet* error correction as a multi-class classification task. The output from the classification task will be used to correct the data.

Both sentences *'girls like flowers'* and *'**the** girls like flowers'* can be accepted as correct, depending on the context - whether the noun refers to a specific group or it is a general statement. Another example like *'he ate*

***the** cake*' and '*he ate **a** cake*' are also grammatically correct depending on the context whether the cake has been introduced before or not.

4.2 *ArtOrDet* Classification

An article or a determiner is followed by an NP. This article often refers to a definite or indefinite element of a class or pointing to something specific or general. There are many examples article/determiner that follows an NP, for example, *the, a, some, any, this, these, that, those,* etc. According to (Huddleston, 1984), one NP can hold up to three determiners e.g. *all her many* ideas. Moreover, each NP has a head which is noun type class. This noun consists of three subclasses including common noun (e.g. book, car, dog), proper noun (e.g. Larry, Sarah, Germany) and pronoun (e.g. you, we, they, them, it). Since we are working with *ArtOrDet* errors, then there is no point of checking NP which contains pronoun subclass because an article can never be followed by pronoun.

We classify these *ArtOrDet* errors into several types which are described in Table 2. The most common error is caused by missing *the* (around 39%). Additionally, unnecessary use of *the* contributes 26% of error. Furthermore, confusion between using *the* or *or a/an* bring 4.3% error. We classified around 15% as undefined error due to several reason. First, the error does not appear in front of the NP itself, sometimes it appears in the middle of the NP. Second, the error appears in other type phrase like adjective phrase, this makes the problem is more difficult to trace. For example, a clause "*...such invention helps to prevent elderly from falling down.*" The word *elderly* is recognized as adjective phrase and the correction happens in front of that word (adding article *the*). Third, the correction involves other articles for example *this, that*, and many more.

Besides the above error, there is another error which we have to handle such as confusion between *a* or *an*. This problem can be solved using a rule-based approach which will be discussed in the next section. To simplify this, we normalize article *a* and *an* into *a*. Later on, after the classification is done, we will use this rule-based to return the correct article.

4.3 Experimental setup

After defining the error types, we split the corpus into training and testing dataset. We select 50 documents from the corpus as a held-out test data and the rest is used for the training data. For the training part, we extract the NP (which is not headed by pronoun) using the information from constituent parse tree and POS tags. Each NP that is extracted represents one training example. Thus, if an NP is incorrect then we label it to one of the label from Table 2. We consider this task as a multi-class classification task, that one NP finds a mapping $f : x \rightarrow \{c_1, c_2, \ldots, c_8\}$ that maps $x \in NPs$ into one of the 8 labels.

For the first experiment, we select two well known

Classification label	Training
Correct NP	97.91%
Missing *the*	0.92%
Missing *a/an*	0.30%
Unnecessary *the*	0.07%
Unnecessary *a/an*	0.61%
Use *the* instead of *a/an*	0.03%
Use *a/an* instead of *the*	0.06%
Undefined	0.11%

Table 3: Training data

classification methods such as LIBLINEAR (Fan et al., 2008) and Naive Bayes (McCallum and Nigam, 1998). Both of these methods are trained using the same training data and features which we are going to discuss in Subsection 4.3.5. In the testing part, our classifier will predict a label for each NP. If the classifier predicts that the observed NP is already correct or it needs to add article *a* then we apply a rule-based approach to make sure it puts the right article (*a/an*). This rule-based will utilize CMU pronouncing dictionary from NLTK to do the checking and put conditional constraints such as checking whether this NP is an acronym or not.

The second and third experiments are inspired by (Dahlmeier et al., 2012; Rozovskaya et al., 2012). We realize that the proportion of observed NP without article error outnumbers the observed NP with an article error (see Table 3). Therefore, this huge proportion of correct NP may affect the classifier accuracy. To justify this claim, we will utilize error inflation method for the second experiment and do re-sampling and undersampling NP as the third experiment.

4.3.1 Naive Bayes

Naive Bayes is a famous classification method which applies Bayes theorem's with naive assumptions. This assumptions believe that all features that are use to describe the data are independent (McCallum and Nigam, 1998). The advantages of this method are fast and easy to implement. This method has shown to be a good classification tool in NLP field (e.g. spam filtering, news classification, etc.). To classify an instance $D = \langle f_1, f_2, \ldots, f_n \rangle$ according to one of the classes $c_j \in C$, we calculate the maximum likelihood estimation of a prior probability c_j times the product of every features$f_{1,\ldots,n}$ given class c_j times as described below:

$$c = \arg\max_{c_j \in C} P(c_j) \prod_i P(f_i|c_j) \quad (1)$$

For this task, we utilize naive bayes package from NLTK. This method is trained using the features which are already described in Table 4.

4.3.2 LIBLINEAR

LIBLINEAR provides a large-scale classification library to handle sparse data that contains a large numbers of instances and features (Fan et al., 2008).

ArtOrDet errors	Proportion	Example(s)
Missing *the*	38.9%	Working class Singaporean would be motivated to work hard as they know ***the*** government would contribute...
Missing *a/an*	12.8%	If China can come up with ***an*** effective policy to change its education system and stimulate innovation
Unnecessary *the*	26%	~~The~~ innovators, who are normally work under Research and Development department, have to recognize...
Unnecessary *a/an*	2.7%	It would no longer be able to ~~a~~ have constant economic growth which places a detrimental effect on the country
Use *the* instead of *a/an*	2.9%	The government budgets should be diverted to other areas of ~~the~~ ***a*** country's development since resources are limited
Use *a/an* instead of *the*	1.4%	As a result of ~~a~~ ***the*** growing aging population...
Undefined	15.3%	...such invention helps to prevent ***the*** elderly from falling down. Of course, ~~it~~ ***this*** is not possible. This caused problem like the appearance of slums which most of the time is not safe due to ~~the~~ ***their*** unhealthy environment

Table 2: *ArtOrDet* errors distribution from NUCLE corpus

It supports two binary linear classifiers such as L2-regularized logistic regression (LR), L1-loss and L2-loss linear SVM. Given a pair training set instance (x_i, y_i), where $i = 1, \ldots, l$, $x_i \in R^n$ and $y \in \{+1, -1\}^l$. This data will be considered as optimization problem:

$$\min_{w} \frac{1}{2} w^T w + C \sum_{i=1}^{l} \xi_i \quad (2)$$
$$\text{subject to } y_i(w^T \phi(x_i) + b) \geq 1 - \xi_i$$

where $C > 0$ as a penalty parameter.

LIBLINEAR not only supports binary class problems but also multi-class problems via one-vs-the-rest strategy. For our purpose, we will use this LIBLINEAR package with C = 0.125. This penalty value is come from the grid search which is provided in the package to find the best parameter C.

Both of these classification methods are evaluated by calculating the number of corrects prediction compare to the annotation label which is defined as:

$$Accuracy = \frac{\#\ of\ correct\ predictions}{\#\ of\ predictions} \quad (3)$$

4.3.3 Error Inflation Method

Since the *ArtOrDet* errors that we have is sparse and increase the errors proportion in the training data can help the classifier to perform better then we apply this error inflation method (Rozovskaya et al., 2012). We select some positive constant (less than 1.0) to reduce the proportion of the correct example and adding this proportion to the other error types by generating the artificial error. We found that probability among the corrections are still similar.

4.3.4 Re-sampling and Undersampling

Besides error inflation method, we are also interested in re-sampling NP with *ArtOrDet* error and undersampling without *ArtOrDet* error. Some combination will be selected to see whether it can help the classifier in detecting and correcting the *ArtOrDet* errors. we select some constant number to re-sample the NP which contains *ArtOrDet* error and some threshold to undersampling the NP which is correct. The results from these two approaches are discussed in the next section.

4.3.5 Feature Extraction

We adopt some features from (Dahlmeier et al., 2012; Rozovskaya et al., 2012) which are described in Table 4. Most of the features are coming from lexical and POS. If the NP contains an article, then we will separate it and consider as as additional feature.

wNb and wNa in Table 4 represent word at position *N* before the NP and word at position *N* after the article position. If there is no article in the beginning of NP then first word in the NP is recognize as $w1a$. pNb and pNa describe the POS of wNb and wNa. NC is a noun compound and this compound is generated by the last two words inside the NP which have noun POS. head of the NP is identified with *headWord* feature and it is determined using the information from dependency tree. NP is a noun phrase which is extracted from the constituent parse tree. $posX$ is a POS feature of X where $x \in \{NC, NP, headWord\}$. *verb* feature and *prep* are determined from the POS information. *wordAfterNP* is activated if there is another word after the NP.

4.4 Results & Discussion

The result from the first experiment can be seen in Table 6. We compare the baseline with Naive Bayes and LIBLINEAR classifier. The baseline that we choose for this task has similar definition with (Rozovskaya and Roth, 2010) which is 'do nothing'. The reason behind of this is because the proportion of NP using correct article is more than 90% and this is better than state-of-the-art classifier for article selection (with article selection, usually the baseline is set by majority class which is zero article). The result shows that LIBLINEAR produces a minor improvement than the baseline. This increase is influenced by the rule based approach that we develop to correct the use of *a* and *an*. Naive Bayes doesn't perform well due to the dependent features that

Feature Type	Description
Observed article	article
Word n-grams	w1b, w2b, w3b, w2b_w1b, w3b_w2b_w1b, w1a, w2a, w3a, w1a_w2a, w1a_w2a_w3a, w1b_w1a, w2b_w1b_w1a, w1b_w1a_w2a, w2b_w1b_w1a_w2a, w3b_w2b_w1b_w1a, w1b_w1a_w2a_w3a
POS features	p1b, p2b, p3b, p2b_p1b, p3b_p2b_p1b, p1a, p2a, p3a, p1a_p2a, p1a_p2a_p3a, p1b_p1a, p2b_p1b_p1a, p1b_p1a_p2a, p2b_p1b_p1a_p2a, p3b_p2b_p1b_p1a, p1b_p1a_p2a_p3a, p1b_w1b, p1b_w1a, p2b_w2b, p2b_w2a
NP	NC, posNC, headWord, posHeadWord, headWord_posHeadWord, w1b_posNP_posHeadWord, w1b_headWord, w1b_headWord_wordAfterNP
Verb	verb, verb_headWord, verb_NC, verb_NP, verb_posNP_headWord, verb_posNP_NC
Preposition	prep, prep_headWord, prep_NC, prep_NP, prep_posNP_headWord, prep_posNP_NC

Table 4: Features set

	1	0.9	0.8	0.7	0.6	0.5
acc.	98.64%	98.63%	98.14%	97.12%	95.10%	92.36%

Table 5: *ArtOrDet* accuracy using error inflation

Method	Accuracy
Baseline	98.5%
Naive Bayes	82 %
LIBLINEAR	98.67 %

Table 6: Classifier performance on correcting *ArtOrDet* errors

Classification label	#	Accuracy
Missing *the*	45	96%
Missing *a/an*	26	38%
Unnecessary *the*	47	100%
Unnecessary *a/an*	4	100%
Use *the* instead of *a/an*	4	0%
Use *a/an* instead of *the*	1	0%
Undefined	5	0%
TOTAL	**132**	**79%**

Table 7: Error Correction distribution

we employs.

Our second experiment tests the use of error inflation method on LIBLINEAR classifier. This test is applied to LIBLINEAR classifier with since it has a higher accuracy than Naive Bayes. The results from this experiment is described in Table 5. The smaller the constant number will result in larger article errors. Nonetheless, if we introduce too many error it will reduce the accuracy.

The last experiment test the effect of re-sampling NP with *ArtOrDet* several error times and reducing the number of observed NP that is already correct can be seen in Table **??**. The re-sampling parameter is put on the first column (5, 10, 15, 20 and 25 times) determine how many duplicates are made for each NP. On the row side we use a threshold to reduce the proportion of the observed NP which is already correct. So for each correct NP, we generate a random number and if it is higher than the threshold, then it is included in the training dataset. Table **??** reveals that re-sampling some NP that has *ArtOrDet* error does not increase the accuracy. On the other hand, reducing the threshold improve the accuracy.

If we look deeper, we found that increasing the threshold and re-sampling may have a positive correlation with correcting the error. However, the number of false positives also increased.

4.5 Further analysis

Inspired by (Gamon et al., 2008) to make two classifiers for detecting and correcting article errors. If we consider that our classifier can detect correctly the error, then we only need to train another classifier to make the correction by using the same features as described in Table 4. The training for this classifier comes from all NP with *ArtOrDet* error. Our result proves that 79% of the *ArtOrDet* can be corrected (see Table 7)

On one hand, our classifier does a good job in a sense of detecting missing article and removing unnecessary article. On the other hand, it is hard to predict either choosing between *a/an* or *the*. We found that our classifier labels this confusion as unnecessary *the* or *a/an*. This means that we have to remove the article for both of these confusions.

This may be caused by lack of training data for particular errors such as confusion between *the* & *a/an*. We realize that this mistake occurs often when the article would appear in front of an adjective - and in our feature sets there is no explicit adjective feature.

5 SVA Correction

5.1 *SVA* Mistake Type

Subject-verb agreement is the fourth most common mistake type in texts written by English language learners. It is also the highest done by machine translation systems, yet still an unsolved problem.
The English verb inflection paradigm is relatively simple, and only the misuse of third person singular and finite form of the verb (the form coinciding with the infinitive form) are of interest for the SVA error correction:

**John and Mary* goes *to work every day.*
**Mary* go *to work every day.*

Nevertheless, it is not a straightforward task, mainly because of the difficulties of linking the corresponding subjects and verbs together. The detection of the disagreement is relatively simple, compared to the task of recognizing the number of the subject and verb.

This mistake type is different in nature form the error types (e.g. determiner and preposition) as the scope of the analysis cannot be determined as easily, therefore it has to be the whole sentence. The verb and its corresponding subject can be quite distant from one another in the sentence, and by no means have predictable positions.

In English the verbs and their subjects have no fixed positions; in indicative sentences the verb most of the times (not immediately) but follows the subject, although not necessarily, e.g. in sentences with expletives the subject follows the verb:

However, there/EXPL are/VERB still many problems/SUBJ hampering engineering design process for innovations.

5.1.1 Issues on the Syntactic Level

There are two types of syntactic phenomena that make the recognition and agreement evaluation of subject-verb difficult.

These issues are explained on dependency parsing examples, but can be generalized to any kind of grammar.

5.1.2 Multiple Subjects

When there are multiple subjects in the sentence, only the first one is labeled as a subject, the ones following it get the conj label. Even if all of them are in singular form, the verb has to be in its plural form, as multiple subjects mean plural number in English. If these type of sentences are not taken care of, that can lead to many missed corrections and to even more faulty ones. Figure 5.1.2 visualizes the problem.

5.1.3 Subject Coreference

If a sentence contains a *wh*-subordinate clause, the verb in the subordinate clause has to agree with the antecedent of the subject, but the subject is a WH-determiner (*that, what, which, who*, etc.) that can refer to both singular and plural antecedents.

The referent (ref) of the head of an NP is the relative word introducing the relative clause modifying the NP is an existing label in dependency parsing, but not available with the parser used here.

There are multiple ways to resolve the coreference, the one simplistic method[1] applied here is based on the assumption that the antecedent of the wh-subject is the closest preceding noun or pronoun to it.

Another competing method is to use the head of the verb in the subordinate clause, which is exactly the antecedent of the wh-subject (see in Figure 5.1.3). This relation is labeled as rcmod, the relative clause modifier.

When the verb is an auxiliary, its head can be a verb (*which have shaped/VBN*), an adjective (*which is effective/JJ*) or a noun (*which is a competitive funding scheme/NN*), whose head is the antecedent of the relative clause.

The second method, apart from being challenging to implement, yields to significantly worse results than the first one, most probably because of the dependency annotation mistakes in the corpus. The other problem with it is, that it requires the subjects and verbs to be paired before they the pairing is done in the pipeline.

5.2 Subject-Verb Pair Extraction

In order to being able to evaluate their agreement, the first task in finding SVA errors is identifying matching subjects and verbs. This is done in two steps:

1. extracting all predicate verbs and subjects from the sentence,
2. identifying which subject(s) belongs to which verb(s).

For recognizing inflected verb forms in **1.** the POS-tags are used; all inflected verb forms (VBZ, VBP, VBD, MD) are extracted from the sentence. As for the subjects, the dependency labels nsubj, nsubjpass, csubj are used to recognize them.

This is also the place where the multiple subject identification and coreference resolution is done. Pronoun- and determiner subjects are classified as singular or plural subjects, based on a finite list. Noun subjects are classified based on their POS-tags: NN and NNP as singular, NNS and NNPS as plural.

Once all subjects and verbs were extracted from the sentence, they have to be paired.

In **2.**, depending on how many subjects and verbs were extracted, POS templates were used to pair them.

It has to be noted here that in dependency parsing the subjects are not always dependent on the predicate verb itself, but rather on the main verb in the sentence, such as in Figure 5.2, so the head of the subject information couldn't be used.

There is no straightforward solution in the constituency parse trees either; it is not sufficient to take the head of the NP under the ROOT as the subject, as this solution wouldn't handle relative clauses properly.

5.2.1 Patterns

Only patterns, which can be almost exhaustively correctly classify subject-verb pairs are used.

Each verb is paired with the subject that is assigned an identical index. The following patterns are used:

```
Subject1  Verb1
Verb1 Subject1
Subject1/2 Verb1 Verb2
Subject1 Verb1 Subject2
Subject1 Verb1 Subject2 Verb2
Subject1 Verb1 Verb2 Subject2
```

[1] In sentences, where the wh-subject is a clausal subject, like *What engineers should do is to invent new machines.* are handled separately.

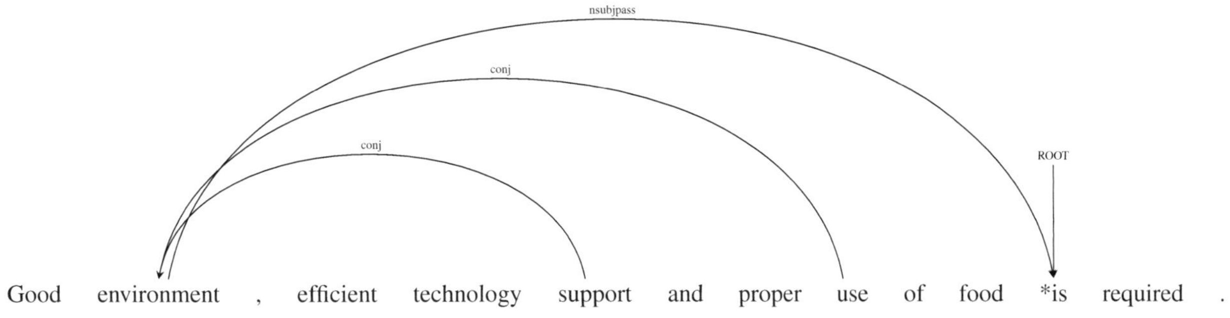

Figure 1: Dependency relations in a sentence with conjunct subjects. Only the relevant dependencies are marked. There is an original SVA mistake (made by the author) in the sentence due to the missed identification of the conjunct subjects.

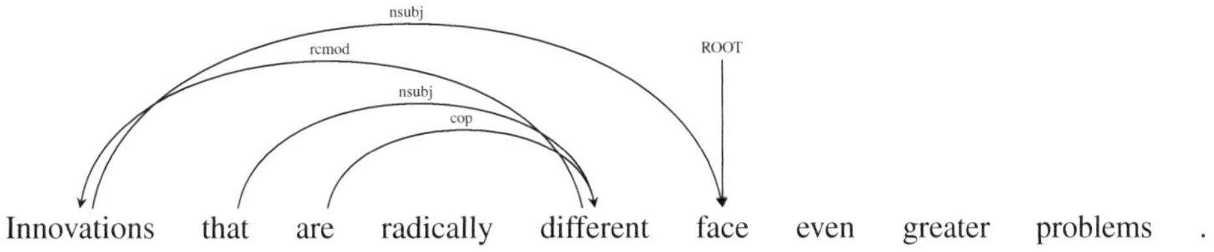

Figure 2: Sentence with subordinate clause. Only relevant dependencies are marked. The subject of the subordinate sentence is headed by the adjective, which is headed by the subject of the main clause.

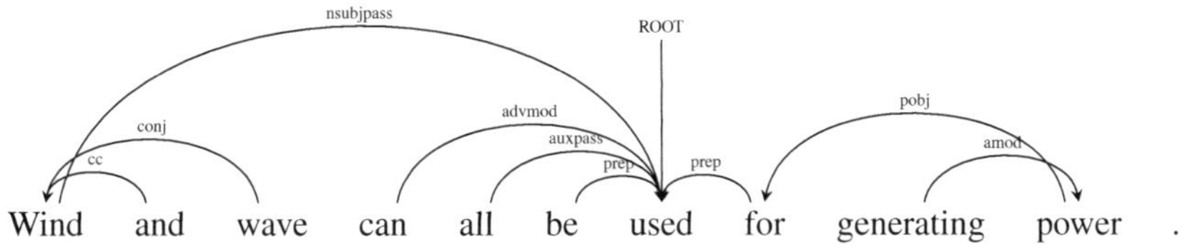

Figure 3: Sentence with labeled dependency relations. The first subject is not headed by the finite verb of the sentence *can*, but rather by the verb in the participial form *used*.

All other patterns (with 5 and more subjects or verbs in the sentence) were discarded from the evaluation, due to the far too many pairing possibilities. These long sentences generally contain a lot of modifiers, and make up 34% of the development data.

5.3 SV-Agreement Evaluation: Rule-based System

After the pairing is complete, only the pairs which include VBP[2]/VBZ[3] tags for the verbs, or verb forms in the past tense of the copula (was/were) are retained for the agreement evaluation.
If the number of the subject and verb don't agree, the verb form gets corrected.

[2]plural verb form

[3]third person singular verb form

5.3.1 Correction

The correction is done by using NodeBox, which is a tool that generates the morphologically correct singular or plural form of a given English verb.

5.4 SVA Results

On development set, only SVA-corrections, with other error types not being corrected we get a precision of 0.18.25% and a recall of 22.20%.

5.4.1 System Error Analysis

The following patterns emerged. False negatives (missed corrections) are mostly, but not exclusively due to non-accurate POS-tags, non-accurate parse trees (including many titles of the documents), dependency on other mistake types: especially on the noun number type mistakes, mistake annotation errors and other specific cases.

6 Integrating the Systems

The systems, handling separately the mistake types, are combined in a sequential order.
The *SVA* mistake type heavily depends on the correction of the other mistake types, most prominently on the noun number (*Nn*) mistakes, as the example sentence below shows.
**This will , if not already , caused/Vform problems as there are/SVA very limited spaces/Nn for us .*
This will , if not already , cause problems as there is very limited space for us .
Although we don't deal with *Nn*-mistakes, the *SVA*-system is still the last in the row. After each iteration, the test data is re-parsed, to become the input for the next system.

7 Joint Results on Blind Data

Our final results (run on the M2 scorer) are as shown in Table 7.

Precision	0.2769
Recall	0.110
F1	0.0211

Table 8: System results on blind data

8 Conclusion

Correcting *ArtOrDet* errors for this task is not an easy job especially the number of NP using correct article is really high (more than 95%). However our LIBLINEAR classifier performance is slightly better than the baseline and Naive Bayes. Besides comparing between Naive Bayes and LIBLINEAR classifiers for this task we also adapt two approaches from (Dahlmeier et al., 2012) and (Rozovskaya et al., 2012). Our result explains that neither re-sampling method nor error inflation method contribute to the increase of accuracy.

There are several directions that can be pursued to improve the classifier accuracy. Adding language model feature which is mentioned by (Gamon et al., 2008; Dahlmeier et al., 2012) might be useful to filter the result. However using language model like Google N-gram corpus would need some extra treatment since the data is really big and need a lot of computation time to build the language model.

The hardest part of the SVA-correction task is to extract the matching subject-verb pairs; with sufficient amount of data annotated for that purpose (there is one out there, for Swedish), the rule-based approach could be turned into a statistical learning one, which might improve the recall of the system. I have found no previous research pointing to this direction. Long and complex sentences, with more than one subject-verb pairs, are frequent in corpora specific to life sciences and technology literature, such as the corpus used in this shared task. The system definitely works better on shorter sentences.

References

Dan Roth Alla Rozovskaya. 2010. Training paradigms for correcting errors in grammar and usage. *Human Language Technologies: The 2010 Annual Conference of the North American Chapter of the ACL*, pages 154–162.

Daniel Dahlmeier, Hwee Tou Ng, and Eric Jun Feng Ng. 2012. Nus at the hoo 2012 shared task. In *Proceedings of the Seventh Workshop on Building Educational Applications Using NLP*, pages 216–224, Stroudsburg, PA, USA. Association for Computational Linguistics.

Ng Hwee Tou Dahlmeier, Daniel. 2012. Better evaluation for grammatical error correction. In *Proceedings of the 2012 Conference of the North American Chapter of the Association for Computational Linguistics: Human Language Technologies, (NAACL 2012)*, pages 568–572, Montreal, Canada.

Ng Hwee Tou Wu Siew Mei Dahlmeier, Daniel. 2013. Building a large annotated corpus of learner english: The nus corpus of learner english. In *To appear in Proceedings of the 8th Workshop on Innovative Use of NLP for Building Educational Applications (BEA 2013)*, Atlanta, Georgia, USA.

Robert Dale, Ilya Anisimoff, and George Narroway. 2012. Hoo 2012: A report on the preposition and determiner error correction shared task. In *Proceedings of the Seventh Workshop on Building Educational Applications Using NLP*, pages 54–62, Montréal, Canada, June. Association for Computational Linguistics.

Rachele De Felice and Stephen G. Pulman. 2007. Automatically acquiring models of preposition use. In *Proceedings of the Fourth ACL-SIGSEM Workshop on Prepositions*, SigSem '07, pages 45–50, Stroudsburg, PA, USA. Association for Computational Linguistics.

Rachele De Felice and Stephen G. Pulman. 2008. A classifier-based approach to preposition and determiner error correction in l2 english. In *Proceedings of the 22nd International Conference on Computational Linguistics - Volume 1*, COLING '08, pages 169–176, Stroudsburg, PA, USA. Association for Computational Linguistics.

Xuelei Miao Yan Song Dongfeng Cai, Yonghua Hu. 2009. Dependency grammar based english subject-verb agreement evaluation. *23rd Pacific Asia Conference on Language, Information and Computation*, pages 63–71.

Mark Dredze and Koby Crammer. 2008. Confidence-weighted linear classification. In *In ICML '08: Proceedings of the 25th international conference on Machine learning*, pages 264–271. ACM.

Rong-En Fan, Kai-Wei Chang, Cho-Jui Hsieh, Xiang-Rui Wang, and Chih-Jen Lin. 2008. Liblinear: A library for large linear classification. *J. Mach. Learn. Res.*, 9:1871–1874, June.

Michael Gamon, Jianfeng Gao, Chris Brockett, Alexandre Klementiev, William B. Dolan, Dmitriy Belenko, and Lucy Vanderwende. 2008. Using contextual speller techniques and language modeling for esl error correction. In *IJCNLP*, pages 449–456.

Na-Rae Han, Martin Chodorow, and Claudia Leacock. 2006. Detecting errors in english article usage by non-native speakers. *Nat. Lang. Eng.*, 12(2):115–129, June.

Rodney D. Huddleston. 1984. *Introduction to the grammar of English / Rodney Huddleston*. Cambridge University Press Cambridge [Cambridgeshire] ; New York.

Stephanie Seneff John Lee. 2008. Correcting misuse of verb forms. *Proceedings of ACL-08: HLT*, 12:174–182.

Dan Klein and Christopher D. Manning. 2003. Accurate unlexicalized parsing. In *ACL*, pages 423–430.

Kevin Knight and Ishwar Ch. 1994. Automated postediting of documents. In *In Proceedings of AAAI*.

Gerard Lynch, Erwan Moreau, and Carl Vogel. 2012. A naive bayes classifier for automatic correction of preposition and determiner errors in esl text. In *Proceedings of the Seventh Workshop on Building Educational Applications Using NLP*, pages 257–262, Stroudsburg, PA, USA. Association for Computational Linguistics.

Christopher D. Manning Marie-Catherine de Marneffe. 2011. Stanford typed dependencies manual.

Andrew McCallum and Kamal Nigam. 1998. A comparison of event models for naive bayes text classification. In *IN AAAI-98 WORKSHOP ON LEARNING FOR TEXT CATEGORIZATION*, pages 41–48. AAAI Press.

Alla Rozovskaya and Dan Roth. 2010. Training paradigms for correcting errors in grammar and usage. In *Human Language Technologies: The 2010 Annual Conference of the North American Chapter of the Association for Computational Linguistics*, HLT '10, pages 154–162, Stroudsburg, PA, USA. Association for Computational Linguistics.

Alla Rozovskaya, Mark Sammons, and Dan Roth. 2012. The ui system in the hoo 2012 shared task on error correction. In *Proceedings of the Seventh Workshop on Building Educational Applications Using NLP*, pages 272–280, Stroudsburg, PA, USA. Association for Computational Linguistics.

Rule-based System for Automatic Grammar Correction Using Syntactic N-grams for English Language Learning (L2)

Grigori Sidorov[†], Anubhav Gupta[‡], Martin Tozer[‡], Dolors Catala[‡], Angels Catena[‡] and Sandrine Fuentes[‡]
[†]Centro de Investigación en Computación, Instituto Politécnico Nacional (IPN), Mexico
[‡] Departament de Filologia Francesa i Romànica, Universitat Autònoma de Barcelona, Spain
`www.cic.ipn.mx\~sidorov`,
`{anubhav.gupta, tozer.martin}@e-campus.uab.cat`,
`{dolors.catala, angels.catena, sandrine.fuentes}@uab.cat`

Abstract

We describe the system developed for the CoNLL-2013 shared task—automatic English L2 grammar error correction. The system is based on the rule-based approach. It uses very few additional resources: a morphological analyzer and a list of 250 common uncountable nouns, along with the training data provided by the organizers. The system uses the syntactic information available in the training data: this information is represented as syntactic n-grams, i.e. n-grams extracted by following the paths in dependency trees. The system is simple and was developed in a short period of time (1 month). Since it does not employ any additional resources or any sophisticated machine learning methods, it does not achieve high scores (specifically, it has low recall) but could be considered as a baseline system for the task. On the other hand, it shows what can be obtained using a simple rule-based approach and presents a few situations where the rule-based approach can perform better than ML approach.

1 Introduction

There are two main approaches in the design of the modern linguistic experiments and the development of the natural language processing applications: rule-based and machine learning-based. In practical applications of machine learning (ML), the best results are achieved by the methods that use supervised learning, i.e., that are based on manually prepared training data for learning. It is also worth mentioning what can be considered a general rule for the combination of these two approaches: a system based on the mixed approach should obtain better results if each part of the system is applied according to its "competence". Specifically, some problems are better solved by the application of the rules—like the rules for choosing the correct allomorph of the article "a" vs. "an", while other problems are better solved by the usage of ML methods—such as deciding the presence or absence of a definite or an indefinite determiner.

This paper describes the system developed for the CoNLL-2013 shared task. The task consists of grammar correction in texts written by people learning English as a second language (L2). There are five types of errors considered in the task: noun number, subject-verb agreement, verb form, article/determiner and choice of preposition. The training data processed by the Stanford parser (de Marneffe et al., 2006) is provided. This data is part of the NUCLE corpus (Dahlmeier et al., 2013). The data also contains the error types and the corrected version.

Development of the system was started only two months before the deadline, so it is also an interesting example of what can be done in a rather short period of time and with relatively little effort: only one person-month joint effort in total.

In our system, we considered mainly the rule-based approach. Note that we used the ConLL data to extract preposition patterns, which can be considered as a very reduced form of machine learning with yes/no classifier, as well as to construct rules directly from the data.

Another feature of our system is the widespread use of the syntactic information present in the provided data. In our previous works, we generalized the use of syntactic information in NLP by introducing the concept of **syntactic n-grams**, i.e. n-grams constructed by following the dependency paths in a syntactic tree (Sidorov et al., 2012; Sidorov et al., 2013). Note that they are not n-grams of POS tags, as could be assumed from the name; the name refers to the manner in which they

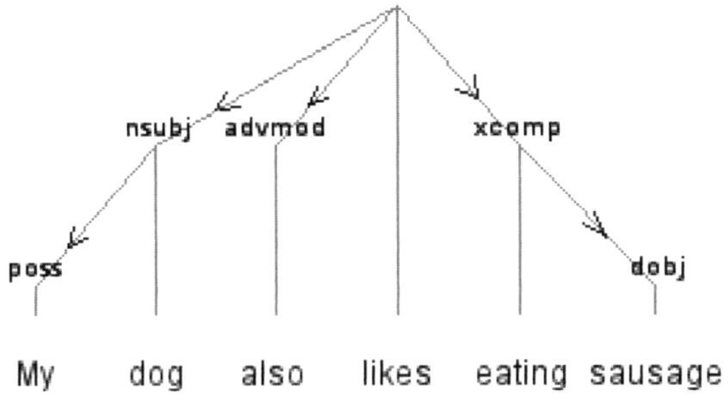

Figure 1: Example of syntactic tree (for extraction of syntactic n-grams).

are constructed. That is to say, in a dependency relation, there is always a head word and a dependent word. In the syntactic tree, this relation is graphically represented by an arrow: head → dependent. As it can be observed in Fig. 1, we can also use the tree hierarchy—the head word is always "higher" in the syntactic tree.

The algorithm for the construction of syntactic n-grams is as follows: we start from the root word and move to each dependent word following the dependency relations. At each step, the sequence of previous elements in the route taken are taken into account. The last n words in the sequence correspond to the syntactic n-gram. This could be reformulated as: we should take the last n words of the (unique) path from the root to the current word.

In other words, we start from the root and reach one of the dependent words. If we want to construct bigrams, then we have a bigram already. If we need other elements of the n-gram, then we move to the word that is dependent and continue to the words that are dependent on it. If a word has several dependent words, we consider them one after another and thus, obtain several syntactic n-grams. Note that the head word always appears before the dependent word in the syntactic n-gram during the construction process.

For example, from the tree presented in Fig. 1, the following syntactic bigrams can be extracted: *likes-also, likes-dog, dog-my, likes-eating, eating-sausage*. Note that only two syntactic 3-grams can be constructed: *likes-dog-my, likes-eating-sausage*. The construction process is the following: we start with the root word *like*. It has several dependent words: *dog, also, eating*. Considering them one after another, we obtain three syntactic bigrams. Then we move on to the word *dog*. It has only one dependent word: *my*. This is another bigram *dog-my*. However, the path from *like* also goes through it, so this is also the 3-gram *like-dog-my*, etc.

The reader can compare these syntactic n-grams with traditional n-grams and consider their advantages: there are a lot less syntactic n-grams, they are less arbitrary, they have linguistic interpretation, etc.

Note that syntactic n-grams can be formed by words (lemmas, stems), POS tags, names of dependency relations, or they can be mixed, i.e., a combination of the mentioned types. Being n-grams, they can be applied in any machine learning task where traditional n-grams are applied. However, unlike traditional n-grams, they have a clear linguistic interpretation and can be considered as an introduction of linguistic (syntactic) information into machine learning methods. Previously, we obtained better results by applying the syntactic n-grams to opinion mining and authorship attribution tasks compared to the traditional n-grams. Further in this paper, it is described how we use syntactic n-grams for the formulation of rules in our system and for the extraction of patterns.

The system described in this paper does not obtain high scores. In our opinion, it could be considered a **baseline system** for the grammar correction task due to its simplicity, its use of very few additional resources and the speed of its development. Concretely, if a more sophisticated system outperforms ours, it reflects well upon that system. If it performs more poorly, its design should be revised. On the other hand, this paper also discusses the few situations where the rule-based system can outperform an ML approach. As we mentioned earlier, the ideal system would combine both these approaches. To quote Tapanainen and Voutilainen (1994), "don't guess if you know".

Further below, we describe the lexical resources that we used, the processing of each type of error and the evaluation of the system.

2 The System's Linguistic Resources

The system consists of several program modules written in the Python programming language. We used only three types of **linguistic resources**:

- The provided corpus NUCLE data was processed with the Stanford parser. It was used for the extraction of patterns to identify preposition errors and for the formulation of rules.

- A list of the 250 most common uncountable nouns[1]. This list was used for processing the possibility of using the nouns in plural form.

- A morphological analysis system for English that in our case was based on the FreeLing morphological dictionary (Padró et al., 2010).

The FreeLing dictionary is a freely available text file which contains more than 71,000 word forms with standard POS tags. It has the following data: for each word form, it contains a list of lemmas and POS tags. An example of the entries:
...abandon abandon VB abandon VBP
abandoned abandon VBD abandon VBN
abandoning abandon VBG
abandonment abandonment NN
abandons abandon VBZ...

This list can also be easily reordered by lemmas. It is therefore very easy to apply this word list to both morphological analysis and generation. The morphological analysis simply consists of searching for a word form in the list, while the morphological generation involves searching the list of lemmas and then finding the word form with the necessary POS tag, i.e., for the generation, the input consists in the lemma and the POS tag. For example, if we want to generate the *VBZ* form of the verb *take*, then we search in the list ordered according to the lemma *take*; there are several forms: *take took VBP, take taken VBN, take takes VBZ* and choose the form that has the POS tag *VBZ*.

3 Error Processing

In accordance with the rules of the ConLL shared task, only five types of errors were considered: noun number, incorrect preposition, choice of determiner or article, subject-verb agreement and verb form. More error types are marked in the corpus, but they are much more complex, being related to the meaning and content.

Let us see examples of the errors:

- Preposition error: "...the need of habitable environment...", where "for" should be used.

- Nn error: "...people are getting more conscious of the damages...", the word "damage" in singular should be used.

- SVA error: "...relevant information are readily available...", where "is" should be used instead.

- Vform error: "The solution can be obtain by using technology...", where "obtained" should appear.

- ArtOrDet error: "...It is also important to create a better material...", where "a" should not be used.

The total number of errors marked in the training and the test data for ConLL 2013 are presented by type in Table 1.

Table 1: Numbers of errors in training and test data listed by type.

Error type	Training	Test
Vform (Verb form)	1,451	122
SVA (Subject-verb agreement)	1,529	124
ArtOrDet	6,654	690
Nn (Noun number)	3,773	396
Prep (Preposition)	2,402	311

Note that the errors related to the noun number should be processed first since later, an agreement error could be produced if the noun number is changed. If the agreement error is introduced by the modification of the noun number, it is not the error committed by the student, however it is considered as such in the current version of the task. Probably, it can be considered as some sort of secondary error. The order in which other errors are processed is irrelevant.

3.1 Noun Number Error Processing

The only rule we implemented in this case was that uncountable nouns do not have a plural. We used a list of the 250 most common uncountable nouns (as mentioned in the Section 2) to determine the possibility of a plural form for a noun. For example: *...ethics, evidence, evolution, failure, faith, fame, fiction, flour, flu, food, freedom...*

We made an exception for the noun "time" and do not consider it as uncountable, because its use in the common expressions such as "many times"

[1]List of 250 most common uncountable nouns. www.englishclub.com>Learn English>Vocabulary>Nouns.

is much more frequent than its use as an uncountable noun as in "theory of time" or "what time is it now?". More sophisticated systems should analyze the contexts obtained from vast data sets (corpora), i.e. consider n-grams or syntactic n-grams. Note that word sense disambiguation would be helpful in the resolution of the mentioned ambiguities. Also, the rule that considers the presence of the dependent words like "many, a lot of, amount of" could be added.

3.2 Subject-Verb Agreement and Verb Form Error Processing

We consider these two types of errors together because they are related to a similar and a rather simple grammatical phenomenon. To correct these errors we used syntactic information to formulate the rules. This is logical because we cannot rely on the context words (neighbours) as they appear in texts (traditional n-grams). Note that the rules are also related to the modal verbs and the passive constructions.

The rules for the agreement are very simple: 1) if the noun is in plural and the VBZ tag is present, then change the tag to VB, 2) if the noun is in singular and the VB tag is present, then change the tag to VBZ. The corresponding morphological generation is also performed.

The rules for verb form correction are as follows: 1) if we have a modal verb, then the depending verb should have a VB tag, 2) if we have an auxiliary verb "have", then the main verb should have a VB tag (perfect tense), etc. Moreover, the FreeLing morphological dictionary is utilized to identify the correct verb form. Note that there are some assumptions here about what drives the verb form, e.g., that a noun or a modal verb are correct and the verb needs to change. This appears to be a reasonable assumption, but may not always be correct.

3.3 Preposition Error Processing

It is well-known that prepositions depend on lexical units that are their heads, see (Eeg-Olofsson and Knutsson, 2003). But what should be done if we want to consider the dependent word? Say, that in the PP attachment task, the lexical unit is the preferred solution as well. In general, it would be an ideal solution in grammar correction, but in the case of our system, very little training data was used. If we consider that the dependent word is a lexical unit, we will have less recall. We are therefore practically obliged to consider that it is a POS tag.

To process the prepositions, we used the training data provided by the organizers. Specifically, we extracted preposition patterns. We apply the concept of syntactic n-grams to include both the head word of the preposition and the dependent word into the pattern. The pattern data corresponds to syntactic n-grams because they are constructed using syntactic dependencies. As we mentioned previously, syntactic n-grams can consist of words, POS tags or a combination. In our case, we used mixed syntactic n-grams: the head word is the lexical unit, while the dependent word is the POS tag, as shown in Table 2.

For example, the first line corresponds to the erroneous phrase "...unwelcomed among public...", where "among" should be substituted by "by". Note that there can be other words between these three words in the surface representation of the sentence, but the parser allows the extraction of the syntactic n-gram, which represents the "pure" pattern.

In order to choose the syntactic n-gram type, our first consideration was that the head word should be a lexical unit (word), because this determines the choice of the preposition. We used a POS tag for the dependent element, because we considered that using a word there would be too specific. Thus, our final syntactic n-gram for the first line was "...unwelcomed among NN...", which should be changed to "...unwelcomed by NN...". The syntactic n-gram for the second line was "...trouble for NN...", which should be changed to "...trouble in NN...", etc. Note that insertion of prepositions is not considered, but deletion can be performed, i.e., changing the preposition to nothing.

The rule for the system is formulated in the following way: if we find a relation "preposition" in the dependency tree, then for the preposition that corresponds to this relation, we search the list of the extracted patterns. If we find the pattern, then we change the preposition. It is quite clear that the training data is too limited to obtain patterns for a great majority of words. Our list contained only 1,896 elements. These patterns should be extracted from a very large corpus or a dictionary.

3.4 Article or Determiner Error Processing

In this case, we found only two clear rules, both related to the article "a": 1) choice of the allo-

Table 2: Examples of patterns for prepositions.

Preposition (error)	Preposition (correction)	Head word (lemma)	Head word (POS)	Dependent word (lemma)	Dependent word (POS)
among	by	unwelcomed	VBN	public	NN
for	in	trouble	NN	development	NN
on	in	practice	NN	October	NNP
on	in	face	VBG	field	NN

morph "a/an", and 2) the fact that the article "a" cannot be used with nouns in plural. Other rules would be too complex for a manually created rule-based system. The first rule takes into the account the immediate neighbor: the choice depends on its phonetic properties. The second rule considers the syntactically related head word, which cannot be in plural if we use the indefinite article.

4 Evaluation of the System

For the evaluation, the organizers provided data similar to the training data from the same NUCLE corpus, which also contained syntactic information. The evaluation results were provided by the organizers using their evaluation script in Python (Dahlmeier and Ng, 2012). The results obtained with this script for our system are: precision 17.4 %, recall 1.8%, and F1 measure 3.3% (the preliminary scores were: 12.4%, 1.2% and 2.2% correspondingly). See the final remarks in this section, where we argue that the real values should be: precision 25%, recall 2.6%, and F1 measure 4.7%.

The results are low, but as we mentioned previously, our system uses a rule-based approach with very few additional resources, so it cannot compete with ML based approaches that additionally rely on vast lexical resources and the Internet. Due to its simplicity, low use of additional resources, and very short development time, we consider our system a possible baseline system for the task. On the other hand, we showed that in some cases the rules should be used as a complementary technique for ML learning methods: don't guess if you know.

The low recall of the system is to be expected as we process only clearly defined errors, ignoring more complex cases.

It is always interesting to perform an analysis of the errors committed by a system. Let us analyze the supposed errors committed by our system for the noun number error type. It performed 18 corrections, 3 of which coincide with the marks in the corpus data. Two of them are clear errors of the system: "traffic jam", where the word "jam" is used in a sense other than that of the "substance", and "many respects", where again the word "respect" has a different meaning to that of the uncountable noun. There are 13 cases listed below, that our system marked as errors, because they are uncountable nouns in plural, but they are not marked in the corpus. Let us consider the nouns in capital letters:

...peaceful(JJ) LIVINGS(NNS)[2]*...,*
...life(NN) QUALITIES(NNS)...,
...Many(JJ) science(NN) FICTIONS(NNS)...,
...does(VBZ) not(RB) have(VB) enough(JJ) LANDS(NNS)...,
...indicates(VBZ) that(IN) the(DT) FOODS(NNS) the(DT) people(NNS) eat(VBP)...,
...problem(NN) of(IN) public(JJ) TRANSPORTATIONS(NNS)...,
...healthcare(NN) consume(VBP) large(JJ) QUANTITIES(NNS) of(IN) energy...,
...this(DT) society(NN) may(MD) lack(VB) of(IN) LABOURS(NNS)...

Note that the words "equipment" and "usage" in plural were marked as errors in the corpus. In our opinion, it is inconsistent to mark these two as errors, and not to mark the words from this list as such. While it is true that their use in plural is possible, it is clearly forced and is much less probable. At least, students of English should learn to use these words in singular only. Some of these mistakes (but not all) were corrected by the organizers for the final scoring data. If we consider all these cases as correctly marked errors, then the precision of our system is around 25%, recall 2.6%, and F1 measure 4.7%.

[2]"LIVINGS" is encountered 5 times and "QUANTITIES" is encountered 2 times

5 Conclusions

In this paper we have described the system presented for the CoNLL-2013 shared task for grammar correction in English (L2). The system uses a rule-based approach and relies on very few additional resources: a list of 250 uncountable nouns, a morphological analyzer and the training data from the NUCLE corpus provided by the organizers. The system uses syntactic n-grams for rule formulation, i.e., n-grams that are constructed by following the dependency paths in a parsed tree.

We analyzed various situations in which a rule based technique can give better results than ML techniques: don't guess if you know. These cases are: 1) two rules for the article "a", and 2) the rules for uncountable nouns (in this case, word sense disambiguation would help to determine if the sense in the text is an uncountable noun or has some other use), and 3) the subject-verb agreement rule. In the case of prepositions, ML learning is definitely better. Otherwise, vast resources would need to be used, which in any case, would resemble machine learning. We are not sure about verb form errors: the rules which we formulated are rather simple, but the performance of various ML methods should be analysed in order to decide which technique is better.

The system is simple and was developed in a very short time. It does not obtain high scores and could be considered as a baseline system for the task.

Acknowledgements

This work was done under partial support of the Mexican Government (CONACYT, SNI, COFAA-IPN, SIP-IPN 20120418, 20121823), CONACYT-DST India ("Answer Validation through Textual Entailment"), Mexico City Government (ICYT PICCO10-120), and FP7-PEOPLE-2010- IRSES: Web Information Quality - Evaluation Initiative (WIQ-EI) European Commission project 269180.

References

Daniel Dahlmeier and Hwee Tou Ng. 2012. Better evaluation for grammatical error correction. In *Proceedings of the 2012 Conference of the North American Chapter of the Association for Computational Linguistics (NAACL 2012)*, pages 568–572.

Daniel Dahlmeier, Hwee Tou Ng, and Siew Mei Wu. 2013. Building a large annotated corpus of learner English: The NUS corpus of learner English.

M.C. de Marneffe, B. MacCartney, and C.D. Manning. 2006. Generating typed dependency parses from phrase structure parses. In *LREC 2006*.

Jens Eeg-Olofsson and Ola Knutsson. 2003. Automatic grammar checking for second language learners – the use of prepositions. In *Proceedings of Nodalida'03*.

Llus Padró, Miquel Collado, Samuel Reese, Marina Lloberes, and Irene Castellón. 2010. Freeling 2.1: Five years of open-source language processing tools. In *Proceedings of 7th Language Resources and Evaluation Conference (LREC 2010)*, ELRA.

G. Sidorov, F. Velasquez, E. Stamatatos, A. Gelbukh, and L. Chanona-Hernandez. 2012. Syntactic dependency-based n-grams as classification features. *LNAI 7630*, pages 1–11.

G. Sidorov, F. Velasquez, E. Stamatatos, A. Gelbukh, and L. Chanona-Hernandez. 2013. Syntactic dependency-based n-grams: More evidence of usefulness in classification. *LNCS 7816 (Proc. of CICLing)*, pages 13–24.

Pasi Tapanainen and Atro Voutilainen. 1994. Tagging accurately - don't guess if you know. In *Proceedings of ANLP '94*.

Memory-based grammatical error correction

Antal van den Bosch
Radboud University Nijmegen
P.O. Box 9103
NL-6500 HD Nijmegen, The Netherlands
a.vandenbosch@let.ru.nl

Peter Berck
Tilburg University
P.O. Box 90153
NL-5000 LE Tilburg, The Netherlands
p.j.berck@tilburguniversity.edu

Abstract

We describe the 'TILB' team entry for the CoNLL-2013 Shared Task. Our system consists of five memory-based classifiers that generate correction suggestions for center positions in small text windows of two words to the left and to the right. Trained on the Google Web 1T corpus, the first two classifiers determine the presence of a determiner or a preposition between all words in a text. The second pair of classifiers determine which is the most likely correction of an occurring determiner or preposition. The fifth classifier is a general word predictor which is used to suggest noun and verb form corrections. We report on the scores attained and errors corrected and missed. We point out a number of obvious improvements to boost the scores obtained by the system.

1 Introduction

Our team entry, known under the abbreviation 'TILB' in the CoNLL-2013 Shared Task, is a simplistic text and grammar correction system based on five memory-based classifiers implementing eight different error correctors. The goal of the system is to be lightweight: simple to set up and train, fast in execution. It requires a preferably very large but unannotated corpus to train on, and closed lists of words that contain categories of interest (in our case, determiners and prepositions). The error correctors make use of information from a lemmatizer and a noun and verb inflection module. The amount of explicit grammatical information input in the system is purposely kept to a minimum, as accurate deep grammatical information cannot be assumed to be present in most real-world situations and languages. The system described in this article takes plain text as input and produces plain text as output.

Memory-based classifiers have been applied to similar tasks before. (Van den Bosch, 2006) describes memory based classifiers used for confusible disambiguation, and (Stehouwer and Van den Bosch, 2009) shows how agreement errors can be detected. In the 2012 shared task 'Helping Our Own' (Dale et al., 2012) memory based classifiers were used to solve the problem of missing and incorrect determiners and prepositions (Van den Bosch and Berck, 2012).

The CoNLL-2013 Shared Task context limited the grammatical error correction task to detecting and correcting five error types:

ArtOrDet	Missing, unnecessary or incorrect article or determiner;
Prep	Incorrect preposition used;
Nn	Wrong form of noun used (e.g. singular instead of plural);
Vform	Incorrect verb form used (e.g. *I have went*);
SVA	Incorrect subject-verb agreement (e.g. *He have*).

The corrections made by the system are scored by a program provided by the organizers (Ng, 2012). It takes a plain textfile as input (the output generated by the system) and outputs a list with correctly rectified errors followed by precision, recall and F-score.

As training material we used two corpora. The Google Web 1T corpus (Brants and Franz, 2006) was used to train the classifiers for the ArtOrDet and Prep error categories. The GigaWord Newspaper text corpus[1] was used to create the data for the classifier for the noun and verb-related error categories. To make the classifiers more compatible

[1] `http://www.ldc.upenn.edu/`

with each other, future versions of the system will all be trained on the same corpus. We also used two lists, one consisting of 64 prepositions and one consisting of 23 determiners, both extracted from the CoNLL-2013 Shared Task training data. Using the Google corpus means that we restricted ourselves to a simple 5-gram context, which obviously places a limit on the context sensitivity of our system; on the other hand, we were able to make use of the entire Google Web 1T corpus. The context for the grammatical error detectors was kept similar to the other classifiers, also 5-grams.

2 System

Our system is based on five memory-based classifiers that all run the IGTree classifier algorithm (Daelemans et al., 1997), a decision-tree approximation of k-nearest neighbour classification implemented in the TiMBL software package.[2] The first two classifiers determine the presence of a determiner or a preposition between all words in a text in which the actual determiners and prepositions are masked. The second pair of classifiers determine which is the most likely correction given a masked determiner or preposition. The fifth classifier is a general word predictor that is used for suggesting noun and verb form corrections.

All classifiers take a windowed input of two words to the left of the focus position, and two words to the right. The focus may either be a position *between* two words, or be *on* a word. In case of a position between two words, the task is to predict whether the position should actually be filled by an determiner or a preposition. When the focus is on the word in question, the task is to decide whether it should be deleted, or whether it should be corrected.

It is important to note that not just one classification is returned for a given context by the IGTree classifier, but a *distribution* of results and their respective occurrence counts. The classifier matches the words in the context to examples in the tree in a fixed order, and returns the distribution stored at that point in the tree when an unknown word is encountered. This is analogous to the backoff mechanisms often used in other n-gram based language modeling systems. When even the first feature fails to match, the complete class distribution is returned. The output from the classifiers is filtered by the error correctors for the correct answers. Filtering is done based on distribution size, occurrence counts and ratios in occurrence counts (in the remainder of the text, where we say frequency we mean occurrence count), and in the case of the noun and verb-related error types, on part-of-speech tags.

The system corrects a text from left to right, starting with the first word and working its way to the end. Each error corrector is tried after the other, in the order specified below, until a correction is suggested. At this point, the correction is stored, and the system starts processing the next word. The other classifiers are not tried anymore after a correction has been suggested by one of the classifiers.

The first two classifiers, **preposition?** and **determiner?**, are binary classifiers that determine whether or not there should be a preposition or a determiner, respectively, between two words to the left and two words to the right:

- The **preposition?** classifier is trained on all 120,711,874 positive cases of contexts in the Google Web 1T corpus in which one of the 64 known prepositions are found to occur in the middle position of a 5-gram. To enable the classifier to answer negatively to other contexts, roughly the same amount of negative cases of randomly selected contexts with no preposition in the middle are added to form a training set of 238,046,975 cases. We incorporate the Google corpus token counts in our model. We performed a validation experiment on a single 90%-10% split of the training data; the classifier is able to make a correct decision on 88.6% of the 10% heldout cases.

- Analogously, the **determiner?** classifier takes all 86,253,841 positive cases of 5-grams with a determiner in the middle position, and adds randomly selected negative cases to arrive at a training set of 169,874,942 cases. On a 90%–10% split, the classifier makes the correct decision in 90.0% of the 10% heldout cases.

The second pair of classifiers perform the multi-label classification task of predicting which preposition or determiner is most likely given a context of two words to the left and to the right. Again,

[2] `http://ilk.uvt.nl/timbl`

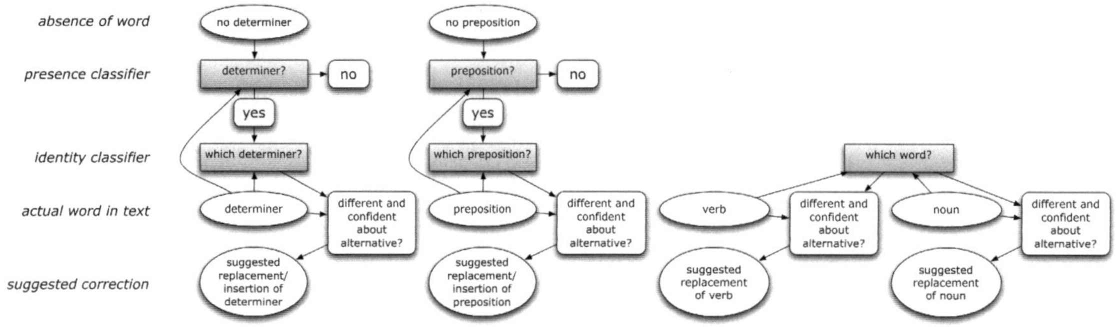

Figure 1: System architecture. Shaded rectangles are the five classifiers.

these classifiers are trained on the entire Google Web 1T corpus, including its token counts:

- The **which preposition?** classifier is trained on the aforementioned 120,711,874 cases of any of the 64 prepositions occurring in the middle of 5-grams. The task of the classifier is to generate a class distribution of likely prepositions given an input of the four words surrounding the preposition, with 64 possible outcomes. In a 90%-10% split experiment on the complete training set, this classifier labels 63.3% of the 10% heldout cases correctly.
- The **which determiner?** classifier, by analogy, is trained on the 86,253,841 positive cases of 5-grams with a determiner in the middle position, and generates class distributions composed of the 23 possible class labels (the possible determiners). On a 90%-10% split of the training set, the classifier predicts 68.3% of all heldout cases correctly.

The fifth classifier predicts the most likely word(s) between a context of two words to the left and two to the right.

- The general word predictor, **which word?**, for the grammatical error types, was trained on 10 million lines of the GigaWord English Newspaper corpus. This amounts to 66,675,151 5-grams. It predicts the word in the middle between the two context words on the left and on the right.

From the predictions of the five classifiers the following eight error correctors are derived. There is no one-to-one correspondence between classifier and corrector. The ArtOrDet and Prep error categories are handled by three separate errors correctors each that handle replacement, deletion, and insertion errors. The three error types Nn, Vform and SVA are handled by just two correctors:

1 missing preposition (Prep)
2 replace preposition (Prep)
3 unnecessary preposition (Prep)
4 missing determiner (ArtOrDet)
5 replace determiner (ArtOrDet)
6 unnecessary determiner (ArtOrDet)
7 noun form (Nn, SVA)
8 verb form (Vform, SVA)

For the latter two error correctors, 7 and 8, we make additional use of a lemmatizer[3] and a singular-plural determiner and generator[4] for noun form errors, and a verb tense determiner and generator[5] for verb form and SVA errors.

The algorithms for the six preposition and determiner correctors will be explained in the rest of this section. The algorithms use the same logic, the difference is in the different lists and parameters used for each error type.

The algorithm for missing preposition (or determiner) is as follows.

1 next word is not a preposition
2 run **positive-negative classifier** P^{+}_{-}
3 if the classification = + (i.e. we expect a preposition), and freq(+):freq(−) > MP_PNR
4 run the **which preposition?** classifier
5 if length distribution <= MP_DS take answer as missing preposition

The parameters (MP_PNR and MP_DS in the above algorithm) are used to control the certainty we expect from the classifier. Their values were determined in our submission to the 2012 'Helping

[3]http://www-nlp.stanford.edu/software/corenlp.shtml
[4]https://pypi.python.org/pypi/inflect
[5]http://nodebox.net/code/index.php/Linguistics

Our Own' shared task (Dale et al., 2012), which focused on determiner and preposition errors (Van den Bosch and Berck, 2012). Similar classifiers were used in this year's system, and the same parameters were used this time.

In step 3 above, we check the ratio between the frequency of the positive answer and the negative answer. If the ratio is larger than the parameter MP_PNR (set to 20) we interpret this as being certain. In step 5, we prefer a small, sharp distribution of answers. A large distribution indicates the classifier not finding any matches in the context and returning a large distribution with all possible answers. In that case, the majority class tends to be the majority class of the complete training data, and not the specific answer(s) in the context we are looking at. To avoid this we only suggest an answer when the distribution is equal to or smaller than a certain preset threshold, MP_DS, which was set to 20 for this task.

The algorithm for replacing propositions (or determiners) proceeds as follows:

1 word in focus is a preposition p
2 run **which preposition?**, classification is p_{alt}
3 if freq(p_{alt}) $>$ RP_F and
4 if word is in distribution and freq(p_{alt}):freq(p) $>$ RP_R, take p_{alt} as a correction

This algorithm shows another parameter, namely a check on frequency (occurrence count). In order to be generated as a correction, the alternate answer must have a frequency higher than RP_F, set to 5 in our system, and the ratio between its frequency and that of the preposition in the distribution that is the same as in the text must be larger than RP_R. This parameter was set to 20.

The algorithm for unnecessary preposition (or determiner) works as follows:

1 word in focus is a preposition
2 run **positive-negative** classifier P^{+}_{-}
3 if classification $= -$ and freq($-$):freq($+$) $>$ UP_NPR
4 the preposition is unnecessary

The next two algorithms show the Nn and Vf correctors. The parameters these correctors use have not been extensively tweaked, but rather use the same settings as used in the preposition and determiner correctors.

The first list shows the algorithm for the noun type error. This error corrector also makes use of a noun inflection module to turn singular nouns into plural and vice versa. The algorithm first looks for the alternative version of the noun in the distribution returned by the classifier given the context. If it is found, and if it is much more frequent in the distribution than the noun form used in the text, a noun form error may have been found. The alternative form found in the distribution is returned as the correction.

1 word in focus w is a noun
2 check singular or plural, determine alternate version w_{alt}
3 run the **which-word?** classifier, resulting in distribution D
4 check if w is in D
5 check if w_{alt} is in D
6 if freq(w) in D < 10 and w_{alt} is in D use w_{alt} as correction

Finally, the verb form error corrector makes use of a verb-tense determiner and generator, and a lemmatizer. The alternative verb forms are generated from the lemma of the verb and the tense of the verb. To prevent the system changing, for example, *give* to *gave*, the generated alternatives are kept in the same tense as the word in the text. This does, however, mean that it will not be able to correct verb tense errors (*I see him yesterday* versus *I saw him yesterday*).

1 word in focus is a verb v
2 determine the lemma of v
3 determine the tense of v
4 generate alternatives in same tense as word, v_{alt}
5 run **which-word?** predictor, resulting in distribution D
6 check if v is in D
7 check which v_{alt} are in D, take highest frequency freq(v_{alt})
8 if freq(v_{alt}):freq(v) > 10: take v_{alt} as a correction of v

3 Results

Table 1 lists the precision, recall and F-score of our system on the test data. The test data (Tetreault, 2013) consisted of 300 paragraphs of English text written by non-native speakers. The system's output is processed by a scorer supplied by the organizers (Ng, 2012). For each sentence, it reports the number of correct, proposed and gold edits, and a running total of the system's precision, recall and F-score.

The system suggested a total of 1,902 edits. Of these, 118 were correct. The total number of correct edits was 1,643. To explain the score obtained by the system, we inspect the kind of errors which it was subjected to, and what kind of errors it did correct and which it missed.

Precision	6.20%
Recall	7.18%
F1	6.66%

Table 1: Summary Score

We see a number of errors which are difficult to correct because they depend on understanding the sentence. Take the following sentence for example:

Surveillance technology such as RFID can be operated twenty-four hours with the absence of operators to track done every detail about human activities .

The gold-edit for this sentence is changing *with* (word 11) to *without*. This edit may be questionable, but questionability aside, it is based on a understanding of what is being talked about in the text. Correcting these kinds of errors falls outside the scope of the system at the moment.

Multi-word edits are also a problem. In *All passengers and pilots were died*, the gold-edit is to change *were died* to *died*. In *The readers are just smiling when they flip the page because it never comes to their mind that one day it might come true*, the gold-edit is to change *are just smiling* to *just smile*. These kind of corrections are missed by our system at the moment due to the rigid one-word, left-to-right checking of the sentence.

Inserting more than one word is also problematic for our system at the moment. Take the following sentence.

Firstly , security systems are improved in many areas such as school campus or at the workplace .

The gold-edit is to insert *on the* before *school*. A potential solution for this problem is to take multiple passes over the sentence, first inserting *on*, followed by *the* in a later pass.

Nevertheless, the system made a number of correct edits as well. The next subsections list examples of each error type and a correction, where applicable.

Missing determiner

In this sentence, the missing determiner before *smart* was corrected by the system.

In spite of that, ***the smart*** *phone is still a device . . .*

In the following sentence however, a determiner is inserted where it is not needed, before *RFID*.

. . . the idea of using ***the RFID*** *to track people . . .*

To illustrate the reasoning of our system, the **determiner?** classifier thinks that it is more than 13 times more likely to find a determiner between *of using* and *RFID to* than not. Of the possible determiners, the determiner *the* has the highest frequency with 38,809 occurrences.

Replace Determiner

Here is an example of a determiner which is corrected:

. . . signal and also ***a⇒the*** *risk that their phone . . .*

It also happens that the right determiner is incorrectly changed into another determiner, as shown in the next example.

. . . this kind of tragedy to happen on ***any⇒the*** *family.*

The determiner *the* had a frequency of more than 6 million in the distribution, compared to only 68,612 for *any*.

Unnecessary Determiner

The system did not detect any unnecessary determiners. It missed, for example, removing the determiner *the* in this setentence:

. . . technology available for the Man 's life .

Replace Preposition

In this example, a preposition was corrected.

. . . to be put ***into⇒under*** *close surveillance . . .*

But in the following sentence

. . . remain functional ***for⇒after*** *a long period of . . .*

the preposition *for* is unfortunately changed to *after*, which in this context is more common.

Unnecessary Preposition

The following is an example of a correct removal of a preposition:

*. . . , many **of** things that are regarded . . .*

Prepositions were also incorrectly removed, as shown in the following example. Here

*. . . that can be out **of** our imaginations . . .*

of is deemed unnecessary.

Missing Preposition

In this example, the missing preposition *on* was inserted after *live*.

*. . . find another planet to live **on** , the earth is . . .*

In the sentence

*. . . especially **in** the elderly and the children . . .*

the system inserts the preposition *in* between *especially* and *and*, which in this case was incorrect.

Noun form

The next example shows a noun form correction.

*. . . brought harmful side **effect⇒effects** to human body*

This can, of course, also go wrong:

*Since RFID **tags⇒tag** attached to the product . . .*

Here the singular form of the noun was deemed correct.

Verb form

Finally, an example of a verb form correction:

*People **needs⇒need** a safe environment to live . . .*

And the final example, an incorrect replacement of *been* to *was*.

. . . that has currently been⇒was implemented

4 Discussion

We have described a memory-based grammar checker specialized in correcting the five types of errors in the CoNLL-2013 Shared Task. The system is built on five classifiers specialized in the error categories relevant for the task. They are trained to find errors in a small local context of two words to the left and two words to the right. The system scans each word in each sentence in the test data and calls the relevant classifier(s) to determine if a word needs to be replaced, deleted, or inserted. The classifiers take word tokens as input; no deep grammatical information was supplied to them. Even though the training data supplied for the task contained syntax trees, they were not used in creating our system. On the other hand, the part-of-speech information in the training data was used to create the lists of prepositions and determiners. Furthermore, a part-of-speech tagger was used to determine if the noun or verb form error corrector was to be applied.

There are several obvious shortcomings to this approach. The most obvious one is that each corrector is applied to single words, using only a small local context of two words to the left and right. This may work fine for missing prepositions and determiners, but for spotting grammatical errors like subject-verb agreement this limited contextual scope is insufficient. It also means that we are only able to correct “single words to single words”. That is, it is not possible to substitute two words for one, and vice versa. One avenue that could be explored is larger contexts. In addition, the classifiers are not limited to words, and contexts with other (contextual) information could be tried as well.

Secondly, the correctors are applied in a strict order one after the other. This should not be a big problem as the classifiers are called separately for their particular part-of-speech category (determiner, preposition, verb, or noun). On the other hand, this puts a lot of weight on the part of speech tagger. Ambiguous or wrong tags could cause the wrong corrector to be tried and even applied, and could miss a potential correct correction.

Furthermore, the corrected words are not fed back into the system. This means that the context after an error still contains that error. This may cause the classifiers to mismatch and miss the next error. It should be noted that the small context of two words to the left and right probably helps to alleviate this problem. However, making the system insert corrections and backtracking a step (or more) could help towards solving the problem of multi-word corrections.

Finally, not all correctors found errors. This may of course depend on the test data, but it seems unlikely that the data contained no 'missing preposition' errors. There is a potential gain in tuning the parameters controlling the error correctors.

4.1 Update

The organizers of the shared task updated the m2-scorer used to calculate the results, resulting in slightly better scores. Table 2 shows the revised score of our system, with the old score between parentheses.

Precision	7.60%	(6.20%)
Recall	9.29%	(7.18%)
F1	8.36%	(6.66%)

Table 2: Revised Summary Score

And to conclude, we continued working on the system and tweaked some of the parameters controlling the preposition and determiner checkers. By allowing the correctors to be applied more often, we see an increase in the number of proposed and correct edits (2,533 and 178 respectively). The downside to this is of course that the number of false positives increases, which decreases the precision of the system.

The tweaked score is shown in table 3, with the revised score between parentheses.

Precision	7.03%	(7.60%)
Recall	10.83%	(9.29%)
F1	8.52%	(8.36%)

Table 3: Tweaked Summary Score

These improved scores give us good hope that the highest scores have not been reached yet.

Acknowledgements

The authors thank Ko van der Sloot for his sustained improvements of the TiMBL software. This work is rooted in earlier joint work funded through a grant from the Netherlands Organization for Scientific Research (NWO) for the Vici project *Implicit Linguistics*.

References

T. Brants and A. Franz. 2006. LDC2006T13: Web 1T 5-gram Version 1.

W. Daelemans, A. Van den Bosch, and A. Weijters. 1997. IGTree: using trees for compression and classification in lazy learning algorithms. *Artificial Intelligence Review*, 11:407–423.

R. Dale, I. Anisimoff, and G. Narroway. 2012. HOO 2012: A report on the preposition and determiner error correction shared task. In *Proceedings of the Seventh Workshop on Innovative Use of NLP for Building Educational Applications*, Montreal, Canada.

Daniel Dahlmeier & Hwee Tou Ng. 2012. Better evaluation for grammatical error correction. In *Proceedings of the 2012 Conference of the North American Chapter of the Association for Computational Linguistics*, pages 568 – 572.

H. Stehouwer and A. Van den Bosch. 2009. Putting the t where it belongs: Solving a confusion problem in Dutch. In S. Verberne, H. van Halteren, and P.-A. Coppen, editors, *Computational Linguistics in the Netherlands 2007: Selected Papers from the 18th CLIN Meeting*, pages 21–36, Nijmegen, The Netherlands.

Hwee Tou Ng & Siew Mei Wu & Yuanbin Wu & Christian Hadiwinoto & Joel Tetreault. 2013. The conll-2013 shared task on grammatical error correction. In *Proceedings of the Seventeenth Conference on Computational Natural Language Learning.*

A. Van den Bosch and P. Berck. 2012. Memory-based text correction for preposition and determiner errors. In *Proceedings of the 7th Workshop on the Innovative Use of NLP for Building Educational Applications*, pages 289–294, New Brunswick, NJ. ACL.

A. Van den Bosch. 2006. All-word prediction as the ultimate confusible disambiguation. In *Proceedings of the HLT-NAACL Workshop on Computationally hard problems and joint inference in speech and language processing*, New York, NY.

A Noisy Channel Model Framework for Grammatical Correction

L. Amber Wilcox-O'Hearn
Department of Computer Science
University of Toronto
amber@cs.toronto.edu

Abstract

We report on the TOR system that participated in the 2013 CoNLL shared task on grammatical correction. The system was a provisional implementation of a beam search correction over a noisy channel model. Although the results on the shared task test set were poor, the approach may still be promising, as there are many aspects of the current implementation that could be optimised. Grammatical correction is inherently difficult both to perform and to evaluate. As such, possible improvements to the evaluation are also discussed.

1 Introduction

Grammatical correction covers many subproblems including spelling correction, lexical choice, and even paraphrasing. There is a sense in which syntax is separable from semantics and discourse. A sentence may be parsable in a language, even if it is nonsensical. On the other hand, many errors that we consider a matter of grammar, such as some instances of determiner choice, are only incorrect because of the semantic or discourse properties of the sentence in its context.

Another complexity is that there are degrees of grammatical correctness. Some sentences are not parsable, but others are just awkward sounding, or unconventional.

So a grammatical error may manifest in a message that doesn't code a meaning in the language at all, and the task becomes inferring a plausible meaning and coding it correctly. This is analogous to non-word spelling errors. Alternatively, it may result in a meaning that is not exactly what was intended. This is more like a real-word spelling error.

In either case, the implication is that in order to detect and correct a grammatical error, we must be able to infer the intended meaning. This points to the depth of the problem.

1.1 Confusion Sets

A common and useful way to construe error correction, including grammatical correction, is to first classify sets of alternatives that are mutually confusable. This is typically done at the lexical level, though the idea is generalizable to multiword expressions, constructions, or phrases. Then the text under examination is searched for instances of members of these confusion sets. Finally a heuristic is used to decide whether one of its alternatives would have been a more appropriate choice in its context. Within this framework, there are different approaches to these steps.

In choosing our confusion sets, we wanted to be flexible and extensible. Therefore, we did not want to depend on corpora of errors with annotated corrections to infer alternatives. So we collected general statistics from corpora that were assumed to be correct, and used those to evaluate proposed corrections to observed sentences. This approach is not unique to this model. It is seen, for example, in (De Felice and Pulman, 2007), (Tetreault and Chodorow, 2008), and (Gamon et al., 2009), among others.

However, the main difference between our system and previous ones is that we do not select our confusion sets in advance of statistical modelling. That is, although the confusion sets we used were based on POS tagsets, there was no classifying or learning to discriminate among members of a confusion set before the task. The aim of this choice was to make our system more general and flexible. We can now modify our confusion sets at runtime without retraining any models. The provisional confusion sets we used are somewhat arbitrary, but this can be changed independently of the rest of the system.

Although our system was not competitive at this

stage, it provides a preliminary basis for further experiments.

The remainder of this paper describes the framework and the initial implementation of that framework that was used in the shared task, as well as future improvements to the model. We also discuss the difficulty in evaluating such systems. All of the code used to generate our submission is freely available for examination and use on GitHub (Wilcox-O'Hearn and Wilcox-O'Hearn, 2013).

2 Overview of the system

We approach grammatical error correction using a noisy channel model. Such a model is also used by (Park and Levy, 2011) and (West, Park, and Levy, 2011). One appealing aspect of this model is that it makes explicit the cost of error, such that a correction must not only be more likely than the observation to be proposed, but it must be more likely even given that errors are less likely than non-errors to a degree specified by the properties of the channel. In practice this can mitigate false positives that result from overconfidence in a language model.

A grammatical error is treated as a transformation of some original, correct sentence, S, generated by a language model M. We attempt to recover the original sentence by hypothesizing possible transformations that could have resulted in the observed sentence S'. If we estimate that it is more likely that S was generated by M and transformed into S' than that S' was generated by M and left unchanged, we propose S as a correction.

In this preliminary implementation of the framework, we use a combination of word and POS n-gram models as the language generation model, while POS tags form the basis of our channel model.

To generate sentence hypotheses that can include multiple interacting errors interleaved with non-errors while putting a bound on the size of the search space, we use a left-to-right beam search. This differs from the beam search used by Dalheimer and Ng (2012a). In their work, the search space is constructed by generating variations of the entire sentence. Just as here, at each iteration, they make every variation appropriate at a single position, but they evaluate the whole sentence containing that correction. Although sentences that require multiple interacting corrections will initially have a low score under this method, a large enough beam width will allow the corrections to be made one at a time without being lost from consideration. In our model, by evaluating partial sentences from left-to-right, we hope to lessen the need for a large beam width, by holding off integration of the continuation of the sentence, and letting it unfold in a way that more closely mimics human sentence comprehension.

2.1 The language model

To model language generation, we used an interpolation of two n-gram models, a trigram model based on regular word types, and a 5-gram model of POS tags. The data for these models was derived by combining the corrected version of the NUCLE corpus (Dalheimer, Ng, and Wu, 2013) with a randomly chosen selection of articles from Wikipedia as provided by the Westbury Lab Wikipedia corpus (Shaoul and Westbury, 2010), which we tokenised using NLTK (Bird, Loper, and Klein, 2009) to match the format of the shared task. The precise set of articles used is included in our GutHub repository (Wilcox-O'Hearn and Wilcox-O'Hearn, 2013). We used SRILM 1.7.0 (Stolcke, 2002) to generate a modest trigram model of 5K words. We then passed the same data through the Stanford POS tagger v3.1.4 (Toutanova, Klein, Manning, and Singer, 2003) and again through SRILM to produce a POS 5-gram model.

2.2 The channel model

The channel model provides a definition of transformations that could have been applied to a sentence before we observed it. Our system considers only transformations of single words, specifically, only single word insertions, deletions, and substitutions. This cannot represent every grammar error we might encounter, but makes a good first approximation, and it represents all errors in this iteration of the shared task. To simplify the description and implementation, we equivalently consider the empty string to be a valid word included in some substitution (confusion) sets, and define the channel as one that sometimes replaces a word with one of the alternatives in its confusion set. The probability of such replacement is a parameter α to be inferred.

As explained in the introduction, one goal of our system is to allow flexible confusion sets that do not need to be fully specified in advance of learning statistics about them. Therefore, we define our confusion sets in terms of the standard POS tagsets as given by the Stanford tagger, using a notion of closed vs. open word classes.

2.2.1 Closed Classes

For our purposes, a closed word class is a set of words that has a relatively small, finite number of members. We composed the following closed classes out of POS tagsets for the purposes of this task:

- DT $\cup \{\epsilon\}$,
- MD $\cup \{\epsilon\}$,
- IN $\cup$ TO $\cup \{\epsilon\}$,
- a hand-built class called AUX, consisting of 'be', 'do', 'have', and 'get' verbs, $\cup$ TO $\cup$ $\{\epsilon\}$.

We then restricted each class to the k most frequently occurring words within it. Our provisional system used $k = 5$.

In the standard tagset, the set TO contains only the word "to". We have put "to" into two different classes, because the same word form represents both the preposition and infinitive verb marker. Although the second such class is labelled "AUX", it does not correspond directly to the standard definition of auxiliary as given by grammars of English. First, "to" does not meet all of the properties of auxiliaries. For example, because it does not occur with a subject, it cannot participate in subject-auxiliary inversion. On the other hand, although modals are traditionally a subclass of auxiliaries, we have left them separate as defined in the tagset.

The intuition guiding those decisions was based on grammatical function and patterns of alternatives. Verb forms in English often consist of a closed class word w, followed by a main verb, the form of which combines with the particular w to indicate the tense and aspect. In other words, w functions as a verb form marker, and doesn't carry other information. Modals, in contrast, have uniform grammatical co-occurrence patterns, essentially all being followed by bare infinitives. They have the semantic function of expressing modality, and are alternatives to one another.

Ultimately, which words are best classed as alternatives should be determined empirically.

2.2.2 Open Classes

We used two open classes specific to this task, verbs and nouns.

The verb errors of this year's task included verb form and subject-verb agreement. Ideally, to find candidates for the confusion set of a verb v, we would want to produce morphological variations of v whose POS tag is different from that of v. This was approximated with the following heuristic. We defined the prefix of v to be the initial characters of v, including least the first character, and not any of the final four, except when the first character was one of those. We collected all words in the vocabulary starting with that prefix, whose stem given by the NLTK Porter stemmer matched the corresponding stem of v and that had appeared at least once with a POS tag indicating a verb of a different form from that of v.

Similarly, the only noun errors under consideration were noun number errors, meaning a change from singular to plural or vice versa. We used the same prefix and stem-matching heuristic as in the verb case to find opposite-numbered nouns for this task.

3 The correction process

In order to detect multiple interacting errors, we would like to consider every possible variation of every word in the sentence. To mitigate the combinatorial expense, we use a beam search as follows.

Proceeding word-by-word through the sentence, we keep a list of the n most likely sentence beginning fragments. Our provisional system used $n = 5$. When we reach the observed word w, then for each sentence fragment s_i in the list, we compute the estimated probability that the correct sentence next contained w' instead of w, using our n-gram probability estimate $P(w'|s_i)$, and that the channel model transformed it to w, by dividing the probability of error α by the number of variations in the confusion set of w', $C(w')$. We also estimate the probability that w was the original word. Because our closed classes each include the empty string, every empty string in the observed sentence could have been produced by the deletion of a member of any of the closed classes. Therefore, we also consider the possibility of inserting each word x, from each closed class. In total, the following probabilities are estimated:

(no error)
$p = P(w|s_i) \times (1 - \alpha)$

and for each word x in each closed class, other than the empty string:

(a deletion, no substitution)
$p = P(xw|s_i) \times \alpha/|C(x)| \times (1 - \alpha)$

and for each variation of w, w':

(a substitution)
$p = P(w'|s_i) \times \alpha/|C(w')|$

and for each variation of w, w', and each word x in each closed class, other than the empty string:

(a deletion and a substitution)
$p = P(xw'|s_i) \times \alpha/|C(x)| \times \alpha/|C(w')|$

The n most likely such extended fragments are then kept for the next iteration. Finally, at the end of the sentence, the sentence with the highest probability is returned as the correction. Probabilities are treated as per-word perplexity in order not to penalise longer sentences.

4 Evaluation

The shared task was evaluated using a section of the NUCLE corpus (see (Dalheimer, Ng, and Wu, 2013)), and the corresponding corrections as annotated by English instructors. The types of corrections ranged from simple and well-defined, such as the addition, removal, or exchange of an article or determiner, to the entire rephrasing of a sentence. Sometimes the corrections were strictly grammatical, in that the original was not well-formed English. Some were more stylistic; what the student had written was awkward, or sounded disfluent, even if it could have been parsed acceptably. This is appropriate and consistent with the nature of the problem. However, it does make evaluation almost as challenging as the task itself.

Often if a sentence has grammatical errors, there are many different ways to repair the error. Teams were encouraged to submit alternative corrections when it was believed that their systems' output ought to be considered valid, even if it did not match the particular annotation given by the grader.

Another problem with the evaluation, however, actually stemmed from the simplification of the task. Because grammatical correction is inherently difficult, and because some of the difficulty increases gradually by type as just described, the task for this year was made more moderate by selecting only 5 error types from the 27 types defined in the corpus. However, this resulted in two difficulties.

The first was that some error types were closely related. Errors of verb form, verb tense, verb modal, and subject-verb agreement may have overlapping interpretation. Those error types are not necessarily distinguishable by our method.

For example, there is a sentence in the test set:

Firstly , security systems are improved in many areas such as school campus or at the workplace .

which is corrected to:

Firstly , security systems have improved in many areas such as school campus or at the workplace .

with the annotation of verb tense error type, and thus not part of this task.

On the other hand, there is also a sentence:

... the electric systems were short circuited...

which is corrected to:

... the electric systems short circuited...

with the annotation of verb form error type, and thus part of this task.

Second, sometimes an annotation not evaluated in this task that resulted in a change of word form was necessarily accompanied by changes to words that were included in the task. This meant that in order for the system to match the gold annotations, it would have to propose a sentence that was grammatically incorrect. This is suboptimal. Although it could sometimes be mitigated by the alternative correction appeal process, that may not have been adequate to address all such occurrences. More accurate scoring might be obtained if only the sentences that do not contain other correction types are included in the test set.

An example of this is the sentence:

Take Singapore for example , these are installed...

The annotation corrects this sentence to:

Take Singapore for example , surveillance is installed...

However, the replacement of *these* with *surveillance* is not in the task, so to get it correct, a system would have to hypothesize:

Take Singapore for example , these is installed...

Evaluation	Prec.	Rec.	F-meas.
Original task	0.1767	0.0481	0.0756
Strict 5 types	0.2079	0.0568	0.0892
With alternatives	0.3067	0.0877	0.1364

Table 1: Results

5 Results

The results of our system were not competitive. Table 1 lists our scores on the original annotation (line 1), and after alternative answers were considered (line 3). It also shows what our system would have scored if only the sentences in the test set which contained no errors types other than those specified for the task were included (line 2).

6 Future Work

There are several simple steps that we expect will improve our system.

First, the language models could be improved. They could use corpora better matched to the data set, and they could have larger vocabulary sizes. We also observe that the POS models, because of their inherently small vocabulary, seem to be impaired by the backoff paradigm. In this case, if a sequence is unattested, it is unlikely that the probability is better estimated by ignoring the beginning of it. Rather, it is likely to indicate an error. Since error detection and correction is precisely what we are attempting, it may be that backoff smoothing is detrimental to the POS models. This hypothesis should be tested empirically.

Second, there are several parameters that could be tuned for better performance, including for example, α, the probability that the channel inserts an error, the beam width n, and the thresholds for the number of alternatives considered in a closed class.

The stemmer we used was not a very sophisticated proxy for morphological analysis, and it made errors in both directions that affected our results.

Finally, there are more classes of error that could be easily included in the sets we have defined. Because they interact, our system may perform better when the allowable transformations are more comprehensive and can complement one another.

Acknowledgments

This work was supported by the assistance of Zooko Wilcox-O'Hearn, who contributed code, analysis, and review, and by Graeme Hirst who provided encouragement and advice.

References

Bird, Steven, Edward Loper and Ewan Klein 2009. *Natural Language Processing with Python.* O'Reilly Media Inc.

Dahlmeier, Daniel, and Hwee Tou Ng. A beam-search decoder for grammatical error correction. *Proceedings of the 2012 Joint Conference on Empirical Methods in Natural Language Processing and Computational Natural Language Learning.* Association for Computational Linguistics, 2012.

Daniel Dahlmeier, Hwee Tou Ng 2012. Better Evaluation for Grammatical Error Correction. *Proceedings of the 2012 Conference of the North American Chapter of the Association for Computational Linguistics (NAACL 2012).* (pp. 568 572). Montreal, Canada.

Daniel Dahlmeier, Hwee Tou Ng, Siew Mei Wu 2013. Building a Large Annotated Corpus of Learner English: The NUS Corpus of Learner English. *To appear in Proceedings of the 8th Workshop on Innovative Use of NLP for Building Educational Applications (BEA 2013).* Atlanta, Georgia, USA.

De Felice, Rachele, and Stephen G. Pulman. 2007 Automatically acquiring models of preposition use. *Proceedings of the Fourth ACL-SIGSEM Workshop on Prepositions. Association for Computational Linguistics*, 2007.

Gamon, Michael, et al. Using contextual speller techniques and language modeling for ESL error correction. *Urbana 51* (2009): 61801.

Hwee Tou Ng, Siew Mei Wu, Yuanbin Wu, Christian Hadiwinoto, Joel Tetreault 2013. The CoNLL-2013 Shared Task on Grammatical Error Correction. *To appear in Proceedings of the Seventeenth Conference on Computational Natural Language Learning.*

Albert Park and Roger Levy 2011. Automated whole sentence grammar correction using a noisy channel model. *Proceedings of the 49th Annual Meeting of the Association for Computational Linguistics: Human Language Technologies.* Volume 1, pp 934-944.

Shaoul, C. and Westbury C. 2010 The Westbury Lab Wikipedia Corpus *Edmonton, AB: University of Alberta* (downloaded from http://www.psych.ualberta.ca/ westbury-lab/downloads/westburylab.wikicorp.download.html)

A. Stolcke 2002 SRILM – An Extensible Language Modeling Toolkit. *Proc. Intl. Conf. on Spoken Language Processing*, vol. 2, pp. 901-904, Denver.

Tetreault, Joel R., and Martin Chodorow. The ups and downs of preposition error detection in ESL writing. *Proceedings of the 22nd International Conference on Computational Linguistics-Volume 1*. Association for Computational Linguistics, 2008.

Kristina Toutanova, Dan Klein, Christopher Manning, and Yoram Singer. Feature-Rich Part-of-Speech Tagging with a Cyclic Dependency Network. *Proceedings of HLT-NAACL 2003*, pp. 252-259.

West, Randy, Y. Albert Park, and Roger Levy. Bilingual random walk models for automated grammar correction of esl author-produced text. *Proceedings of the 6th Workshop on Innovative Use of NLP for Building Educational Applications*. Association for Computational Linguistics, 2011.

L. Amber Wilcox-O'Hearn and Zooko Wilcox-O'Hearn 2013. gc *https://github.com/lamber/gc/tree/d4bc96f03263b8ed00b9629f22dfe0950b37129b*

A Hybrid Model for Grammatical Error Correction

Yang Xiang, Bo Yuan, Yaoyun Zhang*, Xiaolong Wang†,
Wen Zheng, Chongqiang Wei
Intelligent Computing Research Center, Key Laboratory of Network Oriented Intelligent Computation, Computer Science and technology Department,
Harbin Institute of Technology Shenzhen Graduate School,
Shenzhen, Guangdong, 518055, P.R. China
{windseedxy, yuanbo.hitsz, xiaoni5122, zhengwen379, weichongqiang}@gmail.com
wangxl@insun.hit.edu.cn†

Abstract

This paper presents a hybrid model for the CoNLL-2013 shared task which focuses on the problem of grammatical error correction. This year's task includes determiner, preposition, noun number, verb form, and subject-verb agreement errors which is more comprehensive than previous error correction tasks. We correct these five types of errors in different modules where either machine learning based or rule-based methods are applied. Preprocessing and post-processing procedures are employed to keep idiomatic phrases from being corrected. We achieved precision of 35.65%, recall of 16.56%, F_1 of 22.61% in the official evaluation and precision of 41.75%, recall of 20.29%, F_1 of 27.3% in the revised version. Some further comparisons employing different strategies are made in our experiments.

1 Introduction

Automatic Grammatical Error Correction (GEC) for non-native English language learners has attracted more and more attention with the development of natural language processing, machine learning and big-data techniques. The CoNLL-2013 shared task focuses on the problem of GEC in five different error types including determiner, preposition, noun number, verb form, and subject-verb agreement which is more complicated and challenging than previous correction tasks. Other than most previous works which concentrate most on determiner and preposition errors, more error types introduces the possibility of correcting multiple interacting errors such as determiner vs. noun number and preposition vs. verb form.

Generally, for GEC on annotated data such as the *NUCLE* corpus (Dahlmeier et al., 2013) in this year's shared task which contains both original errors and human annotations, there are two main types of approaches. One of them is the employment of external language materials. Although there are minor differences on strategies, the main idea of this approach is to use frequencies as a filter, such as n-gram counts, and take those phrases that have relatively high frequencies as the correct ones. Typical works are shown in (Yi et al., 2008) and (Bergsma et al., 2009). Similar methods also exist in HOO shared tasks[1] such as the web 1TB n-gram features used by Dahlmeier and Ng (2012a) and the large-scale n-gram model described by Heilman et al. (2012). The other type is machine learning based approach which considers most on local context including syntactic and semantic features. Han et al. (2006) take maximum entropy as their classifier and apply some simple parameter tuning methods. Felice and Pulman (2008) present their classifier-based models together with a few representative features. Seo et al. (2012) invite a meta-learning approach and show its effectiveness. Dahlmeier and Ng (2011) introduce an alternating structure optimization based approach.

Most of the works mentioned above focus on determiner and preposition errors. Besides, Lee and Seneff (2008) propose a method to correct verb form errors through combining the features of parse trees and n-gram counts. To our knowledge, no one focused on noun form errors in specific researches.

In this paper, we propose a hybrid model to solve the problem of GEC for five error types.

* Corresponding author

[1] http://clt.mq.edu.au/research/projects/hoo/hoo2012

Machine learning based methods are applied to solve determiner (ArtOrDet), preposition (Prep) and noun form (Nn) problems while rule-based methods are proposed for subject-verb agreement (SVA) and verb form (Vform) problems. We treat corrections of errors in each type as individual sub problems the results of which are combined through a result combination module. Solutions on interacting error corrections were considered originally but dropped at last because of the bad effects brought about by them such as the accumulation of errors which lead to a very low performance. We perform feature selection and confidence tuning in machine learning based modules which contribute a lot to our performance. Also, pre-processing and post-processing procedures are employed to keep idiomatic phrases from being corrected.

Through experiments, we found that the result of the system was affected by many factors such as the selection of training samples and features, and the settings of confidence parameters in classifiers. Some of the factors make the whole system too sensitive that it can easily be trapped into a local optimum. Some comparisons are shown in our experiments section.

No other external language materials are included in our model except for several NLP tools which will be introduced in §**5.2**. We achieved precision of 35.65%, recall of 16.56% and F_1 of 22.61% in the official score of our submitted result. However, it was far from satisfactory mainly due to the ill settings of confidence parameters. Trying to find out a set of optimal confidence parameters, our model is able to reach an upper bound of precision of 34.23%, recall of 25.56% and F_1 of 29.27% on the official test set. For the revised version, we achieved precision of 41.75%, recall of 20.29%, and F_1 of 27.3%.

The remainder of this paper is arranged as follows. The next section introduces our system architecture. Section 3 describes machine learning based modules. Section 4 shows rule based modules. Experiments and analysis are arranged in Section 5. Finally, we give our discussion and conclusion in Section 6 and 7.

2 System Architecture

Initially, we treat errors of each type as individual sub problems. Machine learning based methods are applied to solve ArtOrDet, Prep and Nn problems where similar problem solving steps are shared: sample generation, feature extraction, training, confidence tuning in development data, and testing. We apply some hand-crafted heuristic rules in solving subject-verb agreement (SVA) and verb form (Vform) problems. Finally, results from different modules are combined together. The whole architecture of this GEC system is described in Figure 1.

A pre-processing and a post-processing filter are utilized which include filters for some idiomatic phrases extracted from the training dataset. The Frequent Pattern Growth Algorithm (FP-Growth) is widely used for frequent pattern mining in machine learning. In pre-processing, we firstly apply FP-Growth to gather the frequent items in the training set. Through some manual refinements, a few idiomatic phrases are removed from the candidate set to be corrected. In post-processing, the idiomatic phrase list is used to check whether a certain collocation is still grammatical after several corrections are performed. There are 996 idiomatic phrases in our list which is composed by mainly patterns from the training set and a series of hand-crafted ones. Typical phrases we extracted are *in general*, *have/need to be done*, *on the other hand*, *a large/big number/amount of*, *at the same time*, *in public*, etc.

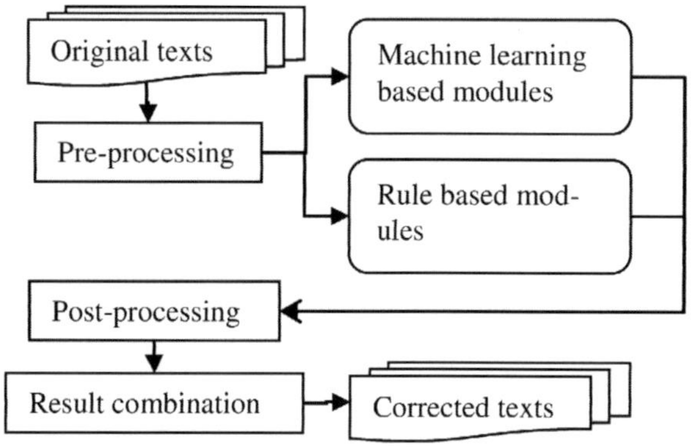

Figure 1. Architecture of our GEC system.

3 Machine Learning Based Modules

For the error types ArtOrDet, Prep and Nn, we choose machine learning based methods because we consider there is not enough evidence to directly determine which word or form to be used. Moreover, it is impossible to transfer all the cases we encounter into rules. In this section, we describe our processing ideas for each error type respectively and then specifically introduce our feature selection and confidence tuning approach.

3.1 Determiners

Determiners in the error type "ArtOrDet" contain articles *a/an*, *the* and other determiners such as *this*, *those*, etc. This type of error accounts for a large proportion which is of great impact on the final result. We consider only articles since the other determiners are rarely used and the usages of them are sometimes ambiguous. Like approaches described in some previous works (Dahlmeier and Ng, 2012a; Felice and Pulman, 2008), we assign three types *a/an*, *the* and *empty* for each article position and build a multi-class classifier.

For training, developing and testing, all noun phrases (NPs) are chosen as candidate samples to be corrected. For NPs whose articles have been annotated in the corpus, the correct ones are their target categories, and for those haven't been annotated, the target categories are their observed article types. Samples we make use of can be divided into two basic types in each category: *with* and *without* a wrong article. Two examples are shown below:

with: ~~*a*~~/<u>*empty*</u> *big apples* ~ *empty* category
without: <u>*the*</u> *United States* ~ *the* category

For each category in *a*, *the*, and *empty*, we use the whole *with* data and take samples of *without* ones from the set of correct NPs to make up training instances of one category. The reason why we make samples of the *without* ones is for the consideration that the classifier would always predicts the observed article and never proposes any corrections if given too many *without* samples, the case of which is mentioned in (Dahlmeier and Ng, 2012a). However, we found that the ratio of *with-without* shows little effect in our model. The article *a* is regulated to *a* or *an* according to pronunciation.

Syntactic and semantic features are considered in feature extraction with the help of WordNet and the ".conll" file provided. We adopt syntactic features such as the surface word, phrase, part-of-speech, n-grams, constituent parse tree, dependency parse tree and headword of an NP; semantic features like noun category and hypernym. Some expand operations are also done based on them (reference to Dahlmeier and Ng, 2012a; Felice and Pulman, 2008). After feature extraction, we apply a genetic algorithm to do feature subset selection in order to reduce dimensionality and filter out noisy features which is to be described in §**3.4**.

Maximum Entropy (ME) has been proven to behave well for heterogeneous features in natural language processing tasks and we adopt it to train our model. We have also tried several other classifiers including SVM, decision tree, Naïve Bayes, and RankSVM but finally find ME performs well and stably. It provides confidence scores for each category which we will make use of downstream.

3.2 Prepositions

Preposition error correction task is similar to the previous one except the different categories and corresponding features. Since there are 36 common prepositions listed by the shared task, originally, we assign 37 types including 36 prepositions and *empty* for each preposition position and build a multi-class classifier. For training, developing and testing, each preposition as well as the empty position directly after a verb is considered as a candidate. Syntactic and semantic features extracted are similar to those in article error correction except for some specific cases for prepositions such as the verbs related to prepositions and the dependency relations. Similarly, we treat those preposition phrases *with* and *without* a certain preposition as the two types of samples in training (as described in §**3.1**). Two examples are listed below:

with: ~~*on*~~/<u>*in*</u> *the 1860s*~ *in* category
without: *have* <u>*to*</u> *be done* ~ *to* category

Through statistics on the training data, we found that most prepositions have very few samples which may not contribute to the performance at all and even bring about noise when assigned to wrong categories. After several rounds of experiments, we finally adopt a classifier with seven prepositions which are frequently used in the whole corpus. They are *on*, *of*, *in*, *at*, *to*, *with* and *for*. As to the classifier, ME also outperforms the others.

3.3 Noun Form

Noun form may be interacting with determiners and verbs which may also have errors in the original text. So errors may occur in the context features extracted from the original text. However, if we use the context features that have been corrected, more errors would be employed due to the low performance of the previous steps. Through statistics, we found that co-occurrence between two types of errors such as SVA and ArtOrDet only accounts for a small proportion. After a few experiments, we decided to give up interacting errors so as to avoid accumulated errors.

This is a binary classification problem. All head nouns in NPs are considered as candidates. Each category contains *with* and *without* samples similar to the cases in §**3.1** and §**3.2**. Features are highly related to the deterministic factors for the head noun form such as the countability, WordNet type, name entity and whether there some specific dependency relations including *det*, *amod* etc.

ME also outperforms other classifiers.

3.4 Feature Selection Using Genetic Algorithm

Features we extracted are excessive and sparse after binarization. They bring noise in quality as well as complexity in computation and need to be selected a priori. In our work, it is a wrapper feature selection task. That is, we have to select a combination of features that perform well together rather than make sure each of them behaves well. This GEC task is interesting in feature selection because word surface features that are observed only once are also effective while we think that they overfit. Genetic algorithm (GA) has been proven to be useful in selecting wrapper features in classification (ElAlami, 2009; Anba-rasi et al, 2010). We used GA to select features as well as reduce feature dimensionality.

We convert the features into a binary sequence in which each character represents one dimension. Let "1" indicates that we keep this dimension while "0" means that we drop it, we use a binary sequence such as "0111000…100" to denote a combination of feature dimensions. GA functions on the feature sequences and finally decides which features should be kept. The fitness function we used is the evaluation measure F_1 described in §**5.3**.

3.5 Confidence Tuning

The Maximum Entropy classifier returns a confidence score for each category given a testing sample. However, for different samples, the distribution of predicted scores varies a lot. For some samples, the classifier may have a very high predicted score for a certain category which means the classifier is confident enough to perform this prediction. But for some other samples, two or more categories may share close scores, the case of which means the classifier hesitates when telling them apart.

We introduce a confidence tuning approach on the predicted results through a comparison between the observed category and the predicted category which is similar to the "thresholding" approach described in Tetreault and Chodorow (2008). The main idea of the confidence tuning algorithm is: the choice between *keep* and *drop* is based on the difference between the confidence scores of the predicted category and the observed category. If this difference goes beyond a threshold *t*, the prediction is kept while if it is under *t*, we won't do any corrections. We believe this tuning strategy is especially appropriate in this task since to distinguish whether the observed category is correct or not affects a lot to the predicted result.

The confidence threshold for each category is generated through a hill climbing algorithm in the development data aimed at maximizing F_1-meaure of the result.

4 Rule-based Modules

A few hand-crafted rules are applied to solve the verb related corrections including SVA and Vform. In these cases, the verb form is only related to some specific features as described by Lee and Seneff (2008).

4.1 SVA

SVA (Subject-verb-agreement) is particularly related to the noun subject that a verb determines. In the dependency tree, the number of the noun which has a relation *nsubj* with the verb determines the form of this verb. Through observation, we find that the verbs to be considered in SVA contain only *be*s (including *am, is, are, was, were*) and the verbs in simple present tense whose POSs are labeled with *VBZ* (singular) or *VBP*(plural).

To pick out the noun subject is easy except for the verb that contained in a subordinate clause. We use semantic role labeling (SRL) to help solve this problem in which the coordinated can be extracted through a trace with the label "R-Argument". The following Figure is an example generated by the SRL toolkit *mate-tools* (Bernd Bohnet, 2010)[2].

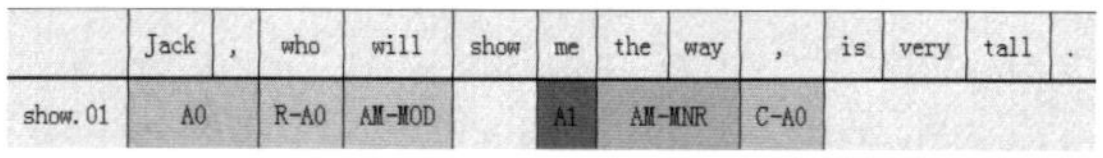

Figure 2. SRL for the demo sentence "Jack, who will show me the way, is very tall." The subject of the verb *show* can be traced through R-A0 -> A0.

However, the performance of this part is partly correlated with the noun form that may have errors in the original text and the wrong SRL result brought about because of wrong sentence grammars.

[2] http://code.google.com/p/mate-tools/

4.2 Verb Form

The cases are more complicated in the verb form error correction task. Modal, aspect and voice are all forms that should be considered for a verb. And sometimes, two or more forms are combined together to perform its role in a sentence. For example, in the sentence:

*He **has been working** in this position for a long time.*

The bolded verb ***has been working*** is a combination of the active voice *work,* the progressive aspect *be+VBG* and the perfect aspect *has+VBN.* It is a bit difficult for us to take all cases into consideration, so we just apply several simple rules and solve a subset of problems for this type. Some typical rules are listed below:

1. The verb that has a dependency relation *aux* to preposition *to* is modified to its base form.
2. The verb that has a dependency relation *pcomp* to preposition *by* is modified to its past form.
3. The verb related to other prepositions (except *to* and *by*) is modified to *~ing* form.
4. The verb depends on auxiliary *do* and modal verb (including its inflections and negative form) is modified to its base form.

We have also tried to use SRL and transitivity of a verb to determine the active and passive voice but it didn't work well.

5 Experiments and Analysis

5.1 Data Description

The *NUCLE* corpus introduced by NUS (National University of Singapore) contains 1414 essays written by L2 students with relatively high proficiency of English in which grammatical errors have been well annotated by native tutors. It has a small proportion of annotated errors which is much lower than other similar corpora (Dahlmeier et al., 2013). In our experiments, we divide the whole corpus into 80%, 10% and 10% for training, developing and testing. And we use 90% and 10% for training and developing for the final test.

5.2 External tools and corpora

External tools we used include WordNet (Fellbaum, 1998) for word base form and noun category generation, Morphg (Minnen et al., 2000)[3] to generate inflections of nouns and verbs, matetools (Bohnet, 2010) for SRL, Stanford-ner (Finkel et al., 2005)[4] for name entity extraction and Longman online dictionary[5] for generation of noun countability and verb transitivity.

We didn't employ any external corpora in our system.

5.3 Experiments

The performance of each machine learning module is affected by the selection of training samples, features and confidence tuning for the maximum entropy classifier. All these factors contribute more or less to the final performance and need to be carefully developed. In our experiments, we focus on machine learning based modules and make comparisons on sample selection, confidence tuning and feature selection and list a series of results before and after applying our strategies.

In our experiment, the performance is measured with precision, recall and F_1-measure where

$$F_1 = \frac{2 \times precision \times recall}{precision + recall}$$

Precision is the amount of predicted corrections that are also corrected by the manual annotators divided by the whole amount of predicted corrections. Recall has the same numerator as precision while its denominator is the amount of manually corrected errors. They are in accordance with those measurements generated by the official m2scorer (Dahlmeier and Ng, 2012c) to a great extent and easily to be integrated in our program.

As we have mentioned in Section 3, we don't employ all samples but make use of all *with* (with errors and annotations) instances and sample the *without* ones (without errors) for training. And the sampling for *without* type is totally random without loss of generality. We apply the same strategy in all of these three error types (ArtOrDet, Prep and Nn) and try several ratios of *with-without* to find out whether this ratio has great impact on the final result and which ratio performs best. We use the 80%-10%-10% data (mentioned in §**5.1**) for our experiments and make comparisons of different ratios on developing data. The experimental results are described in detail in Figure 3.

Confidence tuning is applied in all these three error types which contributes most to the final performance in our model. We compare the results before and after tuning in all sample ratios

[3] http://www.informatics.sussex.ac.uk/research/groups/nlp/carroll/morph.html

[4] http://www-nlp.stanford.edu/software/CRF-NER.shtml

[5] http://www.ldoceonline.com/

that we designed and they are also depicted in Figure 3.

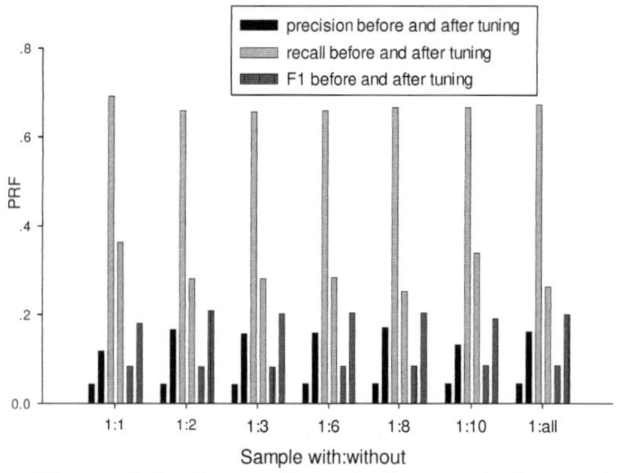

Figure 3-1. Comparisons before and after tuning in ArtOrDet. *1:all* means to use the whole *without* samples.

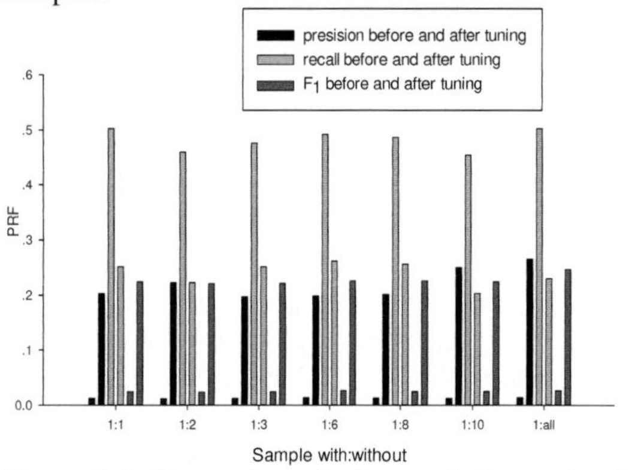

Figure 3-2. Comparisons before and after tuning in Prep.

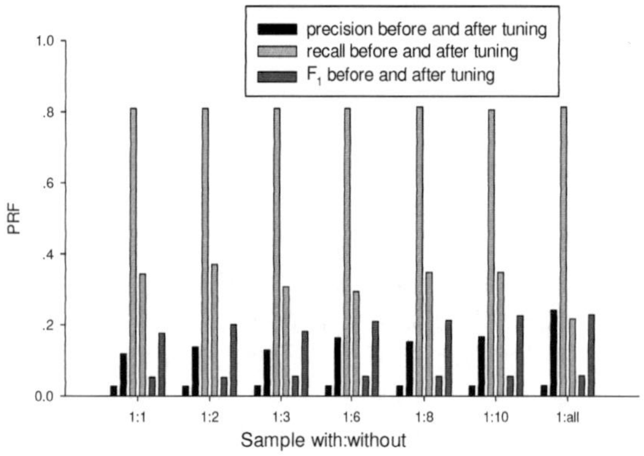

Figure 3-3. Comparisons before and after tuning in Nn.

From the three groups of data in Figure 3, we notice that the ratio of samples has little impact on F_1. This phenomenon shows that our conclusion goes against the previous work by Dahlmeier and Ng (2012a). We believe it is mainly due to our confidence tuning which makes the parameters vary much under different sample ratios, that is, if given the same parameters, the effect of sample ratio selection may become obvious. Unfortunately, we didn't do such a systematic comparison in our work. The improvement under confidence tuning can be seen clearly in all ratios of *with-without* samples. The confidence tuning algorithm employed in our work is better than the traditional tuning methods that assign a fixed threshold for each category or for all categories (about 1%~2% better measured by F_1).

However, although we are able to pick out the training data with a high F_1 through confidence tuning for the developing data, it is difficult for us to choose a set of confidence parameters that also fits the test data well. Given several close F_1s, the numerical values of denominators and numerators which determine the precision and recall can vary a lot. For example, one set that has a high precision and low recall may share the similar F_1 with another set that has a low precision and high recall. Our work lacked of the development on how to control the number of proposed errors to make leverage on the performance between developing set and testing set. It resulted in that the developing set and the testing set were not balanced at all, and our model was not able to keep the sample distribution as the training set. This is the main factor that leads to a low performance in our submitted result which can be clearly seen in Table 1. The upper bound performance of our system achieves precision of 34.23%, recall of 25.56% and F_1 of 29.27%, in which the F_1 goes 7% beyond our submitted system. We notice that results of all metrics of the three error types where machine learning algorithms are applied improve with the simultaneous increase of numerators and denominators. This is especially noticeable in Prep.

For the other two types SVA and Vform, we just apply several heuristic rules to solve a subset of problems and the case of Vform has not been solved well such as tense and voice.

Genetic Algorithm (GA) is applied to process feature reduction and subset selection. This is done in ArtOrDet type in which we extract as many as 350,000 binary features. For error type Prep and Nn, the feature dimensionalities we constructed were not as high as that in ArtOrDet, and the improvements under GA were not obvious which we would not discuss in this work. Through experiments on a few sample ratios, we notice that feature selection using genetic algorithm is able to reduce the feature dimensionality to about 170,000 which greatly lowers down the downstream computational complexity. However, the improvement contributed by GA after confidence tuning is not obvious as that before confidence tuning. We think it is partly because of the bad initialization of GA which is to be improved in our future work. The unfixed parameters may also lead to such a result which we didn't discuss enough in our work. The comparison before and after GA is described in Figure 4.

	Our submission%	Upper bound%
P(Det)	41.38(168/406)	36.44(254/697)
R(Det)	24.35(168/690)	36.81(254/690)
F_1(Det)	30.66	36.63
P(Prep)	13.79(4/29)	26.12(35/134)
R(Prep)	1.29(4/311)	11.25(35/311)
F_1(Prep)	2.35	15.73
P(Nn)	24.81(65/262)	27.27(102/374)
R(Nn)	16.41(65/396)	25.76(102/396)
F_1(Nn)	19.76	26.49
P(SVA)	24.42(21/86)	24.42(21/86)
R(SVA)	16.94(21/124)	16.94(21/124)
F_1(SVA)	20.00	20.00
P(Vform)	19.35(6/31)	19.35(6/31)
R(Vform)	4.92(6/122)	4.92(6/122)
F_1(Vform)	7.84	7.84
P(all)	35.65(272/763)	34.23(420/1227)
R(all)	16.56(272/1643)	25.56(420/1643)
F_1(all)	22.61	29.27

Table 1. Different performances according to different confidence parameters. *Det* stands for ArtOrDet.

Pre-processing and post-processing we propose also contribute to some extent which we could see from Table 2. Some idiomatic phrases are excluded from being corrected in pre-processing which enhances precision while some are being modified in post-processing to improve recall.

	Without pre-processing and post-processing%	Final%
P	33.72(265/768)	35.65(272/763)
R	16.13(265/1643)	16.56(272/1643)
F_1	21.82	22.61

Table 2. Comparison with and without pre-processing and post-processing.

We didn't do much on the interacting errors problem since we didn't work out perfect plans to solve it. So, in the result combination module, we just simply combine the result of each part together.

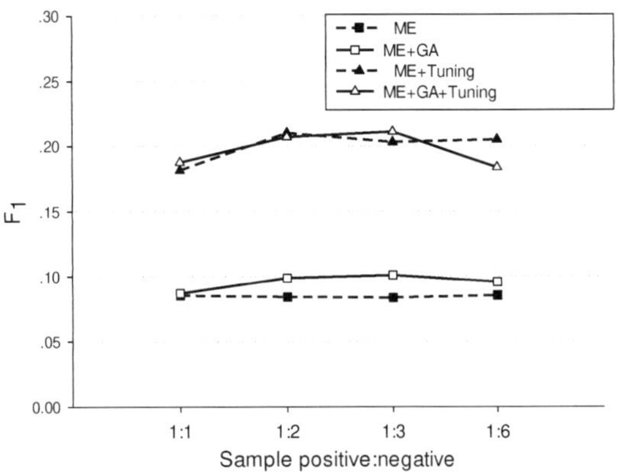

Figure 4. Comparisons before and after Genetic Algorithm on ArtOrDet error type. ME, GA, and Tuning stand for Maximum Entropy, Genetic Algorithm and confidence tuning.

In the revised version, under further corrections for the gold annotations, our model achieves precision of 41.75%, recall of 20.19% and F_1 of 27.3%.

6 Discussion

Which factor contributes most to the final result in the problem of grammatical error correction? Since we didn't include any external corpora, we discuss it here only according to the local classifiers and context features.

Based on our experiments, we find that, in our machine learning based modules, a tiny modification of confidence parameter setting for each category, no matter which type of error, can have great impact on the final result. It results in that our model is much too sensitive to parameters which may easily lead to a poor behavior. Perhaps a sufficient consideration of how to keep the distribution of samples, such as cross-validation, may be helpful. In addition, the selection of classifiers, features and training samples all have effect on the result more or less, but not as obvious as that of the confidence threshold setting.

7 Conclusion

In this paper, we propose a hybrid model combining machine learning based modules and rule-based modules to solve the grammatical error correction task. We are able to solve a subset of the correction problems in which ArtOrDet and Nn perform better. However, our result in the testing data shows that our model is sensitive to parameters. How to keep the distribution of training samples needs to be further developed.

Acknowledgement

This work is supported in part by the National Natural Science Foundation of China (No. 612-72383 and 61173075).

References

Bernd Bohnet. Top Accuracy and Fast Dependency Parsing is not a Contradiction. In *Proceedings of COLING,* 2010.

C. Fellbaum. WordNet: An Electronic Lexical Data-base. *MIT Press*. 1998.

Daniel Dahlmeier, and Hwee Tou Ng. Grammatical error correction with alternating structure optimization. In *Proceedings of ACL*. Association for Computational Linguistics, 2011.

Daniel Dahlmeier, Hwee Tou Ng, and Eric Jun Feng Ng. NUS at the HOO 2012 Shared Task. In *Proceedings of the Seventh Workshop on Building Educational Applications Using NLP*. Association for Computational Linguistics, 2012a.

Daniel Dahlmeier and Hwee Tou Ng. A beam-search decoder for grammatical error correction. In *Proceedings of the EMNLP*. Association for Computational Linguistics, 2012b.

Daniel Dahlmeier and Hwee Tou Ng. Better Evaluation for Grammatical Error Correction. In Proceedings of NAACL, Association for Computational Linguistics, 2012c.

Daniel Dahlmeier, Hwee Tou Ng and Siew Mei Wu. Building a Large Annotated Corpus of Learner English: The NUS Corpus of Learner English. In *Proceedings of the 8th Workshop on Innovative Use of NLP for Building Educational Applications (BEA)*, 2013.

De Felice, Rachele and Stephen G. Pulman. A classifier-based approach to preposition and determiner error correction in L2 English. In *Proceedings of COLING*. Association for Computational Linguistics, 2008.

G. Minnen, J. Carroll and D. Pearce. Robust, applied morphological generation. In *Proceedings of the 1st International Natural Language Generation Conference*, 2000.

Jenny Rose Finkel, Trond Grenager, and Christopher Manning. Incorporating Non-local Information into Information Extraction Systems by Gibbs Sampling. In *Proceedings of ACL* , 2005.

Joel R. Tetreault and Martin Chodorow. The ups and downs of preposition error detection in ESL writing. In *Proceedings of COLING*, Association for Computational Linguistics, 2008.

John Lee and Stephanie Seneff. Correcting misuse of verb forms. In *Proceedings of ACL: HLT*, 2008.

M Anbarasi, E Anupriya, and NC Iyengar. Enhanced prediction of heart disease with feature subset selection using genetic algorithm. *International Journal of Engineering Science and Technology*,Vol.2(10),2010: 5370-5376.

ME ElAlami. A filter model for feature subset selection based on genetic algorithm. *Knowledge-Based Systems*,Vol.22(5), 2009: 356-362.

Michael Heilman, Aoife Cahill, and Joel Tetreault. Precision isn't everything: a hybrid approach to grammatical error detection. In *Proceedings of the Seventh Workshop on Building Educational Applications Using NLP*. Association for Computational Linguistics, 2012.

Hongsuck Seo et al. A meta learning approach to grammatical error correction. In *Proceedings of ACL*. Association for Computational Linguistics, 2012.

N.R. Han, M. Chodorow, and C. Leacock. 2006. Detecting errors in English article usage by non-native speakers. *Natural Language Engineering*, Vol.12(02):115-129.

S. Bergsma, D. Lin, and R. Goebel. 2009. Web-scale ngram models for lexical disambiguation. In *Proceedings of IJCAI*.2009.

X. Yi, J. Gao, and W.B. Dolan. 2008. A web-based English proofing system for English as a second language users. In *Proceedings of IJCNLP*.2008.

KUNLP Grammatical Error Correction System For CoNLL-2013 Shared Task

Bong-Jun Yi, Ho-Chang Lee, and Hae-Chang Rim
Department of Computer and Radio Communications Engineering
Korea University
Anam-dong 5-ga, Seongbuk-gu, Seoul, South Korea
{bjyi,hclee,rim}@nlp.korea.ac.kr

Abstract

This paper describes an English grammatical error correction system for CoNLL-2013 shared task. Error types covered by our system are article/determiner, preposition, and noun number agreement. This work is our first attempt on grammatical error correction research. In this work, we only focus on reimplementing the techniques presented before and optimizing the performance. As a result of the implementation, our system's final F1-score by m2 scorer is 0.1282 in our internal test set.

1 Introduction

As the number of English learners is increasing world widely, the research topic of automated grammar error correction is lively discussed. However, automated grammar error correction is a very difficult field and the result is not satisfactory. Therefore, the shared task about English error correction has been annually held and many researchers are trying to solve this problem.

Helping Our Own (HOO) 2011 is a pilot shared task for automated correction of errors in non-native English speakers' papers. The shared task evaluates the performance of detection, recognition, correction on thirteen types of English grammatical errors by using F1-score. Because each error type has different characteristics, they have to use different approaches to correct appropriate error types.

In *HOO 2012*, only two types of errors, preposition and determiner were handled. This shared task also evaluated the performance of detection, recognition, correction by using F1-score. The best result of the preposition error correction is 0.2371 in F1-score and the determiner error correction is 0.3460 in F1-score. These are remarkable achievement.

This year *CoNLL 2013* shared task covers five types of errors based on the result of *HOO 2012*. These error types are determiner, preposition, noun number, verb form, and subject-verb agreement. Because of the limited amount of time and manpower, we only focus on preposition, determiner and noun number.

2 Previous Works

Most methods for grammar error correction have tried to correct one type of errors. Researchers have never attempted to correct different types of errors at the same time.

In this work, we try to solve the error correction problem based on the previous research presenting good performance.

First, the preposition error correction is based on (Han et al., 2010). They tried to correct the most commonly used 10 preposition errors based on the classification approach. 10 prepositions are *about, at, by, for, from, in, of, on, to, with*. They have implemented 11-way classifier to output 11 types of proper word(10 prepositions + 'NULL') for 11 types of source words. This work assumes that three kinds of corrections exist. If 'NULL' is taken as input and some preposition is produced, it is omission. If some preposition is taken as input and another preposition is produced, it is replacement. If some preposition is taken as input and 'NULL' is produced, it is commission. In the case of replacement, correction precision is 0.817 and recall is 0.132. Furthermore, they reported that the performance is much better when they train the model with well edited error tagged corpus.

(Felice and Pulman, 2008) also used a method based on classification. It is, nevertheless, unusual that they did not use error tagged learner's corpus but error free British National Corpus. Without using an error tagged corpus, they have achieved 51.5% accuracy for error correction.

To improve low recall of Han's method, to construct large training data is the best way. However, it is very costly and hard work to obtain well edited error tagged corpus. By the way, error free corpus like news articles is relatively easy to acquire. We plan to utilize large error free corpus as the training data to overcome the problem of low recall. That plan motivated by Felice's work has not been tried on the proposed system. We will attempt to reimplement the system by utilizing the error free corpus in the near future.

3 System Description

Our system is composed of three components, preposition error corrector, article error corrector, and noun number error corrector. In this work, we do not consider complex cases of grammar errors, thus we assume that the order of correction does not influence the result of correction. And all components are based on the machine learning method.

3.1 Preposition Error Correction

In the training corpus, there are more article errors than preposition errors in number. However, the preposition error correction is much more difficult and the performance of correction is worse than the article error correction.

We select preposition error candidates for replacement or commission or omission as follows.

- Replacement or Commission
  - Preposition : tagged as 'IN' or 'TO' and dependency relation with its parent(DPREL) is identified as a 'prep'
- Omission
  - In front of a noun phrase : the preceding word of the noun phrase is not preposition
  - In front of a verb phrase : the preceding word of the verb phrase including 'VBG'(verb, gerund/present participle) is not preposition

As described above, we use all words(preposition and 'NULL' when omission) in that place as source word for preposition correction.

We have implemented only one classifier that takes a source word as input and produces corrected preposition or 'NULL' as output. We use the part of feature set(Table 1) proposed by (Han et al., 2010) for learning. They are presented in the experiment part.

No.	Feature Name	Description
1	s	the source word
2	wd-1	the word preceding s
3	wd+1	the word following s
4	wd-1,2_s	the two words preceding s and s
5	s_wd+1,2	s and the two words following s
6	3GRAM	the trigram, wd-1, s, wd+1
7	5GRAM	the five-gram, wd-2, wd-1, s, wd+1, wd+2
8	MOD	the lexical head which the preposition modifies
9	ARG	the lexical head of the preposition argument
10	MOD_ARG	MOD and ARG
11	MOD_s	MOD and s
12	s_ARG	s and ARG
13	MOD_s_ARG	MOD, s, ARG
14	MODt_ARGt	POS tags of MOD and ARG
15	MODt_s	the POS tag of MOD and s
16	s_ARGt	s and the POS tag of ARG
17	MODt_s_ARGt	MODt and s and ARGt
18	TRIGRAMt	POS trigram
19	wd_L	3 words preceding s
20	wd_R	3 words following s

Table 1: Set of features proposed by (Han et al., 2010)

Each feature represents the word itself in the Han's work. However, the same word can be extracted again as a different kind of features. In order to distinguish the same word used for the different features, we attach the feature name to the word as postfix. This naming convention can make the feature sparse, but increase the discrimination power and improve the performance of the classifier. In our experiment, we have tested the system with two different sets of features(i.e. raw word and with feature names).

3.2 Article Error Correction

We have implemented the article error corrector just like the preposition error corrector. When we experiment the pilot article correction system just like the preposition correction system, it shows a good performance unexpectedly. There is a little difference in presenting set of features. In preposition error corrector, we add postfix to the set of feature to keep sort of features(e.g. word 'in' as source word feature, postfix is 'S', final feature is 'in_S'). This method gives more discrimination ability to the classifier. But in case of article, using raw word lead to a better result.

3.3 Noun Number Error Correction

Noun number error indicates improper use of singular or plural form of nouns. For example, the singular form 'problem' should be corrected to the plural form 'problems' in the following sentence.

"They are educational and resource problem."

As far as we know, there have been few attempts to correct noun number agreement errors. In this shared task, we propose a novel noun number agreement correction system based on a machine learning method trained with basic features.

In order to extract nouns from the input sentences, we parse the sentence and extract the last noun in every noun phrase for the error correction candidates. If there is a coordinating conjunction in the noun phrase, we split the noun phrase into two parts and extract two candidates.

> [S [NP Relevant **information**] [VP are [ADJP readily ROOT available [PP on [NP [NP the **internet**] and [NP **article**] [PP in [NP **magazines** and **newspapers**] .]]]

Figure 1: Extracting candidates for error correction of noun number(candidates are indicated by bold)

Figure 1 shows the example of selecting candidates for the error correction of noun number. We classify a noun into four classes using features of Table 2 based on the machine learning method. Four classes are NN(plural noun), NNP(plural proper noun), NNS(singular noun), and NNPS(singular proper noun). It is based on the observation that the common noun and the proper noun have many different characteristic. The set of features used for learning is shown in Table 2.

No.	Feature Name	Description
1	p	POS tag for the source word
2	s	the source word
3	DET	the determiner of the noun argument
4	CD	boolean value whether the cardinal number exists
5	UCNT	boolean value whether the noun is uncountable
6	MOD	the lexical head which the noun modifies
7	MMOD	the lexical head which MOD modifies
8	ARG	the lexical head of the noun argument
9	AARG	the lexical head of the ARG argument
10	MOD_s_ARG	MOD, s, and ARG
11	MODt	POS tag for MOD
12	MMODt	POS tag for MMOD
13	ARGt	POS tag for ARG
14	AARGt	POS tag for AARG
15	MODt_p_ARGt	MODt, p, and ARGt
16	MMOD_MOD_s	MMOD, MOD, and s
17	s_ARG_AARG	s, ARG, and AARG
18	MOD_s_ARG	MOD, s, and ARG
19	MM_M_s_A_AA	MMOD, MOD, s, ARG, and AARG
20	MMODt_MODt_p	MMODt, MODt, and p
21	p_ARGt_AARGt	p, ARGt, and AARGt
22	MODt_p_ARGt	MODt, p, and ARGt
23	MMt_Mt_s_At_AAt	MMODt, MODt, s, ARGt, and AARGt

Table 2: Set of features for learning noun number error correction

4 Experiments

4.1 Corpus

We use only NUS Corpus of Leaner English(NUCLE)((Dahlmeier, 2013)) provided from CoNLL 2013 shared task. We construct the development set with first sentences for every 10 sentence and the test set with second sentences and the training set with the rest of sentences. The system is trained to learn error correction with the training set and optimized with the development set and finally evaluated with the test set.

4.2 Preposition Correction Experiment

Table 1 shows 20 types of features used by (Han et al., 2010). We have found that the features consist of various types and the learning world be disturbed by too many features. In our experiment,

Number of feature		20	18	9
Raw Word	Precision	0.0571	0.1194	0.0196
	Recall	0.0402	0.0402	0.1256
	F1-score	0.0472	0.0602	0.0339
With Feature Name	Precision	0.1034	0.1750	0.0208
	Recall	0.0302	0.0352	0.1307
	F1-score	0.0467	0.0586	0.0359

Table 3: The result of preposition error correction

Number of feature		20	18	9
Raw Word	Precision	0.1827	0.3176	0.0914
	Recall	0.1123	0.1264	0.1139
	F1-score	0.1391	0.1808	0.1014
With Feature Name	Precision	0.1942	0.3174	0.1059
	Recall	0.1154	0.1139	0.1061
	F1-score	0.1448	0.1676	0.1060

Table 4: The result of article error correction

Kinds of feature		Basic	Basic& Independent	Basic& Complex
Raw Word	Precision	0.2462	0.1435	0.2469
	Recall	0.0379	0.0811	0.0540
	F1-score	0.0662	0.1036	0.0887
With Feature Name	Precision	0.2413	0.1676	0.2875
	Recall	0.0378	0.0838	0.0621
	F1-score	0.0654	0.1117	0.1022

Table 5: The result of noun number error correction

we exclude wd_L(19), wd_R(20) and employ 18 kinds of features.

We will try to train the correction model by using large amount of error free corpus in order to overcome the problem of low recall. To parse large corpus is very time consuming task. So, in this experiment, we select 9 features which can be extracted without parsing, and test the possibility of using 9 features by training and testing the correction model.

We have performed two different experiments. In the first experiment, we have used the word itself as a feature. In the tables 3˜5, "Raw Word" represents the case when we use just the word itself. In the second experiment, we have used the feature name as the postfix of the feature. In the tables 3˜5, "With Feature Name" represents the case when we attach the feature name to the feature and use it as a feature. For all experiments, we have tried to differentiate the number of features. 20 features are same as Han's work. 18 features are the case when we exclude 2 features(i.e. wd_L(19), wd_R(20)). 9 features are the case when we use only features which do not require parsing.

We have experimented with Maximum Entropy learning method, and fixed the iteration number to 200. Table 3 shows that the precision has highly increased although the recall has decreased when we add the feature name to the set of features used for learning.

When we use 18 features except wd_L(3 words preceding s) and wd_R(3 words following s), the error correction system achieves the best performance. According to the experimental result, we can achieve the better result when we use 18 features and the raw word. But we select final option using 18 features and the word with feature name because of optimization strategies that improve the precision.

4.3 Article Correction Experiment

Table 4 shows that the feature name addition does not improve the precision in the case of article correction, and the set of 18 features achieves the best performance for article correction. Therefore, we just use raw words for features and select 18 features for article correction.

4.4 Noun Number Correction Experiment

In Table 2, features of number 1˜5 belong to the basic feature set and features of number 6˜15 belong to the independent feature set and features of number 16˜23 belong to the complex feature set. The experimental result with various combinations of feature sets shows that the set of basic and complex features achieves the best precision in spite of low recall as shown in Table 5. We use this option and experimentally select the iteration number 700.

5 Conclusions

We develop a grammatical error correction system which can recognize and correct preposition, article, and noun number errors. In this experiment, we have found out the set of good features for preposition and article error correction, and proposed a novel noun number error correction technique based on the machine learning method. For the future work, we will try to utilize large amount of external resources such as well written error free corpus.

References

Daniel Dahlmeier, Hwee Tou Ng, Siew Mei Wu 2013. *Building a Large Annotated Corpus of Learner English: The NUS Corpus of Learner English, Proceedings of the 8th Workshop on Innovative Use of NLP for Building Educational Applications (BEA 2013)*, Atlanta, Georgia, USA.

Rachele De Felice and Stephen G. Pulman 2008. *A classifier-based approach to preposition and determiner error correction in L2 English, Proceedings of the 22nd International Conference on Computational Linguistics (Coling 2008)*, 169–176, Manchester, UK

Na-Rae Han, Joel Tetreault, Soo-Hwa Lee, Jin-Young Ha 2010. *Using an Error-Annotated Learner Corpus to Develop an ESL/EFL Error Correction System, Proceedings of the Seventh International Conference on Language Resources and Evaluation (LREC 2010)*, 763–770, Malta

Author Index